T0258765

Combating Women's Health Issues with Machine Learning

The main focus of this book is the examination of women's health issues and the role machine learning can play as a solution to these challenges. This book will illustrate advanced, innovative techniques/frameworks/concepts/machine learning methodologies, enhancing the future healthcare system. *Combating Women's Health Issues with Machine Learning: Challenges and Solutions* examines the fundamental concepts and analysis of machine learning algorithms.

The editors and authors of this book examine new approaches for different age-related medical issues that women face. Topics range from diagnosing diseases such as breast and ovarian cancer to using deep learning in prenatal ultrasound diagnosis. The authors also examine the best machine learning classifier for constructing the most accurate predictive model for women's infertility risk. Among the topics discussed are gender differences in type 2 diabetes care and its management as it relates to gender using artificial intelligence. The book also discusses advanced techniques for evaluating and managing cardiovascular disease symptoms, which are more common in women but often overlooked or misdiagnosed by many healthcare providers.

The book concludes by presenting future considerations and challenges in the field of women's health using artificial intelligence. This book is intended for medical researchers, healthcare technicians, scientists, programmers and graduate-level students looking to understand better and develop applications of machine learning/deep learning in healthcare scenarios, especially concerning women's health conditions.

Meenu Gupta is Associate Professor in the UIE-CSE Department at Chandigarh University, India. She completed her PhD in Computer Science and Engineering with an emphasis on Traffic Accident Severity Problems from Ansal University, India, in 2020. She has more than 14 years of teaching experience. Her research areas cover machine learning, intelligent systems and data mining, with a specific interest in artificial intelligence, image processing and analysis, smart cities, data analysis and human/brain–machine interaction (BMI). She has edited five books and authored four engineering books. She reviews several journals, including *Big Data*,

CMC, *Scientific Reports* and *TSP*. She is a life member of ISTE and IAENG. She has authored or co-authored more than 30 book chapters and over 80 papers in refereed international journals and conferences.

D. Jude Hemanth is Associate Professor in the Department of ECE at Karunya University, India. He also holds the "Visiting Professor" position in the Faculty of Electrical Engineering and Information Technology at the University of Oradea, Romania. He received his BE degree in ECE from Bharathiar University, India, in 2002, his ME degree in Communication Systems from Anna University, India, in 2006, and his PhD from Karunya University, India, in 2013. His research areas include computational intelligence and image processing, communication systems, biomedical engineering, robotics and healthcare, computational intelligence and information systems, and artificial intelligence. He is also an editor of the *Neuroscience Informatics Journal*.

Biomedical and Robotics Healthcare

Series Editors:

Utku Kose, Jude Hemanth, Omer Deperlioglu

For more information about this series, please visit:
https://www.routledge.com/Biomedical-and-Robotics-Healthcare/book-series/BRHC

Combating Women's Health Issues with Machine Learning

Challenges and Solutions

Edited by
Meenu Gupta and D. Jude Hemanth

CRC Press
Taylor & Francis Group
Boca Raton London New York

CRC Press is an imprint of the
Taylor & Francis Group, an **informa** business

Designed cover image: © Shutterstock

First edition published 2024
by CRC Press
6000 Broken Sound Parkway NW, Suite 300, Boca Raton, FL 33487-2742

and by CRC Press
4 Park Square, Milton Park, Abingdon, Oxon, OX14 4RN

CRC Press is an imprint of Taylor & Francis Group, LLC

© 2024 selection and editorial matter, Meenu Gupta and D. Jude Hemanth; individual chapters, the contributors

ISBN: 978-1-032-45519-8 (hbk)
ISBN: 978-1-032-45752-9 (pbk)
ISBN: 978-1-003-37855-6 (ebk)

DOI: 10.1201/9781003378556

Typeset in Times
by Deanta Global Publishing Services, Chennai, India

Contents

Contributors

Tabrej Ahamad Khan
CSE
Jamia Hamdard
New Delhi, India

Gufran Ahmad Ansari
School of Computer Science, Faculty of
    Science
Dr. Vishwanath Karad MIT World
    Peace University
Pune, India

Naved Alam
ECE
Jamia Hamdard
New Delhi, India

Ritika Arora
CSE
UIET PUSSGRC
Hoshiarpur, Punjab, India

A. Bhardwaj
Department of IPE
Dr B R Ambedkar National Institute of
    Technology
Jalandhar, India

Sharad Chauhan
CSE
Chikitara University Institute of
    Engineering and Technology
Chitjara University
Punjab, India

Arpita Choudhary
Faculty of Pharmaceutical Sciences
Rama University
Kanpur India

Sarika Devi
Quantum School of Health Sciences
Quantum University
Roorkee, India

Hera Fatma
Department of Biotechnology
Dr. Ambedkar Institute of Technology
    for Handicapped
Kanpur, UP, India

A. Gupta
Department of IPE
Dr B R Ambedkar National Institute of
    Technology
Jalandhar, India

Meenu Gupta
CSE
Chandigarh University
Punjab, India

Poonam Joshi
Uttaranchal Institute of Pharmaceutical
    Sciences
Uttaranchal University
Dehradun University

Kalpana Katiyar
Department of Biotechnology
Dr. Ambedkar Institute of Technology
    for Handicapped
Kanpur, UP, India

Harpreet Kaur
CSE
Chandigarh Engineering College
Landran, Mohali, India

Rajdeep Kaur
CSE
Chandigarh University
Punjab, India

Rahul Khurana
CSE
Bharati Vidyapeeth's College of
    Engineering, GGSIPU affiliated
New Delhi, India

Shama Kouser
CSE
Jazan University
Saudi Arabia

R. Kumar
Department of IPE
Dr B R Ambedkar National Institute of
    Technology
Jalandhar, India

Rakesh Kumar
CSE
Chandigarh University
Punjab, India

Umesh Kumar
School of Biosciences
Institute of Management Studies,
    Ghaziabad (University Courses
    Campus)
Ghaziabad, India

S. Lakshmanan
Department of Computer Science and
    Applications
The Gandhigram Rural Institute
    (Deemed to be University)
Dindigul, Tamilnadu, India

M. Mary Shanthi Rani
Department of Computer Science and
    Applications
The Gandhigram Rural Institute
    (Deemed to be University)
Dindigul, Tamilnadu, India

Syed Ali Mehdi
CSE
Jamia Hamdard
New Delhi, India

Rahul Reddy Nadikattu
IT
University of the Cumberlands
USA

P. Nagaraja
Department of Computer Science and
    Applications
The Gandhigram Rural Institute
    (Deemed to be University)
Dindigul, Tamilnadu, India

Nitya Nagpal
CSE
Bharati Vidyapeeth's College of
    Engineering, GGSIPU affiliated
New Delhi, India

Preeti Nagrath
CSE
Bharati Vidyapeeth's College of
    Engineering, GGSIPU affiliated
New Delhi, India

Chaitanya Pandey
CSE
Bharati Vidyapeeth's College of
    Engineering, GGSIPU affiliated
New Delhi, India

C. Prakash
Department of Industrial and
     Production Engineering
Dr. B R Ambedkar National Insititute
     of Technology
Jaladhar, Punjab, India

Arpit Raj
Quantum School of Health Sciences
Quantum University
Roorkee, India

Sapna Rawat
Pharmacy
JBIT College of Pharmacy
Dehradun, Uttarakhand, India

Neeru Saxena
School of Computer Science
Institute of Management Studies,
     Ghaziabad (University Courses
     Campus)
Ghaziabad, India

Surya Saxena
School of Computer Science
Institute of Management Studies,
     Ghaziabad (University Courses
     Campus)
Ghaziabad, Indiia

Salliah Shafi Bhat
Department of Computer Applications
B.S Abdur Rahman Institute of Science
     & Technology
Chennai, India

P. Shanmugavadivu
Department of Computer Science and
     Applications
The Gandhigram Rural Institute
     (Deemed to be University)
Dindigul, Tamilnadu, India

L. P. Singh
Department of Industrial and
     Production Engineering
Dr. B R Ambedkar National Insititute
     of Technology
Jaladhar, Punjab, India

Simran Singh
Department of Biotechnology
Dr. Ambedkar Institute of Technology
     for Handicapped
Kanpur, UP, India

Priti Tagde
Food & Drug Administration
The Madhya Pradesh State Price
     Monitoring Unit
Bhopal, India

Rashmi Vaishnav
School of Computer Science
Institute of Management Studies,
     Ghaziabad (University Courses
     Campus)
Ghaziabad, India

Ajit Kumar Varma
Faculty of Pharmaceutical Sciences
Rama University
Kanpur, India

Pawan Whig
IT
VIPS-TC
New Delhi, India

1 Role of Machine Learning in Women's Health
A Review Analysis

Ritika Arora, Sharad Chauhan and Harpreet Kaur

1.1 INTRODUCTION

Health issues impact human lives. During treatment in hospital, health companies acquire scientific data about affected persons and leverage information from the general population, to determine how to treat that affected person. Data, for this reason, performs an essential position in addressing health problems, and improved records are essential to enhancing patient care. The use of information systems has driven advances in many fields, including computer vision, natural language processing (NLP) and automatic speech reputation (ASR). Such advances have led to the development of effective systems such as self-driving cars, voice-activated private assistants and automated translation). Machine learning (ML) knowledge, which has the capacity to extract records from health data, paired with the centrality of information in healthcare, results in ML research that supports healthcare practices. The development of artificial intelligence (AI) in medicine helps manage the difficulty of managing complex tasks, particularly in the diagnostic or predictive evaluation of clinical statistics. As the generation of healthcare-related statistics expands, greater amounts of scientific clinical data have been collected and could get bigger each year [1]. Diagnostic facts, scientific trial statistics and records on clinical personnel health data collectively form the biggest information database. AI-based technology is capable of devising new algorithms that can be helpful in prognosis and resolving various issues related to health, providing proper treatment of different kinds of diseases and developing new and innovative ideas in medical research, which are resolving issues in women's health.

ML is being employed in medicine, and AI is being used in scientific areas in at least four innovative ways: first, in the managing of patients' health related issues and in predicting treatment fulfilment prior to initiation; second, in trying to manipulate or alleviate headaches; third, in providing help and support to affected persons during their treatment; and fourth, in research aimed towards the pathology or mechanism that is required for ideal treatment of a disease [2].

It has been observed that ML has been utilized in breast imaging when pictures from different mechanisms have been taken, like mammographic, sonographic and

DOI: 10.1201/9781003378556-1

magnetic resonance imaging (MRI), and need to be looked at. Virtual mammography examination with the support of AI are helpful in analysing the task of breast cancer examination and, with the effective use of AI-based decision support systems, is helpful in increasing the overall performance in medical science.

Predictive analysis for osteoporosis has been built that is based on an acclaimed device that uses support vector machine (SVM) algorithms, random forest algorithms, artificial neural network (ANN) and logistic regression. After that, these models have been compared with four traditional scientific evaluation tools: the osteoporosis self-assessment tool, the osteoporosis risk assessment tool, the simple calculated osteoporosis risk estimation and the osteoporosis index of risk.

A comparative analysis based on the performance of various ML and deep learning algorithms in determining the fragility fractures from MRI data was conducted, among different classifiers, random sampling, logistic regression, and the linear discriminants were found to be the best for determining osteoporotic fracture. There are some AI strategies used for managing different types of bone features. The performance based on neuro fuzzy-based systems, SVMs and genetic methods is compared for classifying different types of bone samples. Finally, AI techniques are best at evaluating the bone age of patients suffering from different types of issues [3].

Nowadays, AI-based techniques have been implemented for managing the records from stroke imaging and have been helpful in getting good results. Recently, ML algorithms have been used to find out different types of consequences that are expected in patients suffering from cancer problems. ML use is the first choice for extracting prognostic statistics from mechanically gathered clinical and biochemical records for breast cancer parients [4].

In the recent past, ML algorithms have been used in preventing medicines to expect which patients were at accelerated risk of cardiovascular disorder, colorectal cancer and type 2 diabetes. AI techniques play a critical role in calculating the predicted start time of embryo plantation and the impact of endometriosis on assisted reproductive technologies [5].

1.2   VARIOUS MACHINE LEARNING TECHNIQUES

ML is a branch of computer science that can learn from experience and tell the computer to do that which comes naturally from nature and animals. ML algorithms are based on methods that learn from data instead of predefined equations or models. Various ML techniques are discussed in the sections that follow.

1.2.1   SUPERVISED LEARNING TECHNIQUE

Supervised learning trains a model based upon a well-known input and output to predict future output. Supervised learning makes predictions based on evidence when in the presence of uncertainty. It uses a set of trained input data and a final variable. There are two types of supervised learning techniques to build ML models. These techniques are known as classification and regression.

Classification is based on predicting discrete responses and is used for classifying data. For example, in medical science predicting whether a tumour is cancerous or non-cancerous. In the healthcare industry, a classification technique is used to find out whether a person is suffering from a severe disease or not [6].

Regression is used for predicting continuous responses. If we are required to work on a range of data, then we use regression. For example, if we have data on breast cancer in women from the last ten years, then we use regression. ML mostly uses the regression technique for predicting real-world values.

1.2.2 Unsupervised Learning Technique

Unsupervised learning is used for detecting hidden patterns and detecting internal structures. It works on unlabelled data to find patterns in a particular data set. The clustering of data is based on unsupervised learning. It is used to find hidden data as well as clustering of data [7]. In medical science, if we want to make clusters of diseases based on a similarity parameter, then we use unsupervised learning.

1.2.3 Reinforcement Learning Technique

Reinforcement learning is the science of decision-making. It is a type of ML technique that enables an agent to learn interactively from an environment and takes feedback from its own learning [8]. It learns from its mistakes and corrects itself. The Q-learning technique uses the greedy approach to learn the Q-value, and SARSA uses the action performed by the current policy to learn the Q-value. These two are model-free learning algorithms.

All ML algorithms follow one of the three types of ML techniques as shown in Figure 1.1.

Various popular ML models are used to find solutions with good accuracy. Desired output will be required with any good model so ML techniques are design models that always predict the desired output. The main models based on the

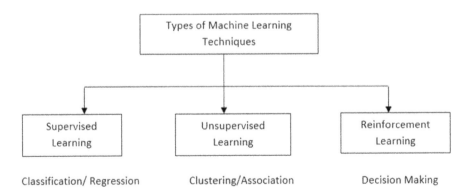

FIGURE 1.1 Various machine learning techniques.

above-mentioned ML techniques are the regression model, the classification model and the clustering model.

Different classification models are k-nearest neighbours (KNN), decision trees, SVMs and neural networks.

Various regression models are linear and non-linear models, stepwise regression, adaptive neuro fuzzy learning and regularization.

Various clustering algorithms are k-means clustering, hierarchical clustering, self-organizing maps and subtractive clustering.

1.3   LITERATURE REVIEW

Mhlanga (2022) discussed the contribution of ML and AI in managing situations in the COVID-19 pandemic. COVID-19 affected the health sector a lot and it shortened life expectancy in developed countries. In their research about the problems raised by COVID-19 in the healthcare sector, the author demonstrates their solutions by using innovative ML methodsand AI. The author has suggested that the government should focus on these technologies for addressing health-related issues and managing goals towards health [9].

Anbu and Sarmah (2017) focused on women's health and predicted health-related issues with the help of ML approaches. In developed countries as well, women are facing various health-related issues, like sexually transmitted infections, unintended pregnancies and other infections. The authors have suggested that some training programmes have been conducted to raise awareness among women in underdeveloped countries. They have suggested ML approaches for classifying women based on their health risk segments. They have used some assessment models for checking the validity of their ML model [10].

Allahem and Sampalli (2022) focused on the detection of premature babies by using ML. The authors have highlighted that the issue of babies born prematurely is present in almost every country. Due to this issue, babies have health-related issues like disabilities and difficulties hearing. The authors have suggested that with ML physicians can check the progress of babies, determine the prematurity in babies in advance and help women in reducing the problems associated with premature birth. Using ML approaches, prematurity can be detected very easily in pregnant women and the authors have tested it with parameters like accuracy and reliability [11].

Doupe et al. (2019) discussed the ML approaches in healthcare that can help researchers in decision-making. The authors have developed an algorithm that can predict outcomes and that contains data selection, preparation, learning and evaluation steps. The authors also undertake a comparative analysis of three ML approaches that can help in predicting the performance of multiple ML methods: decision tree methods, deep learning methods and ensemble methods. This prediction will help decide which patients will be given high priority when being admitted to hospital based on their conditions and seriousness. This estimator developed with the assistance of the ML technique is thus helpful for different researchers and decision-makers [12].

Handing et al. (2022) highlighted the issue of depression in older men and women. People's health is badly affected due to depression, so the authors have suggested an ML method, random forest analysis (RFA), to analyse proactive parameters and risks due to depression in a sample of older people. They have analysed it with the help of a questionnaire. In their findings, they have shown that depression affects a lot of men and women due to their having mobility difficulties. Difficulties carrying out daily activities increase the depression rate also [13].

Kino et al. (2021) highlighted the growth of ML in the computer science field of health and social science. They have shown how ML helps researchers to find new and innovative ways of measuring health outcomes. They worked on social determinants of health (SDH), and ML helps SDH in determining health issues. SDH with the assistance of ML helps manage casual inference, sampling of relevant data and finding out bias in predictions [14].

Zhang and Gou (2022) discussed ML approaches in the health sector for analysing mental health problems in older people. They have highlighted risk factors associated with depression and how ML algorithms can help in identifying risk factors associated with depression. If these risk factors are identified properly, then this will be helpful in the treatment of depression. In their study, they concluded that in the absence of proper support, health issues and mobility are the key features found among older people with depression. ML models can find patterns and relationships in data which helps determine risk factors associated with depression [15].

1.4 ROLE OF MACHINE LEARNING AND THE INTERNET OF MEDICAL THINGS IN HEALTHCARE

ML knowledge of fitness care relies on an ever-evolving patient information set. This data set is used to locate various patterns that are used by doctors and specialists to find new illnesses, risk factor selection among patients and remedy outcomes. Because of an increase in patients and the numerous clinical technologies for managing records, having healthcare devices synchronized from a principal "network" is considered a handy way to manage a large number of records.

The Internet of Medical Things (IoMT) acts as a community of the Iinternet of Things (IoT)-enabled smart gadgets and packages which can speak with other devices with the help of internet services. There are already many scientific gadgets which can exchange information with the help of Wi-Fi and talk with other devices with the help of cloud platforms. Using this facility, it can be possible to manage and monitor clinical histories, remote patient monitoring, monitoring clinical histories, getting useful information from wearable gadgets, etc. Due to the change in time and growth in medical science, new smart wearable devices will be developed, which can amplify the power of IoMT exponentially.

1.4.1 CATEGORIES OF AI USED IN THE HEALTHCARE SECTOR

In recent times, AI technologies have developed particularly fast in the field of healthcare. In the healthcare sector, the operation of smart gadgets cannot be imagined without AI techniques. All fitness gadgets used by people are enabled by AI techniques. AI is used to manage the clinical data containing healthcare records and to streamline the data taken from smart gadgets for extracting useful information. This information is useful to assist physicians in making suitable decisions which are beneficial to patients.

In resolving the above-mentioned issues, various AI terms are used.

1.4.1.1 Neural Networks

Neural networks are described as a collection of algorithms that obtain knowledge in a way that mimics the human brain. They are also known as ANNs. They can also be considered as a series of neurons that works like our brain and are used for collecting and processing data. They have three layers, including an input layer, more than one hidden layer and one output layer. They can help diagnose diseases and manage fitness records and smart gadgets which are helpful in healthcare.

In healthcare, ML and deep learning help manage MRI and other clinical photos coming from different sources. ANNs demonstrate that the process of getting to know how analysing data in the form of large records is helpful. Deep neural networks (DNNs) help scan and diagnose various types of cancers, fractures and different other diseases.

1.4.1.2 Natural Language Processing

NLP is a computer's ability to understand the text and speech of a human being. In the healthcare sector, NLP is used to help in searching, analysing and interpreting a patient's data. With the help of NLP, we can understand the data generated by smart gadgets and manage the electronic health records of patients. Based on this data doctors and surgeons can make useful decisions related to patients' health.

1.4.1.3 Physical Robots

These types of devices are helpful in complex surgeries which are not feasible manually. In recent times, it has been observed that this robot surgery will efficiently reduce human effort and manage surgery effectively. This can aid surgeons during complex methods that require unique actions. It reduces the complications occurred during manual surgery and increases the overall performance of the system.

1.5   USE OF MACHINE LEARNING IN WOMEN'S DISEASE DETECTION AND PREDICTION

Different gadgets for gaining knowledge of approaches were used to discover a disease in its early stages. If diseases are not discovered in early stages then it would be difficult to deal with these diseases in later stages[16]. As a result of these procedures, it can be easier to detect certain kinds of sickness. However, numerous accuracy tiers rely on factors, such as the used set of rules, functions and data used. Together with the significance of diagnosing an ailment at an early stage, the ML knowledge of algorithms to diagnose diseases and the functions that are considered to make preventions from diseases.

1.5.1 CANCER

In the human body, there is a proper count of several cells of every type. If there is an abrupt modification in cell structure in our body, then it causes medical issues and cancer begins as a result. In human beings, if there is no proper development and control of cells, different kinds of signals are generated that order cells. These alert signals will be very useful as they will become defective and then these cells multiply themselves and create a lump referred to as a tumour. To remove these lumps, thermography is a reliable treatment most of the time and is non-invasive and non-ionizing. Recent advancements in thermography have resulted in a more sustainable technique that produces higher quality results, making it more effective than other technology [17]. With the help of these thermographic pictures and the use of function extraction strategies and AI techniques, the presence of cancer cells can be detected easily. There are two strategies, the scale invariant function remodel (SIFT) strategy and the sped-up robust function (SURF) strategy, applied to extract capabilities from images. By using fundamental principal component analysis (PCA), higher interpretations can be taken as it has extra features that allow one to do so [18].

1.5.1.1 Breast Cancer

Breast cancer is a kind of cancer that is often found in women and it affects the health of many women and may lead to loss of life. As technology advances, this kind of cancer can be removed by early detection of these harmful cells through biopsy, ultrasound, mammography and MRI. Using technology, breast cancer is detected by classifying the tumour. These tumours are of two types: benign and malignant. Studies have shown that malignant tumours are more difficult to treat and more harmful than benign tumours. Technology advances day by day, yet it is not easier for physicians to differentiate between these two types of tumours. Our gadgets are more capable of detecting tumour types automatically by using algorithms and enhancing their learning and experiences without being explicitly programmed to do so.

In the past few years, several different ML techniques have been developed for the early detection and prevention of breast cancer and its different types. Detection of breast cancer has three stages: pre-processing, extraction and classification. The feature extraction process is crucial as it assesses the tumour type, whether it is benign or malignant. After this, segmentation is used for extracting pictures capturing the smoothness, intensity and regularity of the tumour [19].

After that, photos are taken and then converted into binary form from which it is very easy to extract beneficial data. It has been observed that converting images into binary form will result in the loss of important features that contain important details. To avoid this, images are stored in greyscale format. Thereafter, with the help of discrete wavelet transformation (DWT), these snapshots are converted from the time to the frequency domain. Based on these values, the machine gets to know algorithms.

1.5.1.2 Lung Cancer

In medical science, it has been observed that lung cancer can affect the windpipe, fundamental airways or lungs. It mostly affects patients with emphysema and previous chest troubles and these patients have a greater chance of developing lung cancer. People who have the habit of chewing tobacco or smoking have the highest probability of developing lung cancer. Air pollution can also be considered another hazard factor for developing it. In the first stage, the cancer starts inside the lungs and then in the second stage, it spreads to different organs of the body. Lung cancer carries the greatest risk of not being diagnosed until the disease spreads to different organs of the body.

For the detection of lung cancer, computerized tomography (CT) reports are more effective than other reports as they are less noisy. These CT reports use greyscale conversion which has less noise. They also use binarization and segmentation strategies which can scan the required shape with less noise. For converting scans into the greyscale format, the average RGB colour format is considered. Segmentation gets rid of needless information from the scans. At feature extraction level, capabilities including region, perimeter and eccentricity are taken into consideration.

A different type of lung cancer is small cell lung cancer (SCLC), but detection of this kind of cancer in the human body is extraordinarily difficult. Here, AI algorithms together with convolution neural networks (CNNs), and primarily ML techniques will be used for detecting SCLC in the human body. But a large data set is required for deep learning algorithms. This is problematic because a large data set is not available. The entropy degradation approach (EDM) may be used to detect SCLC. High-resolution lung CT scans are required for a large data set. EDM incorporates the idea of a shallow neural community in which vectorized histograms are used to detect lung cancer. Then, it uses logistic features for rating transformation. By using this method, SCLC detection in the human body is easier as it is considered a binomial problem, containing two distributions: lung cancer patients as well as healthy people. So, to start with, check that both groups have been provided with the facts. This technique is accurate within reason, however, it currently doesn't provide high-quality results, and a an improvement is required in this area. While this method may be endorsed it would be improved upon by providing a larger schooling set and a deeper community. This shows that, by using CNNs with image processing, lung cancer may be better detected as CNNs are mostly used on CT scan images.

1.5.2 Acute Lymphoblastic Leukaemia

There is one form that is present in almost all cancers, as different types of immature acute lymphocyte blood cells expand and they have an effect on the development of various kinds of blood cells [20]. This type of form is known as acute lymphoblastic leukaemia (ALL). It can spread very fast from week to week or within a given month. There are various symptoms which help in identifying ALL in patients, like the pale colour of pores and skin, feeling very tired, enlargement of lymph nodes and joint pain. ML techniques are used for detecting leukaemia using microscopic images and managing regular monitoring.

For managing leukaemia detection, different ML algorithms are used. Some of these algorithms are KNN, SVM, radial basis function network (RBFN) and multilayer perceptron (MLP). All these algorithms have four stages: pre-processing, feature extraction, classification version construction and evaluation of the classifier.

1.5.3 DIABETES

Diabetes can be considered as a continual type of health problem, and to be managed it must be diagnosed in its early stages and treated with the proper medicine. Diabetes can be due to a high sugar ratio in the blood. Patients with diabetes face different kinds of difficulties. If diabetes is not handled properly then it could lead to many other diseases. Diabetes may be categorized into three kinds: type 1, type 2 and gestational diabetes.

One multivariate technique known as discriminant analysis (DA) is used to label an input that is decided by a chain of differential equations which can be acquired by way of input features. Normally, DA uses feasible objectives that are helpful in locating an associated equation which uses different test samples, and is helpful in solving predictive equations, which is further helpful in understanding the relationship among different features. During pregnancy, some functions are used for classification: glucose awareness, the ratio of sugar level in the blood, diabetes pedigree function (DPF), skin thickening and the affected person's age.

Using ML knowledge of algorithms including Gaussian naive Bayes (GNB), LR, KFLR-means nearest neighbours, CART, RFA and SVM are helpful in predicting diabetes. These include the serum-glucose 1 and serum-glucose 2 stages which help predict type 2 diabetes. In the recent past, different ML approaches have been developed to improve the accuracy of the prediction of diabetes. A backpropagation algorithm is also used to gain knowledge on the prediction of diabetes. This method has various functions that are beneficial for the detection of problems during pregnancies, serum insulin, BMI and DPF and it has principal functions which are considered when monitoring plasma-glucose levels. It has been proved that the help of neural network level of prediction provides more accurate results as compared with other ML algorithms. In the recent past, more development has been achieved in the usage of DNNs for predicting diabetes by training DNNs with fivefold and tenfold validation methods. All the approaches used with the help of neural networks and ML algorithms have shown an accuracy level of approximately 97% in monitoring sugar levels in diabetic patients.

1.5.4 HEART DISEASES

Heart diseases are very common these days due to poor food quality, as there is an excess amount of chemicals mixed into food products. Heart diseases are caused due to high blood pressure and high cholesterol, diabetes, and smoking etc.which might result in blockages within the heart arteries. This kind of chronic coronary heart disease creates an upward push of plaque in the coronary arteries. At first, it develops slowly but it then leads to a coronary heart attack [21]. As a result, there are some symptoms, like peculiar glucose metabolism, extreme blood pressure, dyslipidaemia, etc. Some other causes of heart disease are identified as smoking, loss of physical fitness, age, etc. Some other major symptoms of a heart ailment are problems breathing, weakness in the body, problems in the feet, fatigue, etc. In recent years, the sector of cardiology has used precision medicines, as well as therapeutics in various forms to treat diagnoses. Recently, interventional cardiology has been used to correct heart rhythms and issues which cause cardiovascular diseases. There has also been a lot of work in genomics. These issues were resolved with the help of precision medicine and drug development in the field of cardiology. As technology advances in healthcare informatics, there are more offerings to treat patients suffering from heart disease, such as clinical decision support systems (CDSSs). Developments in devices make them capable enough to know how complex problems can be solved with the help of machines and how feasible solutions can be provided to patients. By integrating these latest technologies in precision medicine and drug development, the CDSS can make complicated clinical selections, understand more about recognizing modern phenotypes and make plans for individual-orientated specialized remedy options [22].

In medical science, blood tests are considered a popular investigation strategy in precision medicine. Advanced glycation end products (AGEs) is considered one of the precision medications other than blood tests that are used to avoid ischemic coronary heart ailment. In recent years, numerous new developments have been made to find the genetic causes of an ailment. In precision cardiology, some main issues that need to be considered are cardiac genetics, cardiac oncology and ischemic heart sickness. There are different methods used for diagnostic and healing purposes in cardiology, including blood sample tests, genetics tests, picture exams or a mixture of these. It has also been observed that some cardiovascular sicknesses are due to genetics. So, to manage it, solutions using precision medication are taken into consideration with extra efficient techniques. CNN, recurrent neural network (RNN), SVM, long short-term memory (LSTM), and deep learning are considered as some strategies which will work efficiently in cardiology sciences.

For diagnosing cardiologic illness, some new technologies are used which consist of different steps, including pre-processing, characteristic selection, selecting valid moves, ML-based classifiers and performance evaluation of classifier. Several preprocessing techniques are mainly used for finding missing values, scalar values and min–max scalar. In this model, a selection of features should be considered as a critical factor because the performance of ML algorithms depends upon it and inappropriate feature selection degrade the performance of the system. Proper selection of features will improve the accuracy of the system and reduce processing time.

1.5.5 CHRONIC KIDNEY DISEASE

Chronic kidney disease (CKD) is considered a kidney issue in which the kidney does not function properly, leading to kidney failure. It is a kind of kidney disorder which continuously creates problems for the kidney and affects its functionality. CDK can be recognized using clinical records, lab examination, image consideration, biopsy, etc. It has been observed that biopsies have a few negative aspects, which include being invasive, expensive, time-consuming and on occasion volatile. Here ML can be applied to conquer the above-mentioned dangers. On some occasions, for sickness predictions, ML can be replaced with SVM as a commonly used classifier. But research has shown that SVM is rarely used for classification in the case of CKD. Various classifiers used in this domain are artificial neural networks, decision trees and logistic regression. Also, it has been observed that artificial neural networks have performed well and perform better when compared to other classifiers.

1.5.6 PARKINSON'S DISEASE

Parkinson's disease (PD) is a type of chronic disease that has progressive movement ailments. The main cause of this disease is a decreased development of dopamine in the body, which is a type of chemical that basically controls movement and proper coordination of the body. The main symptoms of this disease are tremors, tension, slowness of motion and postural instability. Also, a significant symptom of this sickness is abnormal writhing. Various researchers of PD have observed that ML-based techniques can help treat this type of disease and treat patients. Some researchers have made extensive use of voice samples in their research. These samples have proved helpful in differentiating healthful controls in patients suffering from this disease. PD can be considered a type of neurodegenerative disorder which directly affects the mind's cells, with changes in patients' speaking ability and different cognitive elements.

PCA and genetic algorithms (GAs) can be used to obtain the desired function set for this category. From research it has been shown that GAs are derived from Darwin's principle where every variable is taken as a gene and chromosomes are considered as a collection of genes. On these chromosomes, a built-in function is applied and excessive-appearing chromosomes can be used to create offspring. Various functions used to create offspring include mutation and crossover. In this process, the fittest chromosomes will live to tell the tale until they give up. For this concept, GAs will help by providing feature extraction. PCA is a statistical technique and an unsupervised linear conversion approach which is applied to get new styles in high-dimensional statistics.

1.5.7 DERMATOLOGICAL DISEASES

Dermatological diseases are complicated and consist of a large range of features. For proper treatment of these diseases, it is preferred that these are detected at an early stage; otherwise, they will be difficult to manage. Different types include eczema, herpes, cancer and psoriasis. If these dermatological diseases are identified at the start, then people's lives can be saved.

To diagnose these types of diseases, related statistical data is first collected and statistics are augmented for the use of photographs. After that, a model is designed and educated. Finally, the picture is converted into an array of sequences and the educated model is broken down based on its features. It uses the diverse augmentation technique known as the synthetic minority oversampling technique (SMOTE), including greyscaling, growing assessment, converting the colour channel, sharpening, removing the noise and at last smoothing. If provided training with the convolutional neural network over a large data set, then the problem of overfitting occurs. For prediction, an SVM classifier is used. The capabilities in the very last layer may be immediately given to the SVM. It requires some skilled function from the final and last convolution layer for the data set for converting the data set into vector form for saving it in the data set.

1.6   MACHINE LEARNING APPLICATION IN HEALTHCARE

Application of machine learning in healthcare are presented in Figure 1.2 and discussed in detail below.

1.6.1   Use of Machine Learning in Medical Imaging

For diagnosing diseases and sicknesses, medical imaging can be considered an important technique. When recognizing images, the use of devices involves various steps. Once a picture is given as input, it will be segmented into different parts. Thereafter, by using information retrieval techniques, functions may be taken from specified areas. Specified features are then determined after the removal of noise from the image. Finally, the classifier will be used to classify the facts taken from specified areas and to make predictions based on these facts. In the recent past, as medical science has grown, the correct evaluation of an ailment required processing huge portions of clinical statistics. In the field of medication and medical sciences, there are various diseases and sickness which are probably being treated with the help of ML algorithms. Also, in this field, records are distributed based on their developments, examining medical

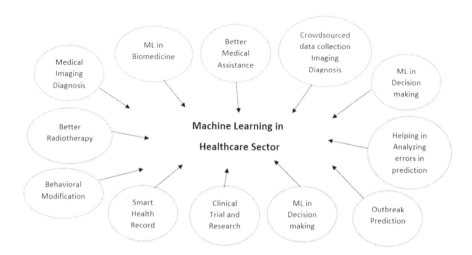

FIGURE 1.2   Role of machine learning in the healthcare sector.

information, sickness prognosis, remedy planning, collection and inspection of records. Thereafter, clinical imaging is used for correcting diagnostics of different illnesses and after extracting proper skillsets, the medical images are implemented [23].

1.6.2 Machine Learning in Biomedicine

Nowadays, devices are being implemented with the help of ubiquitous computing and vital statistics help to solve complicated problems. In biomedicine, ML techniques are used for different purposes collectively to extract features based on protein structure, features from genetic sequences, determining gold preferred diets for patients, medical microbiome profiles, etc. ML is collectively used for processing real-time, excessive-resolution physiological facts in numerous health-related fields. The study of systems in the biomedical field has specifically identified three main processes: (1) systems will be able to improve diagnosis, (2) devices will learn how to reduce the work of researchers, doctors and people involved in the healthcare sector. Normally, these doctors will interpret digital images by using ML algorithms and those images will be given as input, which will bring new development and predictions provided through the set of rules [24]. (3) The system will progress successfully by minimizing errors and improving the accuracy of the system.

1.6.3 Machine Learning in Medical Assistance

The healthcare industry is an important enterprise that provides care to millions of citizens; at the same time, it contributes to the nearby economic system. AI is helping the healthcare enterprise in numerous ways. The information era is revolutionizing the healthcare enterprise by providing a supporting hand. This involves key responsibilities like decision-making, fixing complex issues, object detection and many more activities involved in this field. The benefits of technologies, inclusive of the extended stage of accuracy and excessive level of computation, which takes days for people to solve manually, are being implemented in the healthcare commercial enterprise.

1.6.4 Machine Learning in Decision-making

It has been observed that AI has played a vital role in decision-making in the field of healthcare. An effective use case of AI in decision-making is shown using surgical robots which can be helpful in surgeries. These robots have helped doctors lower error rates and can increase the overall performance of systems by providing suitable assistance promptly. It has been shown that these techniques are helpful in complicated surgical procedures by providing higher flexibility and control compared to other techniques.

1.6.5 Help Analysing Errors in Prescriptions

ML () knowledge can also be useful in analysing the errors in prescriptions. This knowledge will be helpful in inspecting the health records of patients and discovering mistakes in the drugs given to patients.[25].

1.6.6 Machine Learning Primarily Based on Behavioural Modification

It has been found in medical science that behavioural modification plays an important role in preventive medicine. In the healthcare industry, several start-ups are cropping up which identify preventive cancers and other diseases. Somatix is a B2B2C primarily based data analytics agency which is using ML techniques to understand gestures in our daily life and identify the critical changes and unconscious conduct based on these gestures.

1.6.7 Smart Health Records

ML is also helpful in maintaining health and fitness records. In daily life, things are changing very fast so it's not as easy to maintain fitness records without the use of smart gadgets, which can manage all the health records of patients in real time. The predominant tools used when studying healthcare are vector machines, ML-based optical character recognition (OCR) techniques and Google's Cloud Vision API.

1.6.8 Clinical Trial and Research

It has been proven that ML is a popular technique used in medical and clinical trials. As anyone involved in the pharma industry would tell you, medical trials are costly and time-consuming. In medical trials, candidates can assist researchers in drawing a pool from huge records, including preceding physician visits and social media by applying ML-based predictive analytics. ML has been utilized to ensure real-time monitoring and statistics to lessen fact-based errors.

1.6.9 Crowdsourced Data Collection

In recent times, crowdsourcing is all the rage in medical science, allowing researchers and practitioners to get proper entry to a vast number of facts uploaded through humans with their very consent. IBM recently partnered with Medtronic to decipher, gather and make available diabetes data in real time, primarily focused on a crowdsourced data set. With upgrades being made in IoT, the healthcare enterprise continues to be coming across new strategies to assist with the development of analysis and medicine.

1.6.10 Better Radiotherapy

ML can also help with radiology problems. Medical imaging analysis has many discrete variables which could arise at any time. It has been found that many lesions and most cancers' foci cannot be virtually modelled with the usage of complex equations. In the past few years, ML-based algorithms have been able to examine a multitude of various samples, making it less complex to diagnose and discover variables. Clinical assessment is considered one of the most renowned uses of system studying which trains the class of objects together which is helpful in everyday life.

1.6.11 OUTBREAK PREDICTION

Artificial neural networks assist in collecting data and can predict a large range of outbreaks, from malaria to excessive chronic infectious illnesses. Predicting these outbreaks is specifically useful in Global international locations as they lack critical medical infrastructure and academic systems. One of the most useful examples of this network is ProMED-mail, a completely Internet-based reporting platform which provides video demonstrations of diseases as they evolve and suggestions for dealing with these outbreaks in real time [26].

1.7 VARIOUS APPROACHES IN PREDICTING WOMEN'S DISEASES BY MACHINE LEARNING

1.7.1 PREDICTING WOMEN'S HEALTH FROM THEIR SOCIO-ECONOMIC FAME: A GADGET GETTING TO KNOW TECHNIQUE

Socio-economic status (SES) is measured by the social determinants of fitness, determining the likes of women's height, which can be considered as an important parameter of human welfare at various levels using regression techniques. This analysis will be based on different ML algorithms containing various characteristic instructions and their predictive patterns will be assessed via ordinary least squares regression (OLS) [27].

As countries grow economically and population increases, a methodology associated with fitness is recommended, relating to access to especially nutritious food, improved fitness facilities and additional sanitation facilities.

1.7.2 AUTOMATED LABOUR DETECTION MODEL TO DISPLAY PREGNANT WOMEN WITH A HIGH RISK OF PREMATURE LABOUR USING ML TECHNIQUES

Based on an international survey [28], it has been predicted that greater than 0.1% of newborn babies are born early or prematurely. Due to prematurity, newborn babies may suffer from several diseases. Some of them can face lifelong fitness-associated disabilities. If proper monitoring were in place, then physicians could observe the fitness and development of babies and predict whether a pregnant woman is in labour or not, then provide her with proper health facilities, helping to minimize the difficulties faced by pregnant women with premature babies. Different kinds of health issues can be caused by the premature delivery of a foetus. It has been observed that premature delivery can lead to several unusual causes of death for neonates, despite modern-day advanced fitness care technology [28].

Moreover, there are 15 million untimely births yearly worldwide, representing 9.6–11% of all newly born children. Prematurity can be defined as birth before the end of the 37th week of gestation. According to studies, children born prematurely are not usually completely advanced, which could result in severe prenatal health-related issues. For example, because of premature birth, babies can suffer lifelong disabilities, like vision loss or cognitive disabilities. Due to prematurity, babies can also have growth and fitness issues [29]. Other health troubles can include breathing, cardiovascular and neuro-developmental impairments.

1.7.2.1 Various Causes and Suggestions for Premature Births

It has been observed that it's very tough to determine whether a delivery is untimely or not. We can say that it can arise spontaneously for different reasons, and the cause is also generally unidentified. But for a pregnant woman, it can be very difficult to identify and manage a premature birth if there are no medical records available for the same kind of problems.

1.7.2.2 Early Detection and Prevention of Premature Birth

A survey [29] showed that living in rural areas that are far away from hospitals can be the cause of late treatment. This would be a reason that early delivery is difficult to prevent, creating issues related to untimely births for both the foetus and the mother. To avoid premature births and decrease their effects, it is better to understand this difficulty. It has been found that untimely delivery troubles are arising, due to premature birth, which are not identified at early stages of treatment. It has been observed that early detection of labour will help offer better treatment facilities and ensure the proper birth and care of a child. Premature or untimely birth may be detected by tracking the signs and symptoms of early labour according to biochemical and physical signals observed in pregnant women. It has been observed that early detection of prematurity would help decrease issues that arise at later stages and mitigate the health dangers for both the mother and new-born child. We have analysed a method to automatically discover signals with the use of ML techniques.

The main issues of untimely birth are timely detection and prediction of prematurity in women. It can also be suggested that there should be a gadget that constantly detects the uterine contractions of the expectant and detects when she is in labour. Early detection of untimely labour would offer doctors and physicians the opportunity to reduce premature birth effects. We must highlight that the use of ML and DL (deep learing) processes is not limited by the constraints that arose in previous studies of these techniques and thus the reliability and accuracy parameters are enhanced. Here, we have predicted that premature birth is a universal problem for mothers of newborn children and that the health problems that arise as a result will affect their lifestyle. Furthermore, there may be no ultimate answer or therapy for untimely birth because the cause is generally unknown. There is a model that involves proper monitoring of pregnant women who have an excessive danger of untimely birth by using a Wi-Fi frame sensor and cell phone. The designed framework will be effective as it is non-stop, domestic-secure, value-effective and dependable. This model aims to discover labour by using effective ML and DL techniques and a notification will be sent to warn the pregnant woman when uterine Evaluation Health Group (EHG) contractions are detected.

1.7.3 Characterization of COVID-19- Effects and Challenges for Pregnant Women

In the past few years, the novel COVID-19 pandemic remains uncontrollable in all countries. It has been found that due to changes in physiology and immunology associated with respiration in pregnant women, the population is extra defenceless to coronavirus [30]. Recent research has shown that angiotensin-converting enzyme 2 (ACE2), which is related to immaturity inside the placenta, leave women at risk of this ailment, especially in the early months of pregnancy. Advanced tests are implemented in research centres to quickly and correctly diagnose a COVID-19-affected person. Basically, these tests, which are developed by medical experts and specialists, detect deoxyribonucleic acid (DNA) amplification and antibodies, which is probably ambiguous for the general network [31].

In the recent past, several accessible diagnostic exams are conducted for COVID-19, but out of these, there are four techniques we depend on in particular: (1) reverse transcription-polymerase chain reaction (RT-PCR), considered a cutting-edge widespread test, (2) loop-mediated isothermal amplification (LAMP), considered as a simple technique, (3) lateral flow assay and (4) enzyme-linked immunosorbent assay (ELISA) [32].

Nowadays, transmission or attenuated total reflectance (ATR) and Fourier transform infrared spectroscopy (FT-IR) is considered a brand new detection approach for coronavirus illness, infections found in the blood, infected cells, or distinct infections, both bacterial or viral, that are primarily detected in blood records. It has been found that with the help of infrared radiation (IR) spectra, bacterial and viral infections are recorded that are due to molecular and chemical changes in the blood. The FTIR spectrum helps identify COVID-19 in pregnant women. It works by seeing the qualitative changes within the different areas similar to lipids from the blood gathered from patients [19].

1.7.4 Identifying Appendicular Skeletal Muscle Mass for Older Women Using a Machine Learning Approach

Appendicular skeletal muscle mass (ASM) in women between 60 and 70 years is determined with an anthropometric equation which is based totally on the least absolute shrinkage and selection operator (LASSO) regression, which is based on a technique developed from ML [33]. Studies have evaluated ASM via bioelectrical impedance evaluation as a reference. There are some parameters like weight, peak, Body Mass Index (BMI), sitting peak, waist-to-hip ratio (WHR), calf circumference (CC) and five precise measures of limb length which have been added as candidate predictors. LASSO regression is used in machine learning for a selection of subset of variables , and a couple of linear regressions which have been implemented to expand the Bioelctrical impedance analysis (BIA)-measured ASM prediction equation.

It has been observed that the required equation for 60- and 70-year-old women belongs to a size of ASM group which cannot be equipped with BIA, thus early screening of sarcopenia is recommended.

1.8   CONCLUSION

ML can be defined as a versatile, powerful tool which is used by doctors, scientists and researchers. With every new piece of research, a brand new ML software emerges which could prove to be a remedy in healthcare. Improvement in the area of ML is constantly developing, and the clinical business enterprise is keeping a close eye on this development. ML discoveries are helping doctors and physicians to save valuable lives and to predict sicknesses before they arise, which helps to better handle patient care, render patients' recovery process more efficient and much more. Across the world, AI and ML models are developing more and more, which can help improve the healthcare industry. In the recent past, technology has allowed corporations and drug developers to broaden their provision of treatments for vital ailments by making them quicker and more efficient. Different industries can now use developed methods and technologies for their digital medical trials, sequencing and identifying patterns. For enhancing normal fitness, healthcare businesses and medical industries understand that they need to consider the complete person, consisting of their lifestyle and environment. These models, which are based on ML techniques, can identify patients with a high likelihood of developing persistent diseases like heart diseases, diabetes, chronic diseases and many others. It can be found that ML-based technologies are very helpful in predicting women's diseases at an early stage, which will help treat them early and prevent women from serious problems at later stages.

1.9   FUTURE SCOPE

As the growth of smart medical gadgets is not unusual, smart healthcare is turning into a reality. Nowadays, due to innovations, new technologies are developing very fast in the healthcare sector, and the destiny of ML in medical science is promising. This field is capable of handling hundreds of different kinds of records, efficiently watching out for risks and effects and avoiding various problems and issues in healthcare. It can custom-design for human beings each with varying requirements. This ML tool along with AI-based technology helps improve medicinal drug treatment. ML enables modern problem-solving and predicts future difficulties. At some stage, this technology will help predict all difficulties in the healthcare sector.

Doctors and scientists can gather a huge pool of records from the internet, real-time data updates from different social media and exclusive resources in day-to-day life. The advent of new tools allows for the possibility to verify known facts and predict everything from illness outbreaks to critical infectious sicknesses. The effectiveness of ML lies in the useful systems produced in the biomedical field. ML is a crucial innovation in healthcare and biomedical research. Its utility has grown significantly, as it considers data on a very large scale to produce accurate findings and provides additional knowledge to researchers in this field. ML and deep learning are considered effective approaches for epidemiological studies; this field of research is also consolidating the idea of drug prediction. When these options examine men or women's health concerns, they often gain success. This and its predictive analytics, which can play a crucial function in medical studies, will be the main reasons to use ML. Doctors and scientists involved in medical science can pick out from a constrained operating environment or find the level of risk to the life of patients and genetic records. ML suggests that a technologies-based environment will generate different therapy options and predict future useful resources based on an affected person's clinical history. Furthermore, scientific faculties must explore incorporating coursework on ML and its packages in their curriculum. AI, ML and statistics technology should be taught to scientific college students, medical students and fellows for the duration of their education. Innovations in the fields of ML and deep learning will also help predict and manage women's health issues in the future. This area will remain open for new technologies based on ML, which are more helpful in managing women's health issues more efficiently and productively.

REFERENCES

1. G. Winter, "Machine Learning in Healthcare," *Br. J. Heal. Care Manag.*, vol. 25, no. 2, pp. 100–101, 2019, doi: 978-1-5386-0965-1/18.
2. M. A. J. K. Shailaja and B. Seetharamulu, "Machine Learning in Healthcare: A Review," in *Proceedings of the 2nd International Conference on Electronics, Communication and Aerospace Technology (ICECA 2018) IEEE Conference Record # 42487; IEEE Xplore ISBN:978-1-5386-0965-1*, 2018, no. 2, pp. 910–914.
3. S. A. Sharad Chauhan and K. Pahwa, "Telemedical and Remote Healthcare Monitoring using IoT and Machine Learning," in *Computational Intelligence in Healthcare Application, Challenges, and Management*, CRC Press, Taylor and Francis Group, Boca Raton, London, New York, 2023, p. 20.
4. S. Chauhan, R. Arora, and N. Arora, "Researcher Issues and Future Directions in Healthcare Using IoT and Machine Learning," in *Smart Healthcare Monitoring Using IoT with 5G*, Ist., G. C. Meenu Gupta and V. H. C. de Albuquerque, Eds. CRC Press, Taylor and Francis Group, Boca Raton, London, New York, 2021, pp. 177–196.
5. K. Pahwa and S. Chauhan, "Big Data and Machine Learning in Healthcare: Tools Challenges," in *Proc. −2021 3rd Int. Conf. Adv. Comput. Commun. Control Networking, ICAC3N 2021*, 2021, pp. 326–330, doi: 10.1109/ICAC3N53548.2021.9725714.
6. JASON, "Artificial Intelligence for Health and Health Care," *MITRE Corp.*, vol. 7508, no. December, 2017, p. 65, [Online]. Available: https://www.healthit.gov/sites/default / files/jsr-17-task-002_aiforhealthandhealthcare12122017.pdf.
7. E. Sharad, N. Kaur, and I. K. Aulakh, "Evaluation and Implementation of Cluster Head Selection in WSN using Contiki/Cooja Simulator," *J. Stat. Manag. Syst.*, vol. 23, no. 2, pp. 407–418, 2020, doi: 10.1080/09720510.2020.1736324.
8. G. H. Jeong, "Artificial Intelligence, Machine Learning, and Deep Learning in Women's Health Nursing," *Korean J. Women Heal. Nurs.*, vol. 26, no. 1, pp. 5–9, 2020, doi: 10.4069/kjwhn.2020.03.11.
9. D. Mhlanga, "The Role of Artificial Intelligence and Machine Learning Amid the COVID-19 Pandemic: What Lessons Are We Learning on 4IR and the Sustainable Development Goals," *Int. J. Environ. Res. Public Health*, vol. 19, p. 1879, 2022, doi: https://doi.org/10.3390/ijerph19031879.
10. S. Anbu, "Machine Learning Approach for Predicting Women's Health Risk," in *Int. Conf. Adv. Comput. Commun. Syst. (ICACCS −2017)*, 2017, pp. 4–7.

11. H. Allahem and S. Sampalli, "Informatics in Medicine Unlocked Automated Labour Detection Framework to Monitor Pregnant Women with a High Risk of Premature Labour Using Machine Learning and Deep Learning," *Informatics Med. Unlocked*, vol. 28, p. 100771, 2022, doi: 10.1016/j.imu.2021.100771.

12. P. Doupe, J. Faghmous, and S. Basu, "Machine Learning for Health Services Researchers," *Value Heal.*, vol. 22, no. 7, pp. 808–815, 2019, doi: 10.1016/j.jval.2019.02.012.

13. E. P. Handing, C. Strobl, Y. Jiao, L. Feliciano, and S. Aichele, "Articles Predictors of Depression among Middle-aged and Older Men and Women in Europe: A Machine Learning Approach,"*The Lancet Regional*, vol. 18, pp. 1–11, 2022, doi: 10.1016/j.lanepe.2022.100391.

14. S. Kino *et al.*, "SSM – Population Health A Scoping Review on the Use of Machine Learning in Research on Social Determinants of Health: Trends and Research Prospects," *SSM - Popul. Heal.*, vol. 15, p. 100836, 2021, doi: 10.1016/j.ssmph.2021.100836.

15. F. Zhang and J. Gou, "Comment Machine Learning Assessment of Risk Factors for Depression in Later Adulthood," *The Lancet Regional*, vol. 18, no. May, pp. 1–2, 2022, doi: 10.1016/j.lanepe.2022.100399.

16. M. Javaid, A. Haleem, R. Pratap Singh, R. Suman, and S. Rab, "Significance of Machine Learning in Healthcare: Features, Pillars and Applications," *Int. J. Intell. Networks*, vol. 3, no. May, pp. 58–73, 2022, doi: 10.1016/j.ijin.2022.05.002.

17. Z. Rayan, M. Alfonse, and A. B. M. Salem, "Machine Learning Approaches in Smart Health," *Procedia Comput. Sci.*, vol. 154, no. 1985, pp. 361–368, 2018, doi: 10.1016/j.procs.2019.06.052.

18. N. K. Sekhon and G. Singh, "Hybrid Technique for Human Activities and Actions Recognition Using PCA, Voting, and K-means," in *Lecture Notes in Networks and Systems*, 2023, pp. 351–363.

19. M. Idrees and A. Sohail, "Explainable Machine Learning of the Breast Cancer Staging for Designing Smart Biomarker Sensors," *Sensors Int.*, vol. 3, no. September, p. 100202, 2022, doi: 10.1016/j.sintl.2022.100202.

20. E. P. Handing, C. Strobl, Y. Jiao, L. Feliciano, and S. Aichele, "Predictors of Depression among Middle-aged and Older Men and Women in Europe: A Machine Learning Approach," *Lancet Reg. Heal. - Eur.*, vol. 18, pp. 1–11, 2022, doi: 10.1016/j.lanepe.2022.100391.

21. P. Lakshmi and M. Lalli, "A Review And Analysis Of The Role Of Machine Learning Techniques To Predict Health Risks Among Women During Menopause," *Webology*, vol. 18, no. 6, pp. 6439–6450, 2021.

22. S. Jayachandran, M. Biradavolu, and J. Cooper, "Using Machine Learning and Qualitative Interviews to Design a Five-question Survey Module for Women's Agency," *World Dev.*, vol. 161, p. 106076, 2023, doi: 10.1016/j.worlddev.2022.106076.

23. A. K. Dey *et al.*, "SSM – Population Health Using Machine Learning to Understand Determinants of IUD Use in India : Analyses of the National Family Health Surveys (NFHS-4)," vol. 19, no. September, 2022.

24. K. Albert and M. Delano, "Sex Trouble: Sex / Gender Slippage, Sex Confusion, and Sex Obsession in Machine Learning using Electronic Health Records," *Patterns*, vol. 3, no. 8, p. 100534, 2022, doi: 10.1016/j.patter.2022.100534.

25. R. Gill, A. Moudgil, and P. Bajaj, "Hybrid Approach for Emotion Recognition Using CNLSTM in Video Expressions," in *2022 10th International Conference on Reliability, Infocom Technologies and Optimization (Trends and Future Directions) (ICRITO)*, Oct. 2022, pp. 1–5, doi: 10.1109/ICRITO56286.2022.9964701.

26. J. Gumà, "What Influences Individual Perception of Health? Using Machine Learning to Disentangle Self-perceived Health," *SSM – Popul. Heal.*, vol. 16, no. December, 2021, doi: 10.1016/j.ssmph.2021.100996.

27. A. Daoud, R. Kim, and S. V. Subramanian, "Predicting Women's Height from their Socioeconomic Status: A Machine Learning Approach," *Soc. Sci. Med.*, vol. 238, no. August, p. 112486, 2019, doi: 10.1016/j.socscimed.2019.112486.

28. H. Allahem and S. Sampalli, "Automated Labour Detection Framework to Monitor Pregnant Women with a High Risk of Premature Labour using Machine Learning and Deep Learning," *Informatics Med. Unlocked*, vol. 28, 2022, doi: 10.1016/j.imu.2021.100771.

29. A. Jamshidnezhad, Z. Anjomshoa, S. Ahmad, and A. Azizi, "Informatics in Medicine Unlocked The Impact Coenzyme Q10 Supplementation on the Inflammatory Indices of Women with Breast Cancer Using A Machine Learning Prediction Model," *Informatics Med. Unlocked*, vol. 24, no. April, p. 100614, 2021, doi: 10.1016/j.imu.2021.100614.

30. P. Singh and S. Chouhan, "Indian Public Interest and Anxiety Surge in COVID-19 Subsequent to a Strong Epidemic in Italy and Spain through a Survey using Google Trends," in 2021 *3rd International Conference on Advances in Computing, Communication Control and Networking (ICAC3N)*, Dec. 2021, pp. 2082–2084, doi: 10.1109/ICAC3N53548.2021.9725520.

31. K. T. Dhiman and S. Chauhan, "Identification of AI based Techniques for Identification of Covid-19 on Chest Xray Images," *Innov. Comput. Comput. Tech. Icacct-2021*, vol. 2555, no. October, p. 040009, 2022, doi: 10.1063/5.0108974.

32. Z. Guleken *et al.*, "Characterization of Covid-19 Infected Pregnant Women Sera using Laboratory Indexes, Vibrational Spectroscopy, and Machine Learning Classifications," *Talanta*, vol. 237, no. June 2021, 2022, doi: 10.1016/j.talanta.2021.122916.

33. N. Lazzarini *et al.*, "A Machine Learning Approach for the Identification of New Biomarkers for Knee Osteoarthritis Development in Overweight and Obese Women," *Osteoarthr. Cartil.*, vol. 25, no. 12, pp. 2014–2021, 2017, doi: 10.1016/j.joca.2017.09.001.

2 Predicting Anxiety, Depression and Stress in Women Using Machine Learning Algorithms

Kalpana Katiyar, Hera Fatma and Simran Singh

2.1 INTRODUCTION

Human beings are, by nature, pretty aspiring and determined these days, seeking out every possible opportunity to grow professionally. People now perceive stress, dejection, anxiety, disappointment and dissatisfaction as inherent components of their professional lives because they are so prevalent. Given people's extremely busy schedules today, few people dedicate time to talk about depression, anxiety and stress, which are some of the greatest sources of illness globally. Women of all ages, and in particular those living in India, which has a population of 1.39 billion, frequently experience depression. According to the World Health Organization (WHO), depression is the most common mental condition, affecting well over 300 million people globally. Because of the severity of the problem, many health researchers have chosen to concentrate their research in this area. Since it is difficult for machines to distinguish between anxiety, depression and stress, an adequate learning algorithm is needed for a precise diagnosis. WHO claims that in addition to being physically healthy, a healthy person also has a healthy intellect [1]. Depression is a state or feeling of disheartenment, unhappiness, terribleness and low motivation for a long period. It is normal for these feelings to persist for very short intervals, such as a couple of days or a week, but when they persist continuously, you're at risk of a very perilous situation, potentially a loss of life. Today, depression and anxiety are very grave situations that can affect women's family relationships, socio-economic responsibility, careers and sense of dignity or self-esteem. Many aspects possibly cause unusual cases of anxiety and depression in women. According to Bohra et al., depressive disorders afflict roughly 10% of Americans, with two to three times more women than men getting affected [2]. In India, the prevalence of depression ranges from 1.5/1,000 to 37.74/1,000 [2]. In comparison, we found that depression rates are greater in rural areas than in urban areas. According to WHO, it is a near precursor of suicide. Disorders like anxiety

DOI: 10.1201/9781003378556-2

and depression, which are frequently connected, affect up to 20% of people receiving primary healthcare in developing nations, although the signs and symptoms of these illnesses are frequently overlooked. In India, there are disproportionately more female cases of depression disorders [2] [3].

During the years women carry children, they are most at risk of having depressive disorders. A Patient Health Questionnaire serves as the primary diagnostic indicator for depression, which contains a set of 21 questions based on which the scale of depression, anxiety and stress of an individual is evaluated [4]. The signs of generalized anxiety disorder are panic attacks, fast breathing, increased heart rate, nervousness and inability to concentrate. A case of minor or serious depression that develops while pregnant or up to one year after giving birth is referred to as postpartum depression (PPD). PPD has a devastating effect on mothers as well as their children [5] [6]. These problems are not easily diagnosed and the symptoms appear after a long time, often when it is too late; however, with the help of some tools like machine learning (ML) algorithms, which can provide a ray of hope, we can predict these problems at a very early stage.

2.1.1 Problem Arising due to Depression, Anxiety and Stress

The primary indicators of depression in clinical data are memory loss, difficulty concentrating, inability to make decisions, loss of interest in hobbies and activities, including sex, loss of appetite, suicidal thoughts [7], constant thoughts of worthlessness, alarm, weight gain, restlessness and irritation. It is very important not to ignore these symptoms as otherwise, the situation would worsen [8]. Although predicting these problems is challenging, it's necessary because these problems have a significant impact on one's life, relationships and socioeconomic situation.

2.1.2 Motivation for Anxiety, Depression and Stress Prediction

To date, the condition of undetected cases of women experiencing depression, anxiety and stress involves a lack of awareness, suffering from mental health, feeling constant stress and pregnancy-related problems. Women have a higher chance of developing depression disorders [9]. Depression cases are seen more frequently in Indian women. We must talk about depression and anxiety because these difficulties are often invisible and their symptoms are not well known [10,11]. As stated by WHO, the rate of depression is 50% higher in women than men, and in India, these reports are very disheartening [10].

2.2 OBJECTIVE

Many researchers are working on predicting depression, anxiety and stress with the help of ML algorithms, such as logistic regression (LR), artificial neural networks (ANNs), naive Bayes (NB), support vector machines (SVMs), decision trees (DTs), gradient boosting (GB) [12] and random forests (RFs). In this chapter, we aim to identify which algorithm has high accuracy and precision rates in predicting these in women. In any case, early-stage sadness and anxiety predictions are a difficult task, but by using algorithms, we proved successful [13].

2.3 METHODOLOGY

The data set that was utilized in this chapter is collected from DASS-21. DASS-21 contains a set of 21 questions which is classified into three classes – depression, anxiety and stress – and each class is assigned 7 questions. The data sets carry the patient's details.

2.3.1 DATA SET

We identified depression, anxiety and stress with the help of the DASS-21 (scale questionnaire). Data was collected from approximately 50 participants via a Google form.

2.3.2 PARTICIPANTS

About 50 female participants between the ages of 18 and 50 who were either employed or unemployed and had a variety of responsibilities, including professional and household chores, participated in the study.

2.3.3 QUESTIONNAIRE

In this chapter, we used a data set designed in such a format that contains groups of questions collected from DASS-21 that help to predict depression, anxiety and stress. DASS-21 consists of 21 questions divided into three classes – depression, anxiety and stress – and each class has 7 questions, as shown in Figure 2.1 and Table 2.1.

2.3.4 SURVEY OF ANXIETY

In this survey, we found that 28% of people have normal anxiety levels, 18% of people have mild anxiety, 21% of people have average anxiety, 14% of people have critical anxiety and 19% of people have extremely critical anxiety, as shown in Figure 2.2.

2.3.5 SURVEY OF STRESS

In this survey, we found that 30% of people have normal stress levels, 22% of people have mild stress, 26% of people have average stress, 20% of people have critical stress and 2% of people have extremely critical stress, as shown in Figure 2.3.

2.3.6 SURVEY OF DEPRESSION

In this survey, we found that 36% of people don't experience depression 9% of people have mild depression, 33% of people have average depression, 11% of people have critical depression and 11% of people have extremely critical depression, as shown in Figure 2.4.

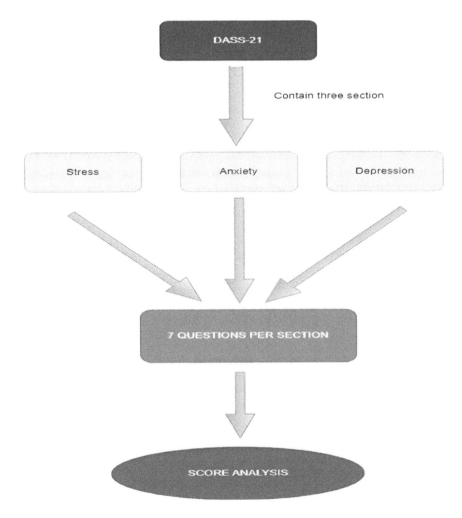

FIGURE 2.1 In this schematic representation, we have taken a total of 21 questions and divided them into three sections of 7 questions that belong to anxiety, stress and depression and calculated the levels of stress, depression and anxiety by calculating their scores.

TABLE 2.1
Analysis of Severity Level Score

Severity	Anxiety Level	Depression Level	Stress Level
Normal	0–8	0–10	0–15
Mild	9–10	11–14	16–19
Average	11–14	15–20	20–26
Critical	15–20	21–28	27–35
Extremely critical	>20	28+	35+

showing different severity levels for anxiety, stress and depression according to the scores obtained.

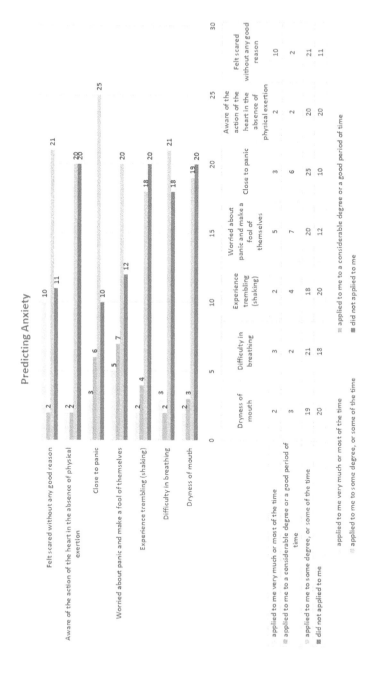

FIGURE 2.2 Predicting anxiety

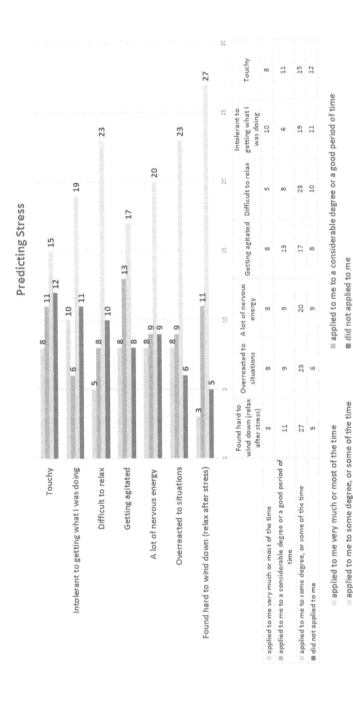

FIGURE 2.3 Predicting stress

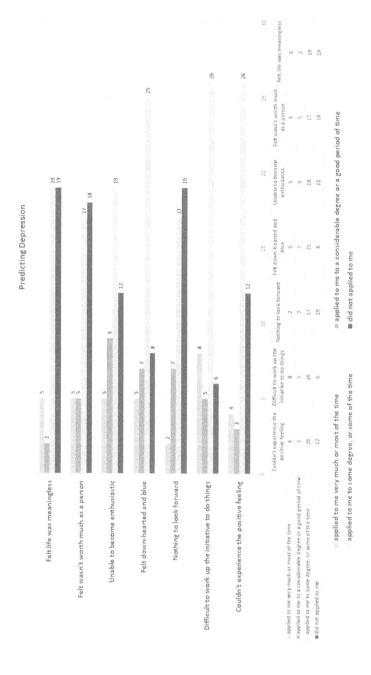

FIGURE 2.4   Predicting depression.

2.3.6.1   Summary of Survey of Anxiety, Stress and Depression

We targeted approximately 300 female students and 23 staff members from Dr. Ambedkar Institute of Technology for Handicapped for a survey to predict anxiety, depression and stress. Approximately 50 people responded to our questions. From this, we can posit that people are negligent about the above-mentioned problems. The impact of this can be observed in the mental health of people. The increase in the number of suicides, unsuccessful marriages and violence is proof of this. As this problem is frequent and most people don't even consider it, as shown in Figure 2.5, we have chosen this topic.

2.4   MACHINE LEARNING

A branch of artificial intelligence called "machine learning" focuses on creating algorithms and statistical models that allow computers to learn from data and make predictions or judgements based on the data. Building models that can naturally recognize patterns and correlations in data without being explicitly trained to do so is the aim of ML. To do this, a ML model is trained on a collection of input data and then used to predict or categorize incoming data [14]. Supervised learning, unsupervised learning and reinforcement learning are the three primary categories of ML.

2.4.1   Supervised Learning

In supervised learning, a model is trained on a collection of labelled data where the right responses are already known. The model's objective is to forecast fresh, unlabelled data.

2.4.2   Unsupervised Learning

In unsupervised learning, a model is trained on a collection of unlabelled data to detect patterns or structures.

2.4.3   Reinforcement Learning

In reinforcement learning, a model is trained to make decisions in a dynamic environment, where the model obtains feedback in the form of rewards or penalties based on its behaviour.

Image identification, natural language processing, recommendation systems, fraud detection and autonomous cars are just a few of the many useful uses of ML.

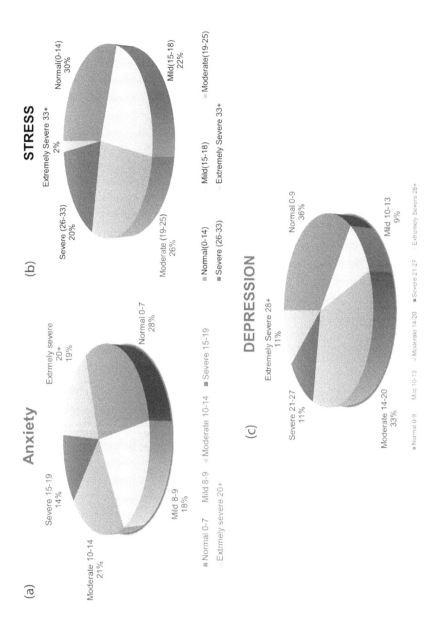

FIGURE 2.5 Summary of survey of anxiety, stress and depression. These figures show the percentage of people falling under different levels of anxiety, stress and depression.

2.4.4 APPLICATION OF MACHINE LEARNING

ML is a multidisciplinary field, which can be applied in various areas, including science and business [15]. Here are a few typical uses for ML:

- *Image and object recognition:* to recognize and categorize items in photos and videos, ML techniques are utilized. This is employed in sectors like security, healthcare and the automobile industry.
- *Natural language processing:* ML algorithms are utilized for natural language processing, which analyses and comprehends spoken language. This is applied to sentiment analysis, virtual assistants and chatbots.
- *Fraud detection:* ML algorithms are capable of seeing trends and anomalies in huge data sets, which are then utilized to spot fraudulent behaviour in financial transactions.
- *Recommendation system:* ML algorithms can examine user behaviour and make suggestions for goods, services and content, depending on their tastes.
- *Predictive analytics:* analytics that anticipates future outcomes from historical data is known as predictive analytics and is employed in various fields, including finance, medicine and marketing.
- *Autonomous vehicles:* self-driving cars can navigate and make judgements based on real-time data, thanks to ML algorithms.

2.5 APPLICABLE ALGORITHMS

For the prediction of depression, anxiety and stress, we can utilize different types ML algorithms like ANN, LR, NB, SVM, DT, GB and RF, which can accurately forecast these types of complications or issues that affect people and have detrimental results.

2.5.1 CONSIDERED LEARNING ALGORITHM

In this chapter, we will discuss NB, LR, ANN and RF.

2.5.1.1 Naive Bayes Algorithm

Based on Bayes' theorem, NB is a ML classification algorithm. It is a commonly used, straightforward yet efficient method for text classification, sentiment analysis and spam filtering. The method chooses the class with the maximum probability as the output after computing the likelihood of each class given the input features. The term "naive" refers to the belief that the features are conditionally independent, meaning that the absence or presence of one feature has no bearing on the likelihood of another [16]. The algorithm must be trained on a data set that contains labelled samples of each class in order to apply NB for classification. The algorithm determines the conditional probability of every feature given to each class during training, as well as the prior probability of each class – the chance of each class happening without taking into account the input characteristics.

The algorithm uses the Bayes theorem to determine the succeeding probability of each class given the input features in order to categorize a new input. The output is chosen to be the class with the highest posterior probability. The NB method is quick and easy to use, and it can function well with little or no training data. However, if the "naive" presumption of feature independence was broken or if the data set had unbalanced class distributions, its performance may decline.

The following is the NB formula:

$$P\left(class \mid features\right) = p\left(class\right) \frac{p(features \mid class)}{p\left(features\right)} \tag{2.1}$$

where

P(class | features) is the posterior probability of the class given the features.
P(class) is the prior probability of the class.
P(features | class) is the likelihood of the features given the class.
P(features) is the marginal probability of the features.

The NB model is uncomplicated, so it is easy to use and especially straightforward when handling large data sets. NB is well known for performing better than the highly developed classification method.

2.5.1.2 Logistic Regression

In ML, the statistical technique of LR is used to estimate the likelihood that an input will belong to one of two groups. It is a kind of regression analysis where the independent variables can either be continuous or categorical and the dependent variable is categorical [17].

The LR process converts the input data into a probability score using a sigmoid function, which is then used to categorize the inputs into one of two classes. Any real-valued input can be mapped by the sigmoid function to a range between 0 and 1, which can be thought of as the likelihood that the input belongs to a positive class. To reduce the discrepancy between the presumed probabilities and the true class labels in the training data, the LR algorithm modifies the weights of the input characteristics during training [18]. Most often, gradient descent optimization or maximum likelihood estimation is used for this. By utilizing methods like one-versus-all or SoftMax regression, LR may also be expanded to tackle multi-class classification issues.

The LR algorithm is straightforward to understand, and is effective for both large and small data sets. It may not function effectively if the relationship is non-linear or when there are interactions between the characteristics because it assumes a linear relation between the input features and the log-odds of the output.

$$\frac{1}{\left(1 + e^{-v}\right)} \tag{2.2}$$

where v is the value.

Value is the actual number you want to change, and e is the base of a natural log (Euler's number or even the EXP () function throughout the spreadsheet). The numbers between –5 and 5 were transformed into the range of 0 to 1 using the logistic function.

2.5.1.3 Random Forest

A ML technique called RF is used for categorization, regression and other tasks. It is an ensemble approach made up of several DTs constructed from various subsets of training data that were chosen at random. To increase accuracy and decrease overfitting, the method combines the predictions of various decision trees.

An outline of the RF algorithm's operation is provided below.

Choose a subset of features at random from the training set. Create a DT that uses a random subset of training data and chosen features. To generate a set of DTs, repeat stages 1 and 2. Run a fresh data point into each of the DTs within the collection, and then combine the findings to generate a prediction. Classification, regression and feature selection are just a few of the ML tasks that may be performed using the robust and flexible RF algorithm. It is extensively utilized in industries and has demonstrated high-quality outcomes in a variety of applications. In RF classification, fewer trees were proposed, as shown in Figure 2.6.

2.5.1.4 Artificial Neural Network

In ANN, an effort to enhance the model from the observed data by a learning algorithm between neuron and adaptive weights along a path. In addition to the learning algorithm, the right cost function must be chosen. A layer of artificial neurons, or computational units that can accept input and apply an activation function as well

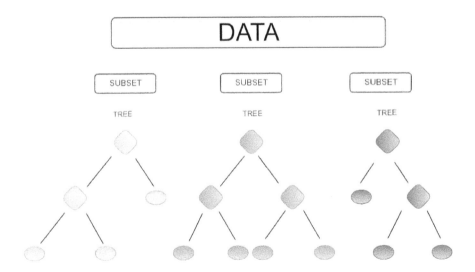

FIGURE 2.6 Random forest algorithm is employed for classification and regression issues in machine learning.

as a threshold to determine whether messages are passed through, is used as the architectural model for an ANN [19]. Fundamentally, brains are organic computer devices. They enable an organism to observe and understand its surroundings, make decisions by synthesizing several streams of information and adapt to a changing environment by turning a flood of complicated and confusing sensory input into coherent cognition and action. In light of this, it is probably not unexpected that the field of creating artificial computational systems, computer science, has long drawn inspiration from biology [20]. ANNs are characterized by having adaptable weights along the routes connecting neurons, which may be adjusted by a learning algorithm that picks up new information from observed data to enhance the model. One must select an acceptable cost function in contrast to the deep learning model itself. The best way to tackle an issue is to learn its optimal solution using the cost function. Using neuron route adaptive weights as the primary goal requires determining the ideal values for all the adjustable model parameters along with algorithm tuning elements like the learning rate [21].

Typically, an ANN is accomplished using optimization methods like stochastic gradient descent or gradient descent. The main goal of these optimization strategies is to obtain an optimized result as near to the ideal result as feasible, which, if successful, indicates that the ANN can tackle the intended issue quickly and effectively. An ANN's architecture is represented by a layer of artificial neurons, or computing units, that can process inputs and implement an activation function and a threshold to determine whether messages are sent [22]. A simple model has three layers: an input layer, a hidden layer and an output layer. One or even many neurons may be present in each stratum. Models can become more intricate and abstract as well as more detailed. By raising the hidden layers, neurons in each layer and/or the number of connections between neurons, models can become more complicated while also becoming more abstract and capable of solving problems [23]. Keep in mind that when model complexity increases, there is a higher possibility of overfitting.

2.6 A MACHINE LEARNING–BASED MODELLING APPROACH PREDICTING GENERALIZED ANXIETY LEVELS IN NON-PREGNANT AND PREGNANT WOMEN DURING THE PANDEMIC

2.6.1 Objective

The COVID-19 outbreak, the ensuing lockdowns and the related safety measures have had a significant negative impact on pregnant and postpartum women's emotional and physical health. The subsequent lockdown between July and December 2020 affected individuals to a greater extent, especially women. A total of 3,569 women (1,937 pregnant and 1,640 postpartum) from five different nations made up the population sample. Seven deep learning algorithms' effectiveness in detecting signs of anxiety and sadness was evaluated, resulting in major use of the GB and RF models [24].

2.6.2 Proposed Techniques

2.6.2.1 Data Set

For this study, regional data sets were used to evaluate the effectiveness of learning algorithms in predicting depressive and perinatal mood disorders during the COVID-19 shutdown in five Gulf nations. Important and fascinating information on the impact of the COVID-19 lockdown on pregnant women is provided by the classification of the participants into several data groups, depending on their region and the general prognosis for the total participants. A total of 3,569 women from five nations – Jordan, Palestine, Lebanon, Saudi Arabia and Bahrain – took part in the study. 1,939 of them were pregnant and 1,630 of them were postpartum. Data sets from July to December 2020, the lockdown period, were collected [24].

2.6.3 Statistical Analysis

Results showed that the mean age of the women was (27.5±5.5) years old. Of the total individuals, 10.6% and 7.7% reported having moderate or severe depression, respectively, and 23.4% and 6.7% reported having moderate or severe anxiety respectively. It was discovered that the rates of anxiety and depression varied, depending on factors such as the country of residence, level of education, economic status, stress at work, social issues, medical conditions, family conflicts, economic difficulties, psychological issues, sleep deprivation and consumption of unhealthy foods. In Israel (18.9%, 24.5%) and Syria (15.6%, 20%), more women were reported to have significant levels of anxiety and depressive symptoms. Also, the findings showed that women who self-reported family issues (34.5%) and sleep deprivation had the greatest rates of depression [24].

2.7 USING ML TOOLS TO DETECT DEPRESSION AND ANXIETY IN POSTPARTUM WOMEN

PPD is one of the most common and severe morbidities to be tackled after delivery, with severe effects on the health of the mother as well as the child [25]. Maternal depression is classified as a mental disease by the Diagnostic Manual DSM-IV and the International Disease Classification ICD-10 with numerous variations. Under PPD symptoms, mothers may have persistent doubts which affect their mental as well as physical health [26]. According to an earlier study, a history of mental illness is one of the key risk elements for PPD. Previous PPD; other mental or depressive conditions; a family history of an affective disease with comparable symptoms of poor post-marital relationship, complications related to pregnancy, including an emergency C-section and unwanted pregnancies; and stressors in a pregnant woman's life can all cause preterm birth [6]. The CC (child care) programme offers the rearrangement of various data kinds and shifts in interpretation and analysis [27].

2.7.1 METHODS

In addition to analytical advancements, the Arksey and O'Malley framework was applied to the scoping review. Also, the procedures follow PRISMA-ScR checklists. To map the body of knowledge on the application of ML in detecting PPD, a scoping review technique was adopted. This methodology incorporated a wider spectrum of research designs and methodologies and provided a descriptive summary of the examined material [25].

2.7.2 CRITERIA

The article reviewed both taken into account omitted based on certain parameters some of which included the effectiveness of the ML data structure or huge data sets method used to forecast PPD were evaluated through the articles. It was released in a journal that underwent peer review. It had been offered in English along with its publication between 2008 and 2020 whereas, the piece that omitted learning implementations in PPD were avoided [25].

2.8 MACHINE LEARNING METHODS FOR PREDICTIVE MODELLING

PPD is a mood disorder found in 13–15% of mothers after childbirth [6]. When it comes to predicting various diseases, ML technology offers several benefits. Artificial learning had specifically been applied to predict outcomes of several body models, including metabolic syndrome, heart failure, cerebral infarction and Alzheimer's disease. By overlaying ROC (receiver operating characteristic curve) plots and comparing predictions for PPD among adolescents and mothers, models have been built utilizing information from Rhode Island Prenatal Threat Assessment Tracking System and c-statistics [7]. These models (known as parallel random access machines or PRAMs) contain data sets like whether a pregnancy was intended, the mother's race, social and economic stature, stressors, stress history, emotional well-being before and after pregnancy and social support. But to date, there aren't any predictive tools for PPD screening that allows prior treatments of the problem on the basis of artificial intelligence techniques [28]. The case study's main goal was to create ML-based PPD prediction models utilizing features on the mother and father based on PRAMS 2013–2014 data sets [6].

2.9 BEST PERFORMING ALGORITHM REPORTED

Based on various data sets collected in Table 2.2, the GB model has the highest accuracy rate (88%), followed by the RF and NB models (85%).

TABLE 2.2
Precision and Accuracy Prediction Data

Model	F1	Accuracy	Precision
ANN	83	77	82
LR	86	76	83
NB	84	75	82
DT	80.5	67	81
Proposed DRNN	96	97	98.5
GB	88	79	86

using the information in Table 2.2, the model with the best accuracy rate is the
GB one (88%) followed by the RF and NB models (85%).

2.10 DRNN-BASED APPROACH

A sophisticated deep learning machine model called deep recurrent neural network
(DRNN) is utilized to predict stress, anxiety and depression in working pregnant
women. Apart from ML and artificial learning algorithms developed for predicting
stressors in women, DRNN is one of the most advanced and recent approaches. The
chances of complications increase in a context with high stress levels. Long-term
strain can raise blood pressure and cause heart rate issues, along with complications in the mother as well as the premature child. The CNN (convolutional neural
network) model can explain the effect of long-term stress on infants and mothers.
The DRNN approach is most often used to fulfil this objective. The major goal of
applying this technique is to improve the model's ability to learn properly and find
the quickest solution to a problem. It also gives the network multiple solid practice
sessions to achieve high performance rates. The LSTM (long short-term memory)
model, which is frequently employed as a mood predictor, is typically an outgrowth
of the RNN (recurrent neural network). To estimate how worried working pregnant
women will be, the system employs a DRNN-based approach technique [10].

2.11 FUTURE PROSPECTS

The future of techniques based on ML has a wide scope. Various ML predictive modelling methods will soon be highly prevalent. Based on various studies, the different
algorithms that have been developed have different uses [12]. The utilization of ML
for the prediction of PPD has in recent years unveiled phenomenal advancements. As
matched with the classical statistic methodologies, larger data sets can be analysed
and performed using ML advanced computations. Overall, it is evident that ML can
considerably increase the early diagnosis of PPD. Lots of research on the utilization of
ML to find possible PPD determinants resulted in affirmative results. Nevertheless, the
study is still restricted, and further research is needed to determine whether ML can
improve the mental health of mothers [25]. It is also suggested that a most-frequently

considered coefficient, or MFCC-based recurring neural network be used in the near future to identify signs of sadness and anxiety and gauge their severity in postpartum and pregnant women [29]. A proposal framework which includes a gender recognition phase and balances the class labels is being planned for future development. Moreover, a web application might be created to automatically identify clinical depression without any help from a doctor [29]. The capability of learning algorithms allows us to analyse intricate non-linear correlations and even combine and pool various data kinds from different sources. The application of ML in healthcare has steadily increased over the past ten years, and its impacts may be seen in a variety of specialities, including oncology, cardiology, haematology, intensive care and psychology.

2.12   CONCLUSION

Stress, anxiety and depression are major, concerning problems in the modern world, especially for pregnant workers, having a stronger negative effect on children and mothers [10]. Therefore, in this chapter, we aimed to provide various algorithms based on ML technology used to predict early stress, depression and anxiety in pregnant, postpartum and working women. This chapter predicts the use and descriptive analysis of various algorithms. To conclude, the use of ML has been a great advantage for detecting stress in pregnant women early on. Additionally, various algorithms have also significantly improved early detection [25]. The study also assessed that these models may be incorporated into medical healthcare databases for the automated prediction of pregnant women's depression and anxiety [24]. Age of onset, racial group, education, number of children born prior, tiny based on the percentile, different strain variables, post-workout for longer than four days, anxiety prior to actual pregnancy, drinking for three months of gestation, smoking habits start changing from the prior trimester of gestation to postnatal period, prenatal BMI and other information implement better are all used in ML-based predictive modelling. So, in future research, this tool may be employed as a screening method for PPD. There are various advantages of this system, which accompanied with integration with the medical system, can excel.

REFERENCES

1. A. Priya, S. Garg, and N. P. Tigga, "Predicting Anxiety, Depression and Stress in Modern Life using Machine Learning Algorithms," *Procedia Comput. Sci.*, vol. 167, no. 2019, pp. 1258–1267, 2020, doi: 10.1016/j.procs.2020.03.442.
2. N. Bohra, S. Srivastava, and M. S. Bhatia, "Depression in Women in Indian Context," *Indian J. Psychiatry*, vol. 57, no. Suppl 2, pp. S239–S245, Jul. 2015, doi: 10.4103/0019-5545.161485.
3. K. Katiyar, "AI-Based Predictive Analytics for Patients' Psychological Disorder – Predictive Analytics of Psychological Disorders in Healthcare: Data Analytics on Psychological Disorders," in M. Mittal and L. M. Goyal, Eds. *Predictive Analytics of Psychological Disorders in Healthcare: Data Analytics on Psychological Disorders*, Singapore: Springer Nature Singapore, 2022, pp. 37–53, doi: 10.1007/978-981-19-1724-0_3.

4. M. K. Nottage *et al.*, "Loneliness Mediates the Association between Insecure Attachment and Mental Health among University Students," *Pers. Individ. Dif.*, vol. 185, no. May 2021, p. 111233, 2022, doi: 10.1016/j.paid.2021.111233.

5. K. Saqib, A. F. Khan, and Z. A. Butt, "Machine Learning Methods for Predicting Postpartum Depression: Scoping Review," *JMIR Ment. Heal.*, vol. 8, no. 11, pp. 1–14, 2021, doi: 10.2196/29838.

6. D. Shin, K. J. Lee, T. Adeluwa, and J. Hur, "Machine Learning-based Predictive Modeling of Postpartum Depression," *J. Clin. Med.*, vol. 9, no. 9, pp. 1–14, 2020, doi: 10.3390/jcm9092899.

7. M. F. Islam. Prediction of Asthma as Side Effect After vaccination, 2018.

8. S. Graham *et al.*, "Artificial Intelligence for Mental Health and Mental Illnesses: An Overview," *Curr. Psychiatry Rep.*, vol. 21, no. 11, p. 116, 2019, doi: 10.1007/s11920-019-1094-0.

9. R. Qasrawi *et al.*, "Machine Learning Techniques for Predicting Depression and Anxiety in Pregnant and Postpartum Women during the COVID-19 Pandemic: A Cross-sectional Regional Study [version 1; peer review: 2 approved]," *F1000Research*, vol. 11, no. 390, 2022, doi: 10.12688/f1000research.110090.1.

10. S. D. Sharma, S. Sharma, R. Singh, A. Gehlot, N. Priyadarshi, and B. Twala, "Stress Detection System for Working Pregnant Women Using an Improved Deep Recurrent Neural Network," *Electron.*, vol. 11, no. 18, 2022, doi: 10.3390/electronics111 82862.

11. K. Kroenke, R. L. Spitzer and J. B. Williams. "The Patient Health Questionnaire-2: validity of a two-item depression screener," *Medical care*, pp. 1284–1292, 2003.

12. R. Kaur, R. Kumar, and M. Gupta, "Predicting Risk of Obesity and Meal Planning to Reduce the Obese in Adulthood using Artificial Intelligence," *Endocrine*, vol. 78, no. 3, pp. 458–469, 2022, doi: 10.1007/s12020-022-03215-4.

13. T. P. S. Oei, S. Sawang, Y. W. Goh, and F. Mukhtar, "Using the Depression Anxiety Stress Scale 21 (DASS-21) Across Cultures," *Int. J. Psychol.*, vol. 48, no. 6, pp. 1018–1029, 2013, doi: 10.1080/00207594.2012.755535.

14. J. Y. Ko, K. M. Rockhill, V. T. Tong, B. Morrow, and S. L. Farr, "Trends in Postpartum Depressive Symptoms – 27 States, 2004, 2008, and 2012," *MMWR. Morb. Mortal. Wkly. Rep.*, vol. 66, no. 6, pp. 153–158, Feb. 2017, doi: 10.15585/mmwr.mm6606a1.

15. N. Hasan and Y. Bao, "Impact of 'e-Learning Crack-up' Perception on Psychological Distress among College Students during COVID-19 Pandemic: A Mediating Role of 'Fear of Academic Year Loss,'" *Child. Youth Serv. Rev.*, vol. 118, no. August, p. 105355, 2020, doi: 10.1016/j.childyouth.2020.105355.

16. T. A. Widiger and P. T. Costa, Eds., *Personality Disorders and the Five-Factor Model of Personality*. American Psychological Association, 2013. [Online]. Available: http://www.jstor.org/stable/j.ctv1chs8rh.

17. D. Bzdok and A. Meyer-Lindenberg, "Machine Learning for Precision Psychiatry: Opportunities and Challenges," *Biol. Psychiatry Cogn. Neurosci. Neuroimaging*, vol. 3, no. 3, pp. 223–230, 2018, doi: https://doi.org/10.1016/j.bpsc.2017.11.007.

18. E. Rejaibi, A. Komaty, F. Meriaudeau, S. Agrebi, and A. Othmani, "MFCC-based Recurrent Neural Network for Automatic Clinical Depression Recognition and Assessment from Speech," *Biomed. Signal Process. Control*, vol. 71, pp. 1–14, 2022, doi: 10.1016/j.bspc.2021.103107.

19. Z. Liu and D. Cui. "Permeable Educational Learning Environments: The Impact of the Space Environment Fosters Student Learning and Engagement," *Educ. Adm.: Theory Pract*, vol. 29, no. 1, pp. 221–237, 2023.

20. D. D. Cox and T. Dean, "Neural Networks and Neuroscience-inspired Computer Vision," *Curr. Biol.*, vol. 24, no. 18, pp. R921–R929, 2014, doi: 10.1016/j.cub.2014.08.026.

21. R. Kaur, R. Kumar, and M. Gupta, "Food Image-based Diet Recommendation Framework to Overcome PCOS Problem in Women using Deep Convolutional Neural Network," *Comput. Electr. Eng.*, vol. 103, no. February, p. 108298, 2022, doi: 10.1016/j. compeleceng.2022.108298.

22. J. M. Jerez *et al.*, "Improvement of Breast Cancer Relapse Prediction in High Risk Intervals using Artificial Neural Networks," *Breast Cancer Res. Treat.*, vol. 94, no. 3, pp. 265–272, 2005, doi: 10.1007/s10549-005-9013-y.

23. K. J. Friston, A. D. Redish, and J. A. Gordon, "Computational Nosology and Precision Psychiatry," *Comput. Psychiatry*, vol. 1, pp. 2–23, 2017, doi: 10.1162/CPSY_a_00001.

24. R. Qasrawi *et al.*, "Machine Learning Techniques for Predicting Depression and Anxiety in Pregnant and Postpartum Women during the COVID-19 Pandemic: A Cross-sectional Regional Study," *F1000Research*, vol. 11, 2022, doi: 10.12688/ f1000research.110090.1.

25. K. Saqib, A. F. Khan, and Z. A. Butt, "Machine Learning Methods for Predicting Postpartum Depression: Scoping Review," *JMIR Ment. Heal.*, vol. 8, no. 11, 2021, doi: 10.2196/29838.

26. A. Srivastava, A. Seth, and K. Katiyar, "Microrobots and Nanorobots in the Refinement of Modern Healthcare Practices," in D. Gupta, M. Sharma, V. Chaudhary and A. Khanna, Eds.*Robotic Technologies in Biomedical and Healthcare Engineering*,United States: CRC Press, Taylor & Francis, 2021, pp. 13–37.

27. S. Katiyar and K. Katiyar, "Recent Trends Towards Cognitive Science: From Robots to Humanoids," in M. Mittal, R. Ratn Shah and S. Roy, Eds. *Cognitive Computing for Human-Robot Interaction*, Amsterdam: Elsevier, 2021, pp. 19–49.

28. A. Prasetyoputri, "Detection of Bacterial Coinfection in COVID-19 Patients Is a Missing Piece of the Puzzle in the COVID-19 Management in Indonesia," *ACS Infect. Dis.*, vol. 7, no. 2, pp. 203–205, 2021, doi: 10.1021/acsinfecdis.1c00006.

29. E. Rejaibi, A. Komaty, F. Meriaudeau, S. Agrebi, and A. Othmani, "MFCC-based Recurrent Neural Network for Automatic Clinical Depression Recognition and Assessment from Speech," *Biomed. Signal Process. Control*, vol. 71, no. PA, p. 103107, 2022, doi: 10.1016/j.bspc.2021.103107.

3 Gender-based Analysis of the Impact of Cardiovascular Disease Using Machine Learning
A Comparative Analysis

Ajit Kumar Varma, Arpita Choudhary and Priti Tagde

3.1 INTRODUCTION

Cardiovascular disease continues to be the leading cause of mortality in adults over 65; it develops in women seven to ten years later than in men. Because of the misconception that women are "protected" from coronary disease, the danger of heart disease in women is underestimated. According to new data from the National Health and Nutrition Examination (NHANES), over the last 20 years, myocardial infarctions were more prevalent in middle aged (35–54) women than in men in the same age range [1]. Recommendations for diagnosing angiograms, interventionist therapies for stable angina pectoris and functional testing for ischaemia are less common for women than for men [2]. Women are less frequently included in clinical studies and receive less intensive treatment regimens as a result of undiagnosed cardiac disease and variations in clinical presentation in women. In order to better their ability to avoid cardiovascular events, women have to devote more attention to growing their self-awareness and understanding their cardiovascular risk factors. In this overview, we emphasize the much more crucial points that are key to primary documentation and successful treatment of women's coronary heart disease (CHD).

3.2 MENOPAUSE'S IMPACT AND ITS EPIDEMIOLOGY

It is believed that a woman's ability to absorb natural oestrogen throughout her fertile years will prevent the onset of atherosclerotic disease. Women experience CHD events before menstruation at a low incidence that is primarily brought on by smoking [3]. In comparison to a typical or late menopause, which happens after the age of 40, early menopause shortens a woman's lifespan by two years [4]. Menopausal age may be more of a cause than a result of a poor cardiovascular risk factor, according to

DOI: 10.1201/9781003378556-3

statistics from the Framingham Heart Study [5]. According to the Women's Ischemia Syndrome Evaluation (WISE) research, the risk of coronary artery disease is more than seven times greater in young women with endogenous oestrogen insufficiency. Oestrogen has an impact on a number of metabolic systems, including lipids, inflammatory indicators and the coagulation system. Additionally, it provides a direct vasodilator impact by stimulating receptors and vessel walls. Intima-media thickness measurements show that women can experience asymptomatic atherosclerosis before menopause, especially when there are several CHD risk factors present [6]. Tests of the vasoreactivity of the brachial artery caused by mediated-flow reveal a gradual decline after menopause. During menopause, involvement-related lesions, which are more combustible, replace the atherosclerotic plaque's original makeup.

3.2.1 VARIOUS KEY CHD RISK FACTORS DIFFER BY GENDER

Menopause's onset is connected with a deteriorating CHD risk profile [7]. When women have CHD that is fully apparent, they are more likely to be older than men and to have higher cardiovascular risks. Although the majority of the traditional risk variables are the same for both men and women, their relative importance and weighting vary. Smoking has a greater negative influence on women than on men at younger ages (50 years) and the number of cigarettes smoked daily has a greater negative impact [3,8]. Smoking makes it more likely for women than men to get their first acute myocardial infarction (AMI). Smoking slows down the endothelium wall's oestrogen-dependent vasodilatation in young premenopausal women [9].

When the spread of body fat shifts from a gynoid to a more android form in the early years after menopause, body weight may increase. In comparison to ageing men, ageing women have central obesity, an increase in visceral fat that happens more frequently after menopause, and a greater prevalence of comorbid risk factors and characteristics of the metabolic syndrome [10]. Type 2 diabetes is rising in prevalence along with weight. Compared to men, women experience diabetes more commonly. According to a meta-analysis of 37 prospective cohort studies, women with diabetes had a 50% higher chance of dying from CHD than men [11]. Many complicated factors, such as more risk factors, more inflammation, fewer coronary arteries, as well as channel size, and typically less active diabetes control in women, contribute to this higher death rate.

Because oestrogen levels diminish throughout the menopausal transition, systolic blood pressure grows more quickly in older women than in younger men [12]. The renin-angiotensin system becomes active after menopause, increasing plasma-renin production. Women who have gone through menopause have increased sympathetic activity and salt sensitivity. Isolated systolic hypertension is significantly associated with left ventricular enlargement, (diastolic) heart failure and strokes in older (>75 years) individuals and is 14% more common in women than in men. Women are more prone than men to have endothelial dysfunction and cardiovascular issues when blood pressure is moderate or borderline (140/90 mmHg) [13]. Chest discomfort, palpitations, headaches and even the emergence of hot flashes can be brought on by hypertension, which frequently develops even during the menopausal transition phase [14]. With good high blood pressure medication, these issues, which are usually associated with menopause, become less prevalent [15]. The likelihood that women, who experience an unusually high number of vaso-vegetative symptoms during the menopausal transition, have a higher risk of CHD is debatable [16].

Men are more likely than women to have hypercholesterolemia as they age. Even though HDL cholesterol values do not alter after menopause, total cholesterol, low-density lipoprotein (LDL) and lipoprotein (a), all increase by 10%, 14% and 14%, respectively. In the event that borderline premenopausal levels were discovered, the lipid profile should be (re)evaluated following menopause. LDL cholesterol levels in women over 65 are greater than in men. Although the Framingham research indicated that women are more at risk for CHD due to low HDL cholesterol than men are [17], women have HDL cholesterol levels 0.26–0.36 mmol/l greater than men do at every age.

Despite the fact that traditionally women have frequently been overlooked in many statin trials, there is no question that LDL lowering resulted in a comparable decline in CHD mortality in women as it did in men in secondary prevention [18]. The main preventative usage of statin medicine in women is still up for debate. Nevertheless, prudence is advised since among some of the age categories examined thus far, women had a lower absolute risk than men. A recent large, Japanese study amply showed the advantages of primary prevention with statins in women over 55 with relatively elevated cholesterol levels [19]. The JUPITER research takes the age difference into account when determining the outstanding outcomes of preventive measures for both men and women [20]. In healthy men under the age of 50 and women over the age of 60, statins have shown to lower hs-CRP levels while keeping LDL levels within the typical range.

3.2.2 ELEMENTS THAT ARE SPECIAL TO WOMEN

It is currently unclear if polycystic ovarian syndrome (PCOS) is a single risk factor for atherosclerosis, although research indicates that hormonal instability in premenopausal women is linked to a heightened risk of atherosclerosis and CHD events [5,21]. PCOS, which affects 8–10% of women, is a significant contributor to infertility. Women who have this condition are much more prone to acquire type 2 diabetes and metabolic syndrome. Examining cardiovascular events in PCOS patients is difficult since they are infrequent in premenopausal women. Postmenopausal women with PCOS were found to have a larger prevalence of CHD risk factors and a higher incidence of adverse CHD events in the WISE study group [22].

Women who are pregnant and already have high blood pressure are more prone to develop early cardiovascular disease and high blood pressure later on. Women who have preeclampsia, which is defined by hypertension (>140/90 mmHg) and proteinuria (0.3 g/24 h), are twice as likely to develop CHD after 20 weeks of pregnancy [23]. The biggest risk is thought to be for women who have placental syndrome together with low foetal development or intrauterine mortality [24].

Hypertensive illnesses are thought to be related to placental defects that lead to abnormal autonomic control, inadvertent generation of vasoactive substances and endothelial dysfunction in the vasculature of both the mother and the fetus. Women with gestational diabetes had a comparable 7–12 times significantly amplified danger of acquiring type 2 diabetes relative to those who had normoglycemic pregnancies [25]. Even though they provide a particularly good chance for improved cardiovascular danger diagnosis and mitigation, illnesses associated with pregnancy have not yet been given the attention they deserve in the most recent recommendations for CHD inhibition in women [26].

3.2.3   ANGINA PECTORIS CLINICAL MANIFESTATIONS AND NON-INVASIVE DIAGNOSTIC PROCEDURES

Women are significantly less dependable than men when it comes to the clinical presentation of coronary artery disease and the interpretation of non-invasive diagnostic methods, particularly in the age range under 55 when the incidence of coronary artery disease is still astonishingly low [27]. Women are more likely than men to experience chest pain symptoms, but these syndromes are less frequently linked to atherosclerosis in the major epicardial coronary arteries [8, 28, 29]. Furthermore, the discomfort caused by myocardial ischaemia may be mimicked by a number of non-cardiac causes of chest pain. In the succeeding five to seven years, women who are detected with non-cardiac chest pain are four times more likely to need repeated hospitalizations and angiograms, and they are twice as likely to report a CHD episode within a time span of 180 days [30]. This suggests that because of the risks they present, women should be protected more rigorously and that traditional diagnostic techniques might not be the most useful for them.

There are no gender-specific Electroencardiography (ECG) interpretation standards, despite the fact that women's resting heart rates are higher and their pulse durations are prolonged. Women's lower levels of exercise, smaller vascular size and non-specific ECG anomalies during rest are the main factors contributing to non-invasive testing's decreased sensitivity and specificity in this group. In younger people, endogenous oestrogen levels may cause ECG anomalies that mimic ischaemia. For the assessment of a walking exercise, women-specific normograms have been created. In both symptomatic and inactive women, a lack of exercise endurance is a trustworthy predictor of five-year death. Women who undergo exercise testing may profit from considering their oestrogen status, history of angina and the existence of significant coronary risk factors [31].

The therapeutic benefit of trauma echocardiography coupled with exercise or dobutamine for the evaluation of anomalies in velocity fluctuations is equal in both sexes. Due to breast attenuation and lower artery diameters, myocardial perfusion imaging studies for women were previously less accurate [1].

The electrocardiographic anomalies, the reduced functional capacity and the complaints of chest pain must be considered when interpreting the scans. Women are more likely than men to acquire microvascular dysfunction and diffuse coronary atherosclerosis without obstructive anomalies [32], and technologies like cardio respiratory magnetic resonance (CMR) and PET may make it simpler to identify these conditions in them. The under diagnosis of these illnesses in female patients may be significantly influenced by the relative scarcity of these imaging modalities. Although calcium scoring with Electron-beam Computed Tomography (EBCT) or multi-detector computed tomography (MDCT) is a very successful therapy for lowering the undesirable chance of obstructive CHD, premenopausal women find it less acceptable due to the (cumulative) radiation dose and for ethical reasons. The lack of arterial calcium has a very high (99%) negative prognostic value for obstructive atherosclerosis in women over 50 who have moderate coronary heart disease risk. Women perform worse on the calcium measure than men across all age categories [33]. Additionally, coronary computed tomographic angiography (CCTA) in the emergency department appears hopeful as a very sensitive diagnostic tool in the early screening of women under 65 who come with signs of acute chest pain, though this method has comparable drawbacks because of radioactive contamination [29].

3.2.4 Women's Acute Coronary Syndromes

There are contradictory findings from numerous research studies on intimate relations variations after acute cardiac crises (ACS). Men and women report experiencing the same chest pain sensations during ST-elevation myocardial infarction (STEMI), despite the fact that women frequently suffer extra vaso-vegetative symptoms that might conceal the heart problems and smaller ST-T abnormalities before admission, particularly when patients are younger [8,34]. In the emergency room, female patients under the age of 55 typically have non-STEMI and unstable angina pectoris misdiagnosed [35]. Due to their higher likelihood of being older and having more risk factors concentrated in one area, women with ACS may have a higher mortality rate [8,9,36]. The higher mortality rate may be made worse by prejudice against women in treatment, differences in vascular flow and structure between men and women and many other factors. Despite the apparent higher incident frequency of non-obstructive arterial disease in women, women with ACS displayed more diffuse and less extensive obstructive coronary artery disease compared to men [8,29].

A recent comprehensive meta-analysis of 11 randomized ACS trials found that the severity of the angiographically confirmed disease and clinical disparities at manifestation account for the majority of the sex-based variations in 30-day mortality among patients with different manifestations of ACS [37]. The difference in outcome measures between men and women may also be due to other vascular biological factors, such as differences in remodelling, functionally distinct variants of the smooth muscle cells within the vessel, smaller vessel size, less collateral flow, a lower coronary flow reserve, a higher level of vascular stiffness, a lower atheroma burden and slower progression in women's walls [29].Men and women should receive distinct kinds of therapy for non-STEMI, despite the fact that early cardiac catheterization therapies such as Percutaneous coronary intervention (PCI) are beneficial for both sexes in STEMI [38]. In individuals with unstable angina or non-STEMI ACS, rapid invasive treatment does not reduce mortality, according to the FRISC II and RITA 3 trials. In low-risk (biomarker-negative) women, early conservative therapy is preferable to early invasive treatment, according to a meta-analysis of eight non-STEMI studies. The 2007 ACC/AHA non-STEMI guidelines change [39] supports this finding.

Despite taking into account risk factors, women are more likely than men to die from coronary artery bypass surgery (CABG), and this disparity is more prominent in younger generations [40]. Only a few of the numerous reasons influencing this gender disparity include the prevalence of hypertensive heart disease, smaller arteries, more urgent therapies for women and concurrent ailments at older ages. Women experienced much worse haemorrhage after PCI, particularly when using glycoprotein IIb/IIIa inhibitors [41]. There are no gender differences in the effectiveness or safety of clopidogrel, according to a meta-analysis of numerous large ACS studies [42].

3.2.5 "Normal" Coronary Angiograms and Chest Pain

In comparison to men, women have ACS more frequently and at younger ages [8] with angiographically "normal" coronary arteries. The fundamental causes of this so-called coronary microvascular insufficiency are complex, and include endothelial reactivity, low endogenous oestrogen levels, coagulation problems, aberrant inflammatory processes and individual differences in how it manifests [29]. Chronic chest pain may also be caused by aberrant cardiac nociception since women feel coronary pain more intensely than men do [43]. It is suggested to refer to this illness as microvascular unstable angina when symptoms of microvascular dysfunction and evidence of ischaemia co-occur. The relationship between capillary failure and epicardial atherosclerosis is still unclear. This sickness' prognosis is worse than previously believed, and it typically needs multiple hospitalizations and coronary angiograms [44]. In order to prevent CHD occurrences in the future, women with a range of risk factors should be quickly treated since they have a worse prognosis.

3.3 DATASETS

Two datasets will be used in this study in order to identify and diagnose heart disease utilizing nine classification algorithms.

3.3.1 Cardiovascular Disease DataSet

With the use of the cardiovascular disease dataset used in this inquiry, heart disease was diagnosed and discovered, and the results were compared to those of previous studies. Information that is both personal and medical is given [1]. Kaggle gathered the data from three sources: subjective, which included patient feedback, examination, which comprised the findings of numerous diagnostic exams, and objective, which also comprised details on cardiovascular issues. The data set was employed for testing, training and validation. The intended information is available to everyone on the internet. The dataset for cardiovascular illnesses is a purified schematic of the CVD (cardiovascular disease) dataset and is organized as follows: (68783, 12), as seen in Tables 3.1 and 3.2.

TABLE 3.1
DataSet in Cardiovascular Conditions [1]

Feature	Information
Age	Age of the patient in years
Gender	Binary category value of 1 for men and 2 for women
Height	Representing the patient's height
Weight	Representing the patient's weight
AP height	Blood pressure in systole
Cholesterol	The level of cholesterol in blood (1: normal, 2: above normal, 3: well above normal)
Glucose	Value in categories for the blood sugar level (1: normal, 2: above normal, 3: well above normal)
Smoke	Smoking (0: no, 1: yes)
Alcohol	Drinking alcohol (0: no, 1: yes)
Physical activity	Type of physical activity
Cardiodisease	Target value determining whether cardiovascular disease is present or not

TABLE 3.2
CVD Class Distribution [1]

Class	Counts
0	34,739
1	34,037

3.3.2 DataSet for Heart Disease

The second sample used in the study, the heart disease data set, contains the most widely used datasets for the prediction of heart diseases and includes the Hungarian Cleveland, Swiss, Long Beach VA and Statlog (Heart) data sets. There are ten characteristics, ten recordings and one target in it. The data was compiled by Anu Siddhartha in 2020. The website of the IEEE Data Gateway make this heart disease data set publicly accessible, and it can be seen in Tables 3.3 and 3.4.

3.3.3 Research Methodology

The logistic regression (LR), k-nearest neighbour (KNN), support vector machine (SVM), decision tree (DT) classifier and naive Bayes (NB) algorithms will be used in this study to categorize the data. To discover the best classifier, it is also necessary to build a network model and assess the effects of different optimizing learning strategies on the recognition of cardiovascular illnesses. Figure 3.1 outlines the steps used to carry out this investigation [1].

TABLE 3.3

Cardiovascular Diseases DataSet [1]

Feature	Data
Age	Age of the patient in years
Gender	Binary category value of 1 for men and 0 for women
Chest pain type	Type of chest discomfort the patient is feeling is divided into four classes
Resting bp s	Blood pressure level
Cholesterol	Level of serum cholesterol in mg/dl
Fasting blood sugar	Sugar level after fasting
Resting ECG	Electrocardiogram results: 0, 1 or 2
Max heart rate	Greatest heart rate
Exercise angina	Exercise-induced angina
Old peak	Comparison of the status of rest and exercise-induced ST depression
ST slope	Peak exercise-related ST segment slope measurement 0 means level, 1 means sloping, 2 means flat and 3 means descending
Target	Binary value 0: normal, 1: patient

TABLE 3.4

CVD Class Distribution [1]

Class	Counts
0	567
1	632

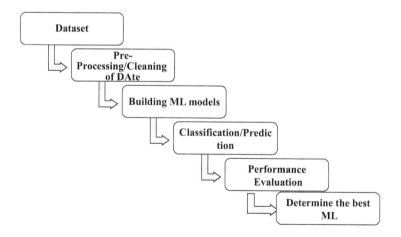

FIGURE 3.1   Research steps

3.3.4 DATA PROCESSING

One of the key phases in enhancing the effectiveness of the models is the attribute selection process, which stores and utilizes only the qualities that are most closely related to one another in order to train the model while rejecting unneeded data to save effort. The dataset was divided using cross-validation into an exercise set and a testing set, 90:10 for each, according to the data analysis.

The body mass index (BMI) was strong-minded during the data processing phase to assess the patient's health. A normal BMI is between 18 and 25, whereas an unhealthy BMI is one that is >25 or <18. The formula below is used to compute the BMI values. The characteristics for height and weight were then eliminated.

BMI = Weight (kg)/Height (cm)

The American Heart Association (AHA) recommends taking systolic and dia-stolic blood pressure readings. A five-point scale is used to rate its seriousness. Each record's blood pressure is computed and the level is recorded [1].

3.4 CLASSIFICATION ALGORITHMS

Algorithms for categorization represent the most widely used machine learning techniques. Reinforcement learning, unsupervised learning and supervised learn-ing are three general categories into which machine learning models can be placed depending on their chosen learning technique. The entire classification procedure trains a system to assign labels to each type of data. Several models are referred to as categorization methods, such as LR, NB, random forest (RF), DT, gradient-boosted trees and linear perceptrons. The efficacy of a few ensemble classifiers and seven classification methods is examined in this study [1].

3.4.1 ARTIFICIAL NEURAL NETWORK

It is a group of algorithms designed to process information and perform human-like functions. The artificial neural network (ANN) is built utilizing a network of weighted connections and neurons to recognize trends and handle artificial intelli-gence (AI) difficulties. Any function, from complicated predictions to classification problems, may be approximated using multilayer networks. In this study, a neural network was employed to diagnose cardiovascular disorders. First, the input layer, also known as the visible layer, is in charge of entering the primary data. This neural network's architecture includes an input layer with the same number of features as there are datasets.

Additionally, there are three hidden layers, one of which is used for computations. Eighteen neurons in the first hidden layer have the activation value "reLU". The layer with 21 neurons that have activation value reLU, known as secret layers, is then exposed. The third concealed layer, which is the layer above that, has eight nodes with the activation value reLU.

The output layer is in charge of generating the required result for the instance with one node with activation value "sigmoid".

3.4.2 Support Vector Machine

The classifiers have gained notoriety ever since they were created, thanks to their exceptional effectiveness, which is on par with that of cutting-edge NNs (neural networks) on challenging tasks using high-processing cost methods. SVMs were first developed as effective tools for categorizing data and identifying trends [45]. Following its debut, researchers started using these algorithms for various classification issues and applications, including speech recognition systems, computer vision and image processing [46, 47].

SVM algorithms are typically employed in classification methods. The SVM develops a hyperplane that separates the data into many categories. Both linear and non-linear issues may be handled with SVM. Finding an N-dimensional hyperplane (where N is the number of features) that categorizes the information or statistics with clarity is the main goal of the SVM. The choice of hyperplanes has a significant effect on the outcome's correctness. It ought to be able to identify the plane where the gaps between its data points in the two groups are the widest. A line dividing two classes serves as the visual representation of the hyperplane. Data points that are located on separate sides of the hyperplane are given opposite classifications.

The hyperplane dimension depends on the number of features. If there are just two features in the input, the hyperplane is a line, and if there are three characteristics, it is a 2D plane. SVM is also utilized to detect anomalies in financial analysis, medical diagnosis and air quality monitoring systems.

3.4.3 Decision Tree Classifier

A categorization method known as DT produces a structure like a tree that may be used to select amongst several actions. A decision-making procedure is a popular machine learning technique that can be used to solve classification and regression problems. Since DT frequently approaches human-level reasoning, it is typically easy to comprehend the data and make some useful conclusions. An illustration of this kind of tree is a DT in which each node stands for a trait, each branch for a guideline and each leaf for the result.

3.4.4 Logistic Regression

To predict the likelihood of the answer characteristics provided, a collection of independent explanatory factors, using LR approach, is often used in computer vision [48]. The binary response parameters are coded as 0 and 1, whereas the binary target variables' values determine how the data is categorized. Ordinal, multinomial and binary or binomial are the several types of LR. The target variable's values can take one of two possible forms in the binary LR: 0 or 1. When the answer parameter, such as class categories, contains three or more unordered possible values to describe the data, the LR is multinomial (A, B, C, D). The categorization is used when an answer parameter, such as student scores, has three or more ordered values (high, mid, low). The LR algorithm responds to abnormalities fast.

3.4.5 K-nearest Neighbour

One of the managed machine learning classification methods is the KNN, which predicts the presence of related things nearby. In other words, related things are situated adjacent to one another. KNN is used to anticipate the target name or label by searching the closest neighbour class. The Manhattan, Euclidean, Minkowski and Hamming distance functions are used to determine the measure of similarity that is used to categorize new instances. The closest neighbour is a straightforward technique that stores all of the existing examples. There are two categories of methods for determining your neighbour's closest neighbour. A structureless NN method is used to classify category object data into training data. The NN technique is built on structures. Data structures such as axis trees, ball trees, k-d trees and orthogonal structure trees are the foundations of structure-based NN method i.e., OST (orthogonal structure tree). In the past, KNN was employed in finance to spot patterns in credit card utilization. KNN algorithms also analyse the data and any suspicious trends found on the website that suggest questionable behaviour.

3.4.6 Naive Bayes

The clustering algorithm described as NB, which assumes that each characteristic that predicts the target value is independent, is built on the Bayes' rule. Based on the probability that the data pertain to a given class, the NB model may determine the class of a particular group of data.

3.4.7 Random Forest

The random forest creates a lot of selection trees during training and posts the outcomes that get the most votes. This technique is used in both regression and categorization assignments.

3.4.8 Voting Classifier

A type of composite machine learning model known as the "majority voting ensemble" or "voting classifier" (VC) combines predictions from many models for training before relying on the simple majority of the contributing models to determine the result. The model performance can be enhanced by using this method. There are two different voting types in the VC. Initially, this kind of hard voting predicts the group or the outcome by using majority of model votes. Second, soft voting forecasts the class or the outcome using the models with the highest probability [48].

3.4.9 GRADIENT BOOSTING CLASSIFIER

A popular machine learning technique for classification issues is steepest descent boosting. Any differentiable loss function may be optimized using gradient boosting (GB), where each prediction corrects the error made by the previous predictor. This approach progressively develops the mechanism before generalizing it. This approach is built on creating a forecast algorithm.

The process begins with the formation and training of a LR on the data collection, followed by evaluation (by calculating the classification error), generation of a judgement call tree and then enhancements. Tree3 is created by merging Tree1 and Tree2. This process is then repeated a predetermined number of times. The projections produced by earlier tree models therefore are averaged together to produce the final model [49].

3.5 EVALUATION METRICS

Group balancing and anticipated results are only two of several factors that might affect the decision-making process when choosing the optimal metrics to assess a single classifier's performance for a particular data set in categorization challenges. A classifier may be evaluated using one performance indicator while being unmeasured by the others, and vice versa. As a result, there is not a common (unified) statistic for describing how well the classifier is performing overall. In this study, a variety of metrics are used to evaluate how well models perform, including accuracy, precision, recall and F1 core. Four different groups provide these measurements:

True positives (TP) are cases when the real class of the event and the model prediction were both 1 (True) (When the model predicts one result but the actual class of the occurrence is 0 (False), this is referred to as a false positive (FP) When the instance's true class is 0 (False) and the model prediction is also 0, this is known as an True Negative (TN). False Negatives (FN) are instances when the model predicted a value of 0 but the instance's actual class was 1 (True) (False).

3.6 RESULT AND DISCUSSION

In the studies described in this part, deep learning networks were used to autonomously identify cardiovascular disease datasets using machine learning methods for classification. To make the findings more understandable, cross-validation (10K-fold), using 90 for teaching and 10 for testing, is used.

Following characteristic choice and data analysis, the classifier's output is displayed, as seen in Table 3.5. The ANN model had a 70% accuracy rate, while the GB model came in second with the greatest performance. The least accurate, at 62%, was DT.

The outcomes of the classification using each characteristic are shown in Table 3.6. In terms of illness prediction, the GB model fared the best, with 72% accuracy, 72% recall, 72% F1score and 73% precision. The accuracy s more than what the research recommended. DT, the model with the worst accuracy, had a score of 63% [47].

TABLE 3.5
Result of the Classifiers (Selected Features) [1]

Models	Precision (%)	Recall (%)	F1Score (%)	Accuracy (%)
KNN	67	67	67	67
SVM	67	65	65	66
DT	64	63	63	63
ANN	70	69	69	69
NB	66	66	65	66
RF	64	64	64	64
LR	65	65	65	65
Voting classifier	68	68	68	68
Gradient boosting	**71**	**71**	**71**	**71**

TABLE 3.6
Result of the Classifiers (All Features) [1]

Models	Precision (%)	Recall (%)	F1Score (%)	Accuracy (%)
KNN	69	69	69	69
SVM	72	70	70	71
DT	62	62	62	62
ANN	72	72	72	72
NB	70	70	70	70
RF	69	69	69	69
LR	72	72	72	72
Voting classifier	72	72	72	72
Gradient boosting	**73**	**72**	**72**	**72**

Tables 3.5 and 3.6 make clear that the outcomes of the models with all features are superior to those of the models with only certain characteristics, which may indicate that the choice and fusion of some features had an impact on the problem's data representation.

Table 3.7, on the other hand, shows the classification outcomes using the dataset for cardiac illnesses [44]. The accuracy of the RF classifier was 94%, followed by the DT classifier at 89%. The results for KNN are displayed in the table, and they are the lowest in this dataset, at 71% for all measures.

Table 3.8 compares the prognosis of cardiovascular disease using various classification and data mining technologies. The figure unequivocally demonstrates that KNN outperformed at 70% when using the same data set used in our analysis. In the same dataset, the NB and LR of this research had accuracy that is higher than at 72% and 74%, respectively [49,50]. The heart diseases dataset from Refs. [48,51] was

TABLE 3.7
Result of the Classifiers Heart Disease Data Set [1]

Models	Precision (%)	Recall (%)	F1Score (%)	Accuracy (%)
KNN	67	67	67	67
SVM	67	65	65	66
DT	62	63	63	63
ANN	70	69	69	69
NB	64	66	65	66
RF	64	64	64	64
LR	65	65	65	65
Voting classifier	68	68	68	68
Gradient boosting	**71**	**71**	**71**	**71**

TABLE 3.8
Result of the Classifiers Heart Diseases Data Set [1]

Previous Work	KNN	RF	SVM	DT	ANN	NB	LR	VC	GB
Using supervised machine learning methods, predict heart disease	67	70	72	73	–	60	72	–	–
Research models with CVD	71	71	73	64	74	72	74	74	74
Research models with heart diseases dataset	72	95	73	90	78	84	86	87	89

one of three research methodologies used in this study, along with deep ANN, VC and GB. The recommended models' performance with the [49,52] dataset properly predicts the sickness; the RF classifier had the best performance (94%).

3.7 CONCLUSION

Women die from cardiovascular disease most often, yet it is not completely under-stood and is undertreated. For healthcare practitioners to enhance therapeutic inter-ventions and results for women, it is essential that they have a better understanding of the variations in angina pectoris and ACS symptoms between men and women, as well as the gender-based interpretation of diagnostic tests. Where required, cardiol-ogy guidelines should place a stronger focus on sex-related disparities. The clinical signs and personal risk factors for CHD that are unique to each woman must also be better understood by the women themselves. Further research will be needed to understand the various biochemical differences between the atherosclerosis of men and women. In this research, a variety of machine learning algorithms were employed to ANN. It can be utilized to detect heart disease, SVM, DT classifiers, LR, KNN, RF, VC, GB classifiers and NB. In the dataset for cardiovascular disease with all criteria, the GB classifier performed better than the RF classifier, while the RF classifier was the best classifier for heart disease. The findings of the study can be utilized to provide suggestions for the improvement of heart disease diagnostics. As a consequence, this may facilitate and speed up medical professionals' assessments of cardiovascular disease diagnosis.

REFERENCES

1. Maas, A.H. and Appelman, Y.E., 2010. Gender differences in coronary heart disease. *Netherlands Heart Journal*, *18*, pp.598–603.
2. Daly, C.A., Clemes, F., Lopez Sendon, J.L., Tavazzi, L., Boersma, E., Danchin, N., Delahaye, F., Gitt, A., Julian, D., Mulcahy, D. and Ruzyllo, W., 2005. On behalf of the Euro Heart Survey investigators The clinical characteristics and investigations planned in patients with stable angina presenting to cardiologists in Europe: from the Euro Heart Survey of stable angina. *European Heart Journal*, *26*, pp.996–1010.
3. Prescott, E., Hippe, M., Schnohr, P., Hein, H.O. and Vestbo, J., 1998. Smoking and risk of myocardial infarction in women and men: Longitudinal population study. *BMJ*, *316*(7137), p.1043.
4. Ossewaarde, M.E., Bots, M.L., Verbeek, A.L., Peeters, P.H., van der Graaf, Y., Grobbee, D.E.and van der Schouw, Y.T., 2005. Age at menopause, cause-specific mortality and total life expectancy. *Epidemiology*, *16*(4), pp.556–562.
5. Mahmood, S.S., Levy, D., Vasan, R.S., Wang, T.J., (2014). The Framingham heart study and the epidemiology of cardiovascular disease: A historical perspective. *The lancet*, *383*(9921), pp. 999–1008.
6. Sutton-Tyrrell, K., Lassila, H.C., Meilahn, E., Bunker, C., Matthews, K.A. and Kuller, L.H., 1998. Carotid atherosclerosis in premenopausal and postmenopausal women and its association with risk factors measured after menopause. *Stroke*, *29*(6), pp.1116–1121.
7. Matthews, K.A., Meilahn, E., Kuller, L.H., Kelsey, S.F., Caggiula, A.W. and Wing, R.R., 1989. Menopause and risk factors for coronary heart disease. *The New England Journal of Medicine*, *321*, pp.641–646.
8. Grundtvig, M., Hagen, T.P., German, M. and Reikvam, A., 2009. Sex-based differences in premature first myocardial infarction caused by smoking: Twice as many years lost by women as by men. *European Journal of Cardiovascular Prevention and Rehabilitation*, *16*, pp.174–179.
9. Vanhoutte, P.M., Shimokawa, H., Tang, E.H. and Feletou, M., 2009. Endothelial dysfunction and vascular disease. *Actaphysiologica*, *196*(2), pp.193–222.
10. Kip, K.E., Marroquin, O.C., Kelley, D.E., Johnson, B.D., Kelsey, S.F., Shaw, L.J., Rogers, W.J. and Reis, S.E., 2004. Clinical importance of obesity versus the metabolic syndrome in cardiovascular risk in women: A report from the Women's Ischemia Syndrome Evaluation (WISE) study. *Circulation*, *109*(6), pp.706–713.
11. Huxley, R., Barzi, F. and Woodward, M., 2006. Excess risk of fatal coronary heart disease associated with diabetes in men and women: Meta-analysis of 37 prospective cohort studies. *BMJ*, *332*(7533), pp.73–78.
12. Barton, M. and Meyer, M.R., 2009. Postmenopausal hypertension. Mechanisms and therapy. *Hypertension*, *54*, p.1118.
13. Vasan, R.S., Larson, M.G., Leip, E.P., Evans, J.C., O'Donnell, C.J., Kannel, W.B. and Levy, D., 2001. Impact of high-normal blood pressure on the risk of cardiovascular disease. *The New England Journal of Medicine*, *345*, pp.1291–1297.

14. Maas, A.H.E.M. and Franke, H.R., 2009. Women's health in menopause with a focus on hypertension. *Netherlands Heart Journal*, *17*, pp.69–73.

15. Ikeda, H., Inoue, T., Uemura, S., Kaibara, R., Tanaka, H. and Node, K., 2006. Effects of candesartan for middle-aged and elderly women with hypertension and menopausal-like symptoms. *Hypertension Research*, *29*(12), pp.1007–1012.

16. Gast, G.C.M., Grobbee, D.E., Pop, V.J., Keyzer, J.J., Wijnands-van Gent, C.J., Samsioe, G.N., Nilsson, P.M. and van der Schouw, Y.T., 2008. Menopausal complaints are associated with cardiovascular risk factors. *Hypertension*, *51*(6), pp.1492–1498.

17. Kennel, W.B., Castelli, W.P., Gordon, T. and McNamara, P.M., 1971. Serum cholesterol, lipoproteins and the risk of coronary heart disease. *Annals of Internal Medicine*, *74*, pp.1–12.

18. Trialists, C.T. and (CTT) collaborators, 2008. Efficacy and safety of cholesterol-lowering treatment: prospective meta-analysis of data from 90,056 participants in 14 randomised trials of statins. *The Lancet*, *366*(9493), pp.1267–1278.

19. Mizuno, K., Nakaya, N., Ohashi, Y., Tajima, N., Kushiro, T., Teramoto, T., Uchiyama, S. and Nakamura, H., 2008. Usefulness of pravastatin in primary prevention of cardiovascular events in women: Analysis of the Management of Elevated Cholesterol in the Primary Prevention Group of Adult Japanese (MEGA study). *Circulation*, *117*(4), pp.494–502.

20. Ridker, P.M., 2008. The JUPITER (Justification for the Use of Statins in Prevention: An Intervention Trial Evaluating Rosuvastatin) Study Group: Rosuvastatin to prevent vascular events in men and women with elevated C-reactive protein. *The New England Journal of Medicine*, *359*, pp.2195–2207.

21. Setji, T.L. and Brown, A.J., 2007. Polycystic ovary syndrome: Diagnosis and treatment. *The American Journal of Medicine*, *120*(2), pp.128–132.

22. Shaw, L.J., Bairey Merz, C.N., Azziz, R., Stanczyk, F.Z., Sopko, G., Braunstein, G.D., Kelsey, S.F., Kip, K.E., Cooper-DeHoff, R.M., Johnson, B.D. and Vaccarino, V., 2008. Withdrawn: Postmenopausal women with a history of irregular menses and elevated androgen measurements at high risk for worsening cardiovascular event-free survival: Results from the National Institutes of Health—National Heart, Lung, and Blood Institute sponsored women's ischemia syndrome evaluation. *The Journal of Clinical Endocrinology & Metabolism*, *93*(4), pp.1276–1284.

23. Brett, S.E., Jiang, B.Y., Turner, C., Ritter, J.M. and Chowienczyk, P.J., 2006. Elevation of plasma homocysteine by methionine loading increases the diastolic blood pressure response to exercise. *Journal of Hypertension*, *24*(10), pp.1985–1989.

24. McDonald, S.D., Malinowski, A., Zhou, Q., Yusuf, S. and Devereaux, P.J., 2008. Cardiovascular sequelae of preeclampsia/eclampsia: A systematic review and meta-analyses. *American Heart Journal*, *156*(5), pp.918–930.

25. Bellam, L., Casas, J.P., Hingorani, D. and Williams, D., 2009. Type 2 diabetes mellitus after gestational diabetes: A systematic review and meta-analysis. *Lancet*, *373*(9677), pp.1773–1779.

26. Mosca, L., Banka, C.L., Benjamin, E.J., Berra, K., Bushnell, C., Dolor, R.J., Ganiats, T.G., Gomes, A.S., Gornik, H.L., Gracia, C. Gulati, M. and Wenger, N.K., 2007. Expert Panel/Writing Group; American Heart Association; American Academy of Family Physicians; American College of Obstetricians and Gynecologists; American College of Cardiology Foundation; Society of Thoracic Surgeons; American Medical Women's Association; Centers for Disease Control and Prevention; Office of Research on Women's Health; Association of Black Cardiologists; American College of Physicians; World Heart Federation; National Heart, Lung, and Blood Institute; American College of Nurses. *Circulation*, *115*(11), pp.1481–1501.

27. Johnson, B.D., Kelsey, S.E. and Merz, C.N.B., 2004. Clinical risk assessment in women: Chest discomfort. Report from the WISE study. *Coronary Disease in Women: Evidence-Based Diagnosis and Treatment*, pp.129–141.
28. Pepine, C.J., Kerensky, R.A., Lambert, C.R., Smith, K.M., von Mering, G.O., Sopko, G., et al., 2006. Some thoughts on the vasculopathy of women with ischemic heart disease. *Journal of the American College of Cardiology*, 47(suppl), pp.S30–S35.
29. Shaw, L.J., Bugiardini, R.and Merz, C.N.B., 2009. Women and ischemic heart disease: Evolving knowledge. *Journal of the American College of Cardiology*, 54(17), pp.1561–1575.
30. Robinson, J.G., Wallace, R., Limacher, M., Ren, H., Cochrane, B., Wassertheil-Smoller, S., Ockene, J.K., Blanchette, P.L. and Ko, M.G., 2008. Cardiovascular risk in women with non-specific chest pain (from the Women's Health Initiative Hormone Trials). *The American Journal of Cardiology*, 102(6), pp.693–699.
31. Morise, A.P., Olson, M.B., Merz, C.N.B., Mankad, S., Rogers, W.J., Pepine, C.J., Reis, S.E., Sharaf, B.L., Sopko, G., Smith, K. and Pohost, G.M., 2004. Validation of the accuracy of pretest and exercise test scores in women with a low prevalence of coronary disease: The NHLBI-sponsored Women's Ischemia Syndrome Evaluation (WISE) study. *American Heart Journal*, 147(6), pp.1085–1092.
32. Reis, S.E., Holubkov, R., Conrad Smith, A.J., Kelsey, S.F., Sharaf, B.L., Reichek, N., Rogers, W.J., Merz, C.N., Sopko, G. and Pepine, C.J., 2001. WISE Investigators: Coronary microvascular dysfunction is highly prevalent in women with chest pain in the absence of coronary artery disease: Results from the NHLBI WISE study. *American Heart Journal*, 141(5), pp.735–741.
33. Warnes, C.A., Williams, R.G., Bashore, T.M., Child, J.S., Connolly, H.M., Dearani, J.A., Del Nido, P., Fasules, J.W., Graham, T.P., Hijazi, Z.M. and Hunt, S.A., 2008. ACC/ AHA 2008 guidelines for the management of adults with congenital heart disease: A report of the American college of cardiology/American heart association task force on practice guidelines (writing committee to develop guidelines on the management of adults with congenital heart disease) developed in collaboration with the American society of echocardiography, heart rhythm society, international society for adult congenital heart disease, society for cardiovascular angiography and interventions, and ....*Journal of the American College of Cardiology*, 52(23), pp.e143–e263.
34. Dey, S., Flather, M.D., Devlin, G., Brieger, D., Gurfinkel, E.P., Steg, P.G., FitzGerald, G., Jackson, E.A., Eagle, K.A. and GRACE investigators, 2009. Sex-related differences in the presentation, treatment and outcomes among patients with acute coronary syndromes: The Global Registry of Acute Coronary Events. *Heart*, 95(1), pp.20–26.
35. Pope, J.H., Aufderheide, T.P., Ruthazer, R., Woolard, R.H., Feldman, J.A., Beshansky, J.R., Griffith, J.L. and Selker, H.P., 2000. Missed diagnoses of acute cardiac ischemia in the emergency department. *New England Journal of Medicine*, 342(16), pp.1163–1170.
36. Milcent, C., Dormont, B., Durand-Zaleski, I. and Steg, P.G., 2007. Gender differences in hospital mortality and use of percutaneous coronary intervention in acute myocardial infarction: Microsimulation analysis of the 1999 nationwide French hospitals database. *Circulation*, 115(7), pp.833–839.
37. Berger, J.S., Elliott, L., Gallup, D., Roe, M., Granger, C.B., Armstrong, P.W., Simes, R.J., White, H.D., Van de Werf, F., Topol, E.J. and Hochman, J.S., 2009. Sex differences in mortality following acute coronary syndromes. *JAMA*, 302(8), pp.874–882.
38. Clayton, T.C., Pocock, S.J., Henderson, R.A., Poole-Wilson, P.A., Shaw, T.R.D., Knight, R. and Fox, K.A.A., 2004. Do men benefit more than women from an interventional strategy in patients with unstable angina or non-ST-elevation myocardial infarction? The impact of gender in the RITA 3 trial. *European Heart Journal*, 25(18), pp.1641–1650.

39. Donoghue, M.O., Boden, W., Braunwald, E., Cannon, C.P., Clayton, T.C. and de Winter, R.J., 2008. Early invasive versus conservative treatment strategies in women and men with unstable angina and non-ST-elevation myocardial infarction. *JAMA*, *300*, pp.71–80.

40. Vaccarino, V., Abramson, J.L., Veledar, E. and Weintraub, W.S., 2002. Sex differences in hospital mortality after coronary artery bypass surgery: Evidence for a higher mortality in younger women. *Circulation*, *105*(10), pp.1176–1181.

41. Alexander, K.P., Chen, A.Y., Newby, L.K., Schwartz, J.B., Redberg, R.F., Hochman, J.S., Roe, M.T., Gibler, W.B., Ohman, E.M. and Peterson, E.D., 2006. Sex differences in major bleeding with glycoprotein IIb/IIIa inhibitors: Results from the CRUSADE (Can Rapid risk stratification of Unstable angina patients Suppress Adverse outcomes with Early implementation of the ACC/AHA guidelines) initiative. *Circulation*, *114*(13), pp.1380–1387.

42. Berger, J.S., Bhatt, D.L., Cannon, C.P., Chen, Z., Jiang, L., Jones, J.B., Mehta, S.R., Sabatine, M.S., Steinhubl, S.R., Topol, E.J. and Berger, P.B., 2009. The relative efficacy and safety of clopidogrel in women and men: A sex-specific collaborative meta-analysis. *Journal of the American College of Cardiology*, *54*(21), pp.1935–1945.

43. Phan, A., Shufelt, C. and Merz, C.N.B., 2009. Persistent chest pain and no obstructive coronary artery disease. *JAMA*, *301*(14), pp.1468–1474.

44. Gulati, M., Cooper-DeHoff, R.M., McClure, C., Johnson, B.D., Shaw, L.J., Handberg, E.M., Zineh, I., Kelsey, S.F., Arnsdorf, M.F., Black, H.R. and Pepine, C.J., 2009. Adverse cardiovascular outcomes in women with nonobstructive coronary artery disease: A report from the Women's Ischemia Syndrome Evaluation Study and the St James Women Take Heart Project. *Archives of Internal Medicine*, *169*(9), pp.843–850.

45. Cortes, C. and Vapnik, V., 1995. Support-vector networks. *Machine Learning*, *20*(3), pp.273–297.

46. Aida-zade, K., Xocayev, A. and Rustamov, S., 2016. Speech recognition using Support Vector Machines. In *2016 IEEE 10th International Conference on Application of Information and Communication Technologies (AICT)*, pp.1–4.

47. Tian, Y., Li, E., Yang, L. and Liang, Z., 2018. An image processing method for green apple lesion detection in natural environment based on GABPNN and SVM. In *2018 IEEE International Conference on Mechatronics and Automation (ICMA)*, pp.1210–1215.

48. Brownlee, J., 2020. How to develop voting ensembles with python.*Machine Learning Mastery*, Apr. 16. https://machinelearningmastery.com/voting-ensembles-with-python/ (accessed Jul. 08, 2021).

49. Princy, R.J.P., Parthasarathy, S., Jose, P.S.H., Lakshminarayanan, A.R. and Jeganathan, S., 2020. Prediction of cardiac disease using supervised machine learning algorithms. In *2020 4th International Conference on Intelligent Computing and Control Systems (ICICCS)*, pp.570–575.

50. Kaur, R., Kumar, R. and Gupta, M., 2022. Food image-based nutritional management system to overcome polycystic ovary syndrome using deep learning: A systematic review. *International Journal of Image and Graphics*, *22*(4), 2350043, https://doi.org /10.1142/S0219467823500432.

51. Kaur, R., Kumar, R. and Gupta, M., 2022. Predicting risk of obesity and meal planning to reduce the obese in adulthood using artificial intelligence. *Endocrine*, *78*(3), pp.458–469.

52. Kaur, R., Kumar, R. and Gupta, M., 2022. Food image-based diet recommendation framework to overcome PCOS problem in women using deep convolutional neural network. *Computers and Electrical Engineering*, *103*, p.108298.

4 Lifestyle and Dietary Management Associated with Chronic Diseases in Women Using Deep Learning

Rajdeep Kaur, Rakesh Kumar and Meenu Gupta

4.1 INTRODUCTION

According to the World Health Organization (WHO), women and girls are at risk of poor health due to discrimination and gender inequality. Women and girls often have a more challenging time than men and boys accessing health information and services [1]. In addition, women may suffer a variety of gynaecological problems in their lives, such as during pregnancy, menopause and pre-menstruation. Non-communicable diseases, including cancers, respiratory diseases, cardiovascular diseases, depression, diabetes, dementia and musculoskeletal disorders, are the leading causes of mortality and disability among women. To optimize the improvement of women's health, enough resources must be given to the prevention, management and treatment of non-communicable diseases in women [2]. Maxwell et al. [3] highlighted the effect of obesity on women's health. They emphasized the need to lower the risk of non-communicable illnesses by managing weight, minimizing excess weight, and improving inadequate nutrition in women considering becoming pregnant . Obesity is linked to a higher chance of developing several cancers, including colon cancer in premenopausal women and endometrial cancer in postmenopausal women. Other cancers that are high risk include, breast, oesophageal, ovarian and renal cancers. In obese women, conservative or surgical obesity management can minimize cancer risk. Obesity, a dietary disorder, is exhibiting a worrisome trend, not only because it affects a large amount of the population, but also because it has begun to emerge earlier in life. Obesity is mostly caused by excessive eating and insufficient exercise. If people consume large quantities of energy, especially fat and carbohydrates, and do not burn it via physical activities like yoga, workouts and other forms of exercise, then a large portion of excess energy is turned into fat and

DOI: 10.1201/9781003378556-4

TABLE 4.1
Obesity Levels Using BMI [5]

BMI (kg/m^2)	Obesity Classification
<18.5	Underweight
18.5–24.9	Normal weight
25–29.9	Overweight
30.0–34.9	Obesity level I
35.0–39.9	Obesity level II
≥40	Obesity level III

stored in the body. There are several causes of obesity, and it is linked to thousands of dangerous diseases. It is among the most prevalent health issues in the world [4]. Thus, quick intervention is necessary to prevent obesity. People are classified as overweight or obese according to their Body Mass Index (BMI), which is calculated by dividing their weight in kilogrammes by their height in metres squared (kg/m^2), as shown in Table 4.1.

In recent years, the use of artificial intelligence (AI) in medicine has risen fast, particularly in diagnostics and healthcare systems. Today's AI technology can generate algorithms for disease diagnosis, therapy and medical research. In this chapter, we describe the current state of AI research on gynaecologic cancers, obesity, women's health issues and lifestyle modifications to prevent these diseases. AI models are used to identify or predict various women-related diseases. A deep learning (DL) approach is used by different researchers in women's health for different purposes such as calculating the amniotic fluid index automatically from ultrasound images [], breast cancer [7, 8], pregnancy-related prenatal abnormalities and cervical cancer in women [9], predicting the mode of delivery [10] and cervical lesion diagnosis [11]. Breast cancer is the second leading cause of cancer-related deaths among women nationwide. In recent years, the survival rate of breast cancer patients has increased due to early detection and improved prognosis because of the use of AI in healthcare. However, to conduct legitimate state-of-the-art research, significant AI research requires a large amount of high-quality data. The integration of AI is crucial to advance cancer research in the age of the Fourth Industrial Revolution, or Industry 4.0. Researchers shouldn't be discouraged from creating superior automated AI models to combat diseases, particularly breast cancer, by the lack of readily available data, since there are various approaches available to generate synthetic data. The various keywords related to women's health issues and machine learning (ML) techniques are shown in Figure 4.1.

This chapter is divided into five sections. Section 4.2 outlines research studies that sought to predict women's health problems. Section 4.3 describes the proposed methodology and illustrates the ML workflow for predicting women's health problems. In Section 4.4, a case study is presented in which multiple ML models are used to predict breast cancer. This study concludes in Section 4.5.

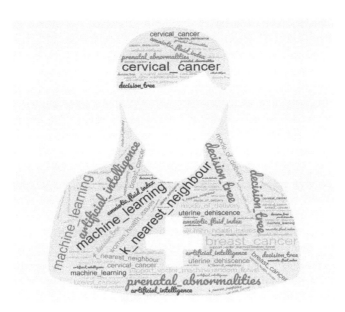

FIGURE 4.1   Keywords related to various women health issues and ML techniques.

4.2   BACKGROUND STUDY

This section provides an extensive analysis of the various AI-based management techniques used to address women's health problems. The review process is presented in three phases. The first phase includes a survey of various researchers' opinions on applying ML techniques to predict women's health issues. In the second phase, studies that use ML models to predict obesity are presented. The third phase includes articles that use AI strategies for life management and prevention of such diseases.

4.2.1   USING ML MODELS TO PREDICT DISEASES RELATED TO WOMEN'S HEALTH

Parvathi et al. [9] focused particularly on providing women with preventative and diagnostic healthcare. Two important health concerns, foetal anomalies in pregnant women and cervical cancer in women, were investigated to assist doctors and patients in taking preventative action. The authors proposed ML algorithms be used to assess and anticipate irregularities. A web application was created to ease communication among the many data factors and produce precise predictions of foetal abnormality from cardiotocography (CTG) images. The methodologies of linear, logistic and correlation analysis were used to create this query. Kadry et al. [7] proposed a model to examine the performance of pre-trained DL models. VGG16, VGG19, ResNet18 and ResNet50, with classifiers k-nearest neighbours (KNN), random forest (RF) and decision tree (DT), were used to detect breast cancer from the benchmark data set. The exploratory results of this study confirmed that VGG16, when combined with DT, improves detection by 95.5%. The suggested work not only improved precision but also sensitivity, specificity and F1 scores. Wu et al. [8] proposed ML models that predict the occurrence of cancer symptoms, which might help make clinical decisions that improve the quality of cancer care. These models intended to create and verify a variety of classification models employing ML techniques to predict the occurrence of breast cancer–related lymphedema among Chinese women. The multi-layer perceptron (MLP) and logistic regression models provided the greatest discrimination for the prediction, while the KNN and support vector machine (SVM) models demonstrated satisfactory validation efficacy in the ML validation data set. Fernandez et al. [10] proposed RF, SVM and multilayer perceptron be utilized to predict the mode of delivery and to create a clinical decision support system. The modes of delivery can be categorized into three: euthymic vaginal delivery, caesarean section and instrumental vaginal delivery. These models were evaluated using a large clinical database encompassing 25,038 records with 48 attributes of women who gave birth at the Obstetrics and Gynaecology Service of the University Clinical Hospital. The performance of the three developed algorithms was comparable, with each system achieving a classification accuracy of at least 90% between caesarean and vaginal delivery modes and an accuracy of about 87% between instrumental and euthocic delivery modes. Dong et al. [11] developed a Dense-U-Net DNN-based AI model (dropout + max pooling) to identify cervical lesions from colposcopy-captured images. The data set used to train the AI model includes 2,475 participants with 13,084 images of colposcopy. Furthermore, the comparison between the Dense-U-Net model and manual diagnosis revealed that the model was accurate, efficient and quick at classifying and detecting cervical lesions by colposcopy. Overall, the effectiveness and accuracy of diagnoses were excellent, although they might be improved upon. In several diagnostic tests, the model outperformed a professional with some expertise, which proves the model's relevance from a clinical point of view.

Cho et al. [6] proposed a DL-based approach for automatically calculating the amniotic fluid index from ultrasound images. The suggested network, designated AF-net, was influenced by three common convolution neural network (CNN) structures: U-net, M-net and DeepLab. A total of 435 images were obtained from the Department of Obstetrics & Gynaecology at Yonsei University in Seoul, to train and evaluate the proposed model. All weights were set as a normal distribution with a standard deviation of 0.01 and a zero-centred mean. The cost function was minimized by utilizing the Adam Optimizer with an initial learning rate of 0.00001. The suggested technique produced a dice similarity, mean absolute error, a mean relative error for the AFI value as 0.877 ± 0.086, 2.666 ± 2.986 and 0.018 ± 0.023, respectively. Kement et al. [12] proposed an ML model which can be utilized to anticipate uterine dehiscence and assist in determining the likelihood of rupture. Thus, complications resulting from early caesarean births can be minimized. For classification, logistic regression, multilayer perceptron, SVM, RF and naive Bayes (NB) techniques were applied. The NB algorithm provided the most accurate predictions as compared to the other models. Inan et al. [13] presented a study which makes it possible to generate high-quality breast cancer data by synthesizing existing data on the disease. It analysed the ability of deep generative models, such as the tabular variational autoencoder and the conditional generative adversarial network, to create high-quality synthetic tabular data of breast tumours and aid in the detection and prognosis of breast cancer. It tested the efficiency of many cutting-edge ML and DL classifiers trained on synthetically manufactured data and then evaluated on genuine data. The proposed integrated strategy can effectively generate high-quality synthetic data for the breast cancer domain, which can be used to develop high-quality AI models for early detection and accurate prognosis of breast cancer. Birchha et al. [14] proposed a study to analyse the performance of an ML classifier using an averaged-perceptron model on a Wisconsin data set for breast cancer. The initial concern was whether the averaged-perceptron classifier can outperform the other classifiers in terms of accuracy and whether it helps to decrease false-positive or false-negative breast cancer predictions. The learning categorization algorithms provided by the averaged-perceptron model were useful in the early diagnosis of breast cancer. The objective of the study was to explore the averaged-perceptron accuracy score of 0.984 with no false-negative predictions. The summary of the various research papers on women's health issues and ML techniques is mentioned in Table 4.2.

4.2.2 Using ML Models to Predict Obesity

Ferdowsy et al. [15] demonstrated ML-based models for predicting obesity. Several age groups, including both obese and non-obese people, were questioned to gather information. These researchers used nine different ML algorithms to create projections for obesity and evaluated the outcomes using performance criteria like accuracy and recall, among others. In comparison to other classifiers, the precision of the logistic regression approach was the greatest. Ma et al. [16] presented a study that found a link between obesity and the onset of polycystic ovary syndrome (PCOS) and demonstrated that obesity significantly affects the metabolic abnormalities of PCOS patients. The goal of the study was to describe and evaluate medical approaches to identifying, evaluating and treating obesity in PCOS patients.

Palechor et al. [17] presented a data set with 17 variables to predict obesity levels. The data were labelled with several obesity categories, including underweight, overweight and obesity (further categorized as Type-I, Type-II and Type-III). This information was used to develop ML models for assessing an individual's level of obesity, which was then used to build recommender systems for tracking obesity levels. Barber et al. [18] investigated in depth the major factors contributing to the relationship between obesity and PCOS. The association between weight gain and obesity as a PCOS risk factor was also studied in the paper. A healthy lifestyle and weight loss were the most effective treatments for women with obesity and PCOS. Cena [19] conducted a study on obesity and a rise in infertility cases. A drop in fertility rates was linked to the sharp rise in obesity and overweight prevalence. Weight loss was the most important factor affecting fertility and pregnancy outcomes. This study concluded that being overweight has a negative impact on fertility and pregnancy outcomes.

TABLE 4.2
Summary of the Research Papers on Women Health Issues and ML Techniques

Author, Year	Women Health Issue	ML Technique	Outcome
Parvathi et al. [9] 2023	Pregnancy-related prenatal abnormalities and cervical cancer in women	Linear regression, logistic regression and correlation analysis	Foetal anomaly and cervical cancer prediction from the CTG scan can be improved using approximate query processing techniques
Kadry et al. [7], 2023	Breast cancer	Pretrained DL techniques (VGG16, VGG19, ResNet18, ResNet50 with different classifiers (RF, DT, KNN)	VGG16 with DT classifier outperformed and achieved 95.5% accuracy
Wu et al. [8], 2022	Occurrence of breast cancer-related lymphedema	MLP, logistic regression, KNN, SVM models	MLP and logistic regression models performed better than other ML models
Fernandez et al. [10], 2022	Decision support system to predict the mode of delivery	SVM, multilayer perceptron and RF	Accuracy for predicting the caesarean and vaginal deliveries is $\geq 90\%$ and for instrumental and eutocic delivery approximately 87%
Dong et al. [11], 2022	Cervical lesion diagnosis	Dense U-net model (dropout + max pooling)	AI model outperformed a professional with some expertise
Cho et al. [6], 2021	Prediction of amniotic fluid index from ultrasound images	AF-net designed from U-net, DeepLab and M-net	Minimize sonographers' efforts as well as probability of human mistake by providing a high-quality AFI line candidate that is near to the ideal line as defined by AFI
Kement et al. [12], 2022	Uterine dehiscence prediction	Multilayer perceptron, logistic regression, SVM, RF and NB algorithm	NB performs better than other algorithms
Inan et al. [13], 2023	Breast cancer	Tabular variational autoencoder and conditional generative adversarial network	Tabular variational autoencoder outperformed in generating synthetic breast tumour data
Birchha et al. [14], 2023	Breast cancer	Averaged perceptron ML classifier	AP classifier achieved the highest accuracy

Smethers et al. [20] discussed how obesity could be treated by reducing body weight. It presented a study on clinical research which shows how lowering energy density promotes weight loss. This study provided a summary of dietary goals and weight-loss recommendations that can be used to help patients form sustaining and gratifying low-energy-dense eating habits. Dugan et al. [21] proposed a model for ML that predicts childhood obesity. To predict obesity, six ML models were utilized, including NB, RF, iterative dichotomiser 3 (ID3), random tree, J48 and NB. For training the models, the CHICA data set was used. The classification model ID3 had the best performance results, with 85% accuracy and 89% sensitivity.

4.2.3 Using ML to Monitor Physical Activity and Food Intake

Rahman et al. [22] created a sensor-based wearable device to track physical activity to fight obesity, utilizing ML boosting techniques like gradient boosting (GB), extreme gradient boosting (XGB), cat boosting, light GB classifiers etc. In addition to this, daily physical activity data were included in this study, which was collected from 30 participants. Furthermore, physical activities were classified by ML algorithms, with 90% accuracy. Jung [23] discussed the nutrient-rich diet recommendations to prevent obesity based on scientific knowledge. Dietary recommendations were generated using an effective clustering algorithm with similarity correlation and collaborative filtering. A mobile service for nutritional control was developed to prevent obesity. Consequently, the average accuracy of the menu recommendations for users was above 80%. Kumar et al. [24] discussed a perceptron model with multiple layers for classifying food categories and predicting their caloric content. The proposed model was able to provide meal suggestions for the treatment of obesity and disorders related to it. For image classification, extracted features were sent to the multi-perceptron model. In addition, the classification of food images and calorie computation using the multi-perceptron model were compared with the SVM model. Shen et al. [25] proposed an ML model for food image recognition to estimate the nutrients in food to keep a balanced diet, which helps control obesity. In this work, the CNN model was created by enhancing the Inception V3 and V4 models using the FOOD-101 food picture data set. Augmentation and multi-crop methods increased the outcomes. Pouladzadeh et al. [26] presented a method that estimates the number of calories in a food item by analysing the food image. It was also estimated to find out the quantity of food based on the portion and volume of the food from the food image. The model was designed to help dieticians to treat obese people. In this study, a food identification SVM classifier was trained to determine the volume and depth information using side views of the meal. Sefa-Yeboah et al. [27] designed a potential tool based on a genetic algorithm for tracking the energy balance of users and predicting the intake of calories required to meet daily calorie requirements for obesity management. A sample of 30 volunteers from Ghana University was used to test the proposed model. The model was able to predict the macro- and micronutrient requirements of the user.

4.3 PROPOSED METHODOLOGY

Data collection and pre-processing of the data are important phases in ML models. Pre-processing of the data can be achieved using different approaches like data reduction, data cleaning and data transformation. Data reduction aims to minimize the original data by removing features that are redundant, unimportant for decision-making or have a linear connection with other variables. This makes the data less dimensional and enables the algorithms to run more quickly and effectively [10]. Data cleansing is the process of fixing or removing from a data set erroneous, flawed, badly structured, duplicated or inadequate information. When combining many data sources, data duplication and labelling mistakes are prevalent. Even if the results and algorithms appear to be right, they are not reliable if the data is wrong. Different data sets will require different data cleansing processes. The process of changing, cleaning and classifying data into a format that can be utilized to create the ML model is known as data transformation. Data transformation is necessary when data must be converted to meet the format of the destination system. After data processing, apply an ML algorithm to train the model for the predictions. There are many ML algorithms out there, but it is hard to tell which one is better than the rest as ML methods depend on the data set given. Researchers use the RF, SVM, decision trees and KNN ML classifiers to make predictions and to support healthcare systems. The evaluation parameters to analyse the performance of these classifiers are accuracy, precision, recall and F1 score.

In addition to ML classifiers, medical image segmentation plays a vital role in detecting and classifying medical images fast and effectively. Accurate image segmentation algorithms are necessary for intelligent ML techniques for computer-aided diagnostics to automatically identify and detect diseased tissues and defective organs. Better diagnosis leads to better therapy, which increases the patient's survival rate. U-Net is gaining popularity in healthcare systems due to its capacity to accurately detect and categorize medical images quickly. U-Net is a DL architecture used for medical image segmentation tasks, such as tumour and organ identification, that are essential for identifying, diagnosing and treating diseases. To evaluate the segmentation results, the dice similarity, accuracy, sensitivity and specificity can be used as assessment measures. Dice similarity indicates the degree of similarity between a segmented output and a ground truth. Figure 4.2 shows the workflow of the ML model to predict the various health issues in women.

Furthermore, the importance of healthcare, diet and physical activity in people's lives has recently increased. AI and its subfields (ML and DL) play a vital role in nutrition and healthcare systems. AI supports users in living a healthy lifestyle by boosting the intelligence of fitness equipment, gadgets, wearables and mobile applications. The role of AI in lifestyle management is shown in Figure 4.3. The modern application of AI also includes changing people's habits. AI can simply monitor your fitness goals and repetitive workout routines. It then uses the information to direct you along your fitness journey.

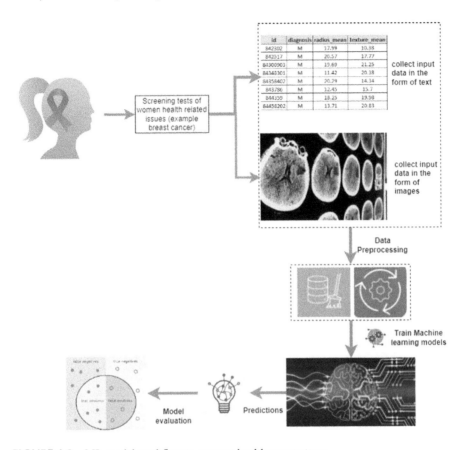

FIGURE 4.2 ML model workflow to support healthcare systems.

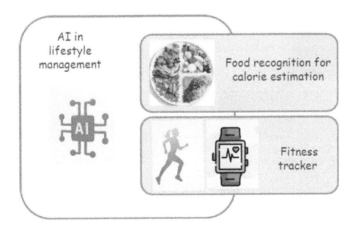

FIGURE 4.3 Role of AI in lifestyle management (food calories estimation and physical activity tracker).

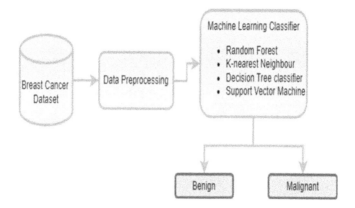

FIGURE 4.4 Breast cancer detection ML model workflow.

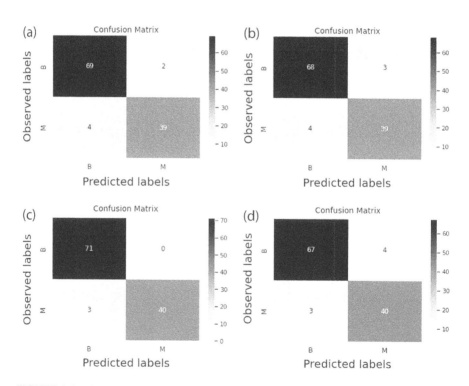

FIGURE 4.5 Confusion matrix: (i) RF, (ii) KNN, (iii) SVM, (iv) DTC.

4.4 BREAST CANCER DETECTION USING ML MODELS: A CASE STUDY

This chapter includes a thorough analysis of research articles that use ML models to predict various cancers or health problems in women, as well as articles that highlight lifestyle modification to prevent these health problems. A case study is undertaken using prior studies to predict types of breast cancer. The data set includes breast cancer attribute information collected from the UCI ML repository [28]. This data set is used to evaluate different ML models such as RF, KNN, SVM and decision tree classifier (DTC). This data set provides observations on 569 women with breast cancer and includes 31 attributes, one of which is the label for the data's breast cancer type. Correlation between the different attributes of the breast cancer data set is extracted and analysed to combine the highly corrected features. The data set was split after pre-processing into training and testing sets at a ratio of 80:20. Then RF, KNN, SVM and DTC classifiers are applied to predict the type of cancer (benign and malignant). The workflow to predict the type of breast cancer is shown in Figure 4.4.

In this case study, precision, recall and F1 score are used to assess the performance of the various classifiers. These performance metrics are computed using the confusion matrix shown in Figure 4.5.

RF, KNN, SVM and DTC achieved 94.7%, 93.8%, 97.3% and 93.8%, respectively, as shown in Table 4.3 and Figure 4.6. The SVM model achieved the highest accuracy. The classification report, which includes precision, recall and F1 score of the above-mentioned models, is shown in Table 4.4.

TABLE 4.3
Accuracy of Breast Cancer Detection Classifiers

Algorithm	Accuracy (%)
RF	94.7
KNN	93.8
SVM	97.3
DTC	93.8

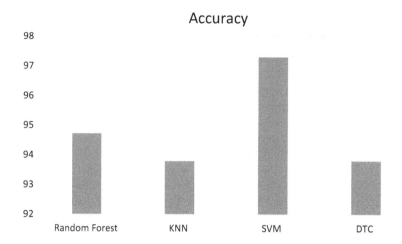

FIGURE 4.6   Accuracy comparison of breast cancer detection classifiers.

TABLE 4.4

Precision, Recall and F1 Score of Breast Cancer Detection Classifiers

Algorithm	Class	Precision (%)	Recall (%)	F1 Score
RF	B	0.95	0.97	0.96
	M	0.95	0.91	0.93
KNN	B	0.94	0.96	0.95
	M	0.93	0.91	0.92
SVM	B	0.96	1.00	0.98
	M	1.00	0.93	0.96
DTC	B	0.96	0.94	0.95
	M	0.91	0.93	0.92

4.5   CONCLUSION

Women experience more chronic health problems, like menopause, breast cancer, ovarian cancer, PCOS and other conditions related to women's health and pregnancy; as such, they require more access to healthcare. These issues have a negative influence on women's mental and physical well-being. Additionally, women who are obese have a higher chance of developing a variety of serious and deadly diseases. Obesity shortens lifespans, lowers the quality of women's lives and increases the cost of healthcare on a personal, societal and international scale. In the past decade, the usage of AI in healthcare has increased significantly. This chapter demonstrates the present state of AI research for women's health and gynaecologic oncology. It provides a thorough analysis of the research papers included in the present literature.

It describes the ML models used to predict chronic disorders, various cancers, obesity, etc., as well as the application of AI in lifestyle management to track diets and physical activity. Data collection and pre-processing are crucial stages in ML models and may be accomplished using a variety of strategies, including data reduction, data cleaning and data transformation. There are numerous ML algorithms available; however, it is difficult to say which one is superior because ML techniques depend on the data set that is provided. The RF, SVM, DT and KNN ML classifiers are utilized by researchers to create predictions and support healthcare systems. To identify types of breast cancer, a case study is conducted. The types of breast cancer (benign and malignant) are then predicted with RF, KNN, SVM and DTC classifiers. The SVM model has the greatest accuracy of 97.3%. In terms of ML models, there is still an opportunity for advancement. As DL technology progresses and more complicated types of analysis are possible, ML models may become more accurate and reliable. In addition, new data sources, such as genetic data, can be combined with current imaging data to offer further cancer diagnostics and prognostic information.

REFERENCES

1. "Gender and health," [Online]. Available: https://www.who.int/health-topics/gender.
2. S. A. E. Peters, M. Woodward, V. Jha, S. Kennedy, and R. Norton, "Women's health: A new global agenda," *BMJ Glob. Heal.*, vol. 1, no. 3, pp. 1–8, 2016, doi: 10.1136/bmjgh-2016-000080.
3. C. V. Maxwell *et al.*, "Management of obesity across women's life course: FIGO best practice advice," *Int. J. Gynecol. Obstet.*, vol. 160, no. S1, pp. 35–49, 2023, doi: 10.1002/ijgo.14549.
4. F. Ferdowsy, K. S. A. Rahi, M. I. Jabiullah, and M. T. Habib, "A machine learning approach for obesity risk prediction," Curr. *Res. Behav. Sci.*, vol. 2, no. May, p. 100053, 2021, doi: 10.1016/j.crbeha.2021.100053.
5. A. Pantanowitz *et al.*, "Estimation of Body Mass Index from photographs using deep Convolutional Neural Networks," *Informatics Med. Unlocked*, vol. 26, no. September, p. 100727, 2021, doi: 10.1016/j.imu.2021.100727.
6. H. C. Cho *et al.*, "Automated ultrasound assessment of amniotic fluid index using deep learning," *Med. Image Anal.*, vol. 69, p. 101951, 2021, doi: 10.1016/j.media.2020.101951.
7. V. Rajinikanth, "Classification of breast thermal images into and healthy / Cancer data engineering group using pre-trained deep learning schemes," *Procedia Comput. Sci.*, vol. 218, no. 2022, pp. 24–34, 2023, doi: 10.1016/j.procs.2022.12.398.
8. X. Wu *et al.*, "Comparison of machine learning models for predicting the risk of breast cancer-related lymphedema in Chinese women," *Asia-Pacific J. Oncol. Nurs.*, vol. 9, no. 12, p. 100101, 2022, doi: 10.1016/j.apjon.2022.100101.
9. A. J. Parvathi, H. Gopika, J. Suresh, S. L. Sree, and S. Harikumar, "Machine learning based approximate query processing for women analytics health analytics," *Procedia Comput. Sci.*, vol. 218, pp. 174–188, 2023, doi: 10.1016/j.procs.2022.12.413.
10. A. De Ramón Fernández, D. Ruiz Fernández, and M. T. Prieto Sánchez, "Prediction of the mode of delivery using artificial intelligence algorithms," *Comput. Methods Programs Biomed.*, vol. 219, 2022, doi: 10.1016/j.cmpb.2022.106740.
11. B. Dong *et al.*, "Classification and diagnosis of cervical lesions based on colposcopy images using deep fully convolutional networks: A man-machine comparison cohort study," *Fundam. Res.*, no. xxxx, 2022, doi: 10.1016/j.fmre.2022.09.032.

12. M. Kement, C. E. Kement, M. K. Kokanali, and M. Doganay, "Prediction of uterine dehiscence via machine learning by using lower uterine segment thickness and clinical features," *AJOG Glob. Reports*, vol. 2, no. 4, p. 100085, 2022, doi: 10.1016/j.xagr.2022.100085.

13. M. S. K. Inan, S. Hossain, and M. N. Uddin, "Data augmentation guided breast cancer diagnosis and prognosis using an integrated deep-generative framework based on breast tumor's morphological information," *Informatics Med. Unlocked*, vol. 37, no. July 2022, p. 101171, 2023, doi: 10.1016/j.imu.2023.101171.

14. V. Birchha and B. Nigam, "Performance analysis of averaged perceptron machine learning international conference on machine learning and data engineering classifier for breast cancer detection averaged perceptron Nigam b machine learning classifier for B," *Procedia Comput. Sci.*, vol. 218, no. 2022, pp. 2181–2190, 2023, doi: 10.1016/j.procs.2023.01.194.

15. F. Ferdowsy, K. S. A. Rahi, M. I. Jabiullah, and M. T. Habib, "A machine learning approach for obesity risk prediction," *Curr. Res. Behav. Sci.*, vol. 2, no. August, p. 100053, 2021, doi: 10.1016/j.crbeha.2021.100053.

16. R. Ma *et al.*, "Obesity management in polycystic ovary syndrome: Disparity in knowledge between obstetrician-gynecologists and reproductive endocrinologists in China,"*MC Endocrine Disorders*, vol. 21, pp. 1–10, 2021.

17. F. M. Palechor and A. de la H. Manotas, "Dataset for estimation of obesity levels based on eating habits and physical condition in individuals from Colombia, Peru and Mexico," *Data Br.*, vol. 25, p. 104344, 2019, doi: 10.1016/j.dib.2019.104344.

18. T. M. Barber, P. Hanson, M. O. Weickert, and S. Franks, "Obesity and polycystic ovary syndrome: Implications for pathogenesis and novel management strategies," *Clin. Med. Insights Reprod. Heal.*, vol. 13, p. 117955811987404, 2019, doi: 10.1177/1179558119874042.

19. H. Cena, L. Chiovato, and R. E. Nappi, "Obesity, polycystic ovary syndrome, and infertility: A new avenue for GLP-1 receptor agonists," *J. Clin. Endocrinol. Metab.*, vol. 105, no. 8, 2020, doi: 10.1210/clinem/dgaa285.

20. A. D. Smethers and B. J. Rolls, "Dietary management of obesity: Cornerstones of healthy eating patterns," *Med. Clin. North Am.*, vol. 102, no. 1, pp. 107–124, 2018, doi: 10.1016/j.mcna.2017.08.009.

21. T. M. Dugan, S. Mukhopadhyay, A. Carroll, and S. Downs, "Machine learning techniques for prediction of early childhood obesity," *Appl. Clin. Inform.*, vol. 6, no. 3, pp. 506–520, 2015, doi: 10.4338/ACI-2015-03-RA-0036.

22. S. Rahman, M. Irfan, M. Raza, K. M. Ghori, S. Yaqoob and M. Awais, "Performance analysis of boosting classifiers in recognizing activities of daily living" *Int. J. Environ. Health Res.*, vol.17, no. 3, pp. 1082, 2020.

23. Jung, H. and Chung, K., "Knowledge-based dietary nutrition recommendation for obese management", *Inf. Technol. Manag.*, vol. 17, pp. 29–42, 2016.

24. R. D. Kumar, E. G. Julie, Y. H. Robinson, S. Vimal, and S. Seo, "Recognition of food type and calorie estimation using neural network," *J. Supercomput.*, vol. 77, no. 8, pp. 8172–8193, 2021, doi: 10.1007/s11227-021-03622-w.

25. Z. Shen, A. Shehzad, S. Chen, H. Sun, and J. Liu, "Machine learning based approach on food recognition and nutrition estimation," *Procedia Comput. Sci.*, vol. 174, pp. 448–453, 2020, doi: 10.1016/j.procs.2020.06.113.

26. P. Pouladzadeh, S. Shirmohammadi, and R. Al-Maghrabi, "Measuring calorie and nutrition from food image," *IEEE Trans. Instrum. Meas.*, vol. 63, no. 8, pp. 1947–1956, 2014, doi: 10.1109/TIM.2014.2303533.

27. S. M. Sefa-Yeboah, K. Osei Annor, V. J. Koomson, F. K. Saalia, M. Steiner-Asiedu, and G. A. Mills, "Development of a mobile application platform for self-management of obesity using artificial intelligence techniques," *Int. J. Telemed. Appl.*, vol. 2021, 2021, doi: 10.1155/2021/6624057.

28. O. L. M. William, H. Wolberg, and W. Nick Street, "Breast cancer Wisconsin (diagnostic) data set," 1992 [Online]. Available: http://archive.ics.uci.edu/ml/.

5 Gender Differences in Diabetes Care and Management Using AI

Pawan Whig, Shama Kouser,
Tabrej Ahamad Khan, Syed Ali Mehdi,
Naved Alam and Rahul Reddy Nadikattu

5.1 INTRODUCTION

The worldwide prevalence of type 2 diabetes mellitus (T2DM) is growing. In 2015, around 415 million individuals were impacted, with a predicted total of over 650 million by 2040. T2DM is a growing epidemic with enormous implications for global healthcare systems, as well as for the people impacted, as shown in Figure 5.1. To curb this enormous growth, effective preventative techniques at a population level are required (Whig, Velu, & Naddikatu, 2022). These treatments have the potential to significantly lower the number of diabetic patients in the future. Many studies have successfully examined various lifestyle and pharmaceutical intervention techniques without taking gender or ethnicity into account (Alkali et al., 2022).

Several features of gender, however, have been recognized as risk issues for T2DM, including pathogenesis, onset age, identification, weight and organization of T2DM. Furthermore, the America Diabetes Association's (ADA) guidelines on diabetes risk consider gender, and men are recognized as being at risk of diabetes (Whig, Kouser, Velu, et al., 2022; Whig, Velu, & Sharma, 2022). According to similar guidelines, high-risk populations for T2DM growth, such as Americans, Hispanics, Native Americans, Asian Americans, and individuals who provide a calming presence, should be screened for early diabetes. The non-Hispanic white population has the lowest diabetes prevalence (Whig, Velu, & Bhatia, 2022).

Screenings for diabetes among Asian individuals should commence at lower Body Mass Index (BMI) thresholds compared to other populationsdue to higher levels of visceral fat accumulation. The majority of participants in weight loss research are women. Women may be more concerned about their weight and exhibit higher rates of weight management engagement, leading them to pursue medical care for weight reduction treatment (Whig, Velu, & Nadikattu, 2022).

DOI: 10.1201/9781003378556-5

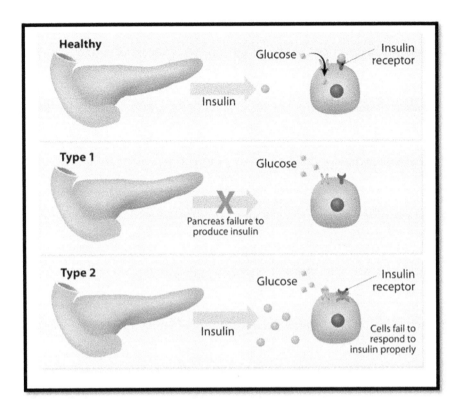

FIGURE 5.1 Type 2 diabetes mellitus (T2DM). Figure 5.1 is a medical illustration that represents the pathophysiology of type 2 diabetes mellitus. At the centre of the image, there is a large circular shape that represents the body. Above this shape, there is an arrow that points to a smaller circular shape, which represents the pancreas. Inside the pancreas, there are smaller shapes that represent the Islets of Langerhans, where the insulin-producing beta cells are located.

The highest effectiveness was observed in severely overweight patients who underwent surgical interventions, often seen among individuals with a high body mass, particularly females. Diabetes risk was lowered by nearly 60% when lifestyle changes were implemented. The flowchart for identification of type 1 and type 2 DM is shown in Figure 5.2. There is currently no physiological basis for significant gender difference in weight reduction; however, some studies show that women shed less weight than men, particularly visceral fat (Jupalle et al., 2022).

Although a patient's gender has significant effects on different elements of T2DM therapy, these factors do not influence therapeutic choices (Tomar et al., 2021). As a

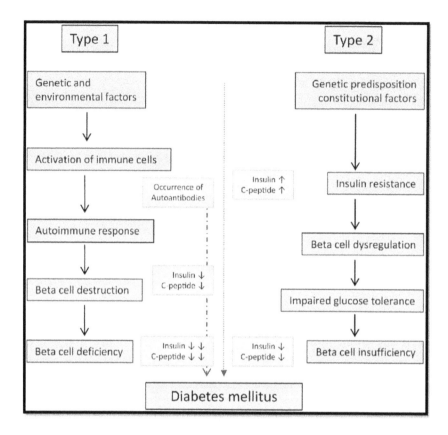

FIGURE 5.2 Flowchart for identification of type 1 and type 2 diabetes. Figure 5.2 is a flowchart that outlines the process of identifying type 1 and type 2 diabetes. The flowchart starts with the initial step of measuring blood glucose levels. If the blood glucose levels are elevated, the next step is to determine if the patient has symptoms of diabetes, such as increased thirst, frequent urination and unexplained weight loss.

result, this study discusses and highlights how gender and ethnicity are critical factors in the prevention of T2DM.

Diabetes is one of the most serious health crises of the twenty-first century. In 2015, diabetes was the sixth largest cause of death globally and its future trend is shown in Figure 5.3. In 2011, diabetes was the fourth largest cause of death among non-communicable diseases (NCDs) globally (Whig, Nadikattu, & Velu, 2022). In 2011, diabetes was the sixth largest cause of death in women globally. Access to healthcare is dependent on the availability and cost of the required services, physical accessibility and acceptance rates. Diabetes-related morbidity and death are heavily influenced by access to healthcare (Anand et al., 2022). Existing research indicates that there are gender inequalities in how diabetes is treated. Women were less likely than men to receive the recommended treatment, and women received less intensive therapy and monitoring.

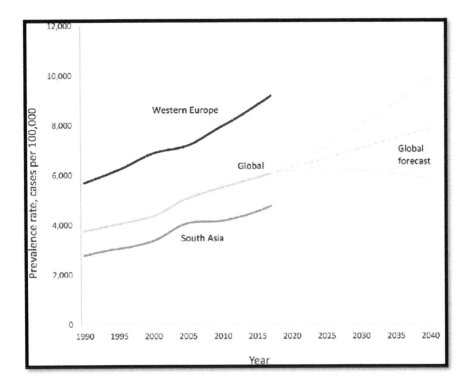

FIGURE 5.3   Diabetes future trend. A diabetes future trend diagram may show the projected increase or decrease of diabetes prevalence over time, based on factors such as population growth, ageing, lifestyle changes and medical advancements. It may also include statistics and data on diabetes-related complications, such as cardiovascular disease, kidney failure and amputations, as well as the economic and social burden of the disease.

5.2   APPROACHES

If older material was very important to this study, it was examined. Relevant material was comprehensively reviewed, and a manual search was conducted to locate additional pertinent information on the subject matter. In a story synthesis method, outcomes are described descriptively rather than systematically.

Sex differences are biological distinctions between men and women. These disparities between men and women are caused by changes in sex chromosomes and their effect on organ systems (Velu & Whig, 2022). Gender disparities emerge from social influences.

Gender disparities are caused by variances in behaviour, being subjected to specific environmental influences, diet, lifestyle and stress, as well as differing attitudes towards treatment and prevention. It is frequently impossible to distinguish between "sex" and "gender" consequences since they are interconnected throughout life (Khera et al., 2021).

5.3   CHANGES IN LIFESTYLE

Few preventative studies and systematic reviews address possible gender differences in diabetes prevention, as shown in Figure 5.4. A meta-analysis of studies revealed comparative effectiveness in reducing therisk of diabetes and achieving weight loss in both men and women who received lifestyle interventions for a duration of two years following the intervention. After one and three years, the risk was reduced by approximately 40%, with a considerable weight loss of nearly 2.5 kg after three years (Velu & Whig, 2021). As a result, encouraging healthy behaviour is critical, with specific emphasis placed on lifestyle changes that are sometimes overlooked in certain genders, such as a good diet in men and physical exercise in women. Furthermore, there was no relationship with gender and the taking of oral medications.

Interestingly, there is a newly published Indian trial of individuals over the age of 50 who got a stepwise intervention strategy that began with lifestyle improvements and then progressed to medication, if needed. Men had a 37% drop in diabetes incidence, while women had a less significant drop of 24%.

There were no significant differences between genders discovered; however, do after six months and one year, men appear to meet their physical activity goals much more frequently than women do. Initially, women reported that they would have more obstacles in participating in the study (Nadikattu et al., 2020). According to the

FIGURE 5.4   Gender differences in diabetes prevention

researchers, this had an impact on recruiting and lifestyle improvements. In addition to the findings, it was observed that among the educated participants, the female representation was significantly higher, accounting for 63% of the educated population. This indicates a notable gender disparity in educational attainment, with a higher proportion of women engaging in educational activities. The substantial female presence in the educated population highlights the progress made in promoting gender equality and empowering women through education. However, further analysis and exploration are warranted to understand the underlying factors contributing to this gender imbalance and to ensure equal opportunities for both men and women in educational pursuits..

In the Diabetes Prevention Program (DPP) intervention group, intensive lifestyle change lowered diabetes risk. Various components of DPP are shown in Figure 5.5. Even though women met much more lifestyle change objectives than men, diabetes incidence was comparable. Among men, several factors, such as elevated cholesterol levels and taller stature were associated with increased risk factors, while women exhibited higher BMI and lower levels of physical activity. After one year, there was no difference in the gender of participants who had lost less than 3% of their body weight. A Weight reduction ranging from 3–7% led to a decrease in 2-hour glucose levels and improved insulin resistance in males likened to females.Furthermore a weight loss exceeding 7% also demonstrated positive effects. The insulin resistance relation with age is shown in Figure 5.6.

The Da Qing Study's lifestyle intervention group observed a possible advantage was the cardiovascular condition of those who participated [Lean & Sattar, 2019]. This may be partly explained by men's higher smoking prevalence compared to women's lower prevalence. However, this is simply speculation and was not addressed in depth in the original paper. Furthermore, just a small number of participants were considered over a long period; varied behaviours and cultural and ethnic characteristics must be considered before making broad conclusions (Whig

FIGURE 5.5   Diabetes prevention program

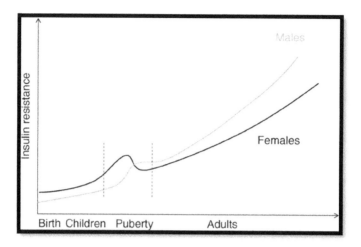

FIGURE 5.6   Insulin resistance relation with age

& Ahmad, 2014). As previously stated, ethnic disparities, in addition to gender difference, must be taken into account in weight reduction and lifestyle management programmes. In a supplimenatry study, it was noted that black women exhibited comparatively lower rates of successful weight reduction through lifestyle intervention compared towomen from other ethnic groups. Furthermore, compared to non-Hispanic white participants, this cultural group had a more recent arrival, lower income levels, and a majority representation of women. Attendance barriers among underprivileged patients might be a major explanation for this, although this was not studied further (Khera et al., 2021).

5.4   SYMPTOMS

Diabetes symptoms are determined by your blood sugar level as shown in Figure 5.7.

The signs of both types of diabetes can be alike, such as augmented dehydration, recurrent micturition, unexplained weight loss, fatigue, mood swings, vision problems and susceptibility to infections, including vaginal infections. Both types of diabetes can also lead to the presence of ketones in urine.

5.5   CAUSES

It is vital to understand how the body typically uses glucose to understand diabetes, as shown in Figure 5.8.

Insulin is released by the pancreas into the bloodstream, facilitating the entry of glucose into cells for energy utilization. Glucose comes from the food we eat and the liver stores glucose for later use. The specific factors involved are still unknown.

FIGURE 5.7   Diabetes symptoms

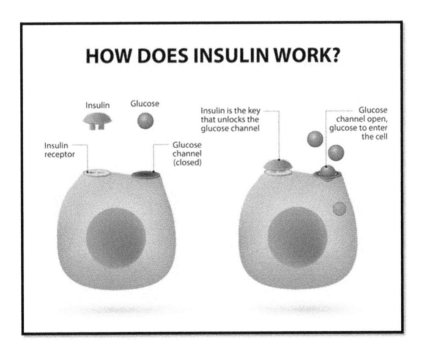

FIGURE 5.8   How insulin functions.

5.6   RISK ELEMENTS

Figure 5.9 shows that depending on the type of diabetes, the risk factors differ. However, not everyone with these autoantibodies will necessarily develop diabetes.

There are several risk factors associated with diabetes:

1. *Age:* As individuals get older, their risk of developing type 2 diabetes increases.
2. *Family history:* A family history of diabetes can increase an individual's risk of developing the disease.
3. *Obesity:* Being overweight or obese can increase an individual's risk of developing type 2 diabetes.
4. *Sedentary lifestyle:* A lack of physical activity can increase an individual's risk of developing type 2 diabetes.

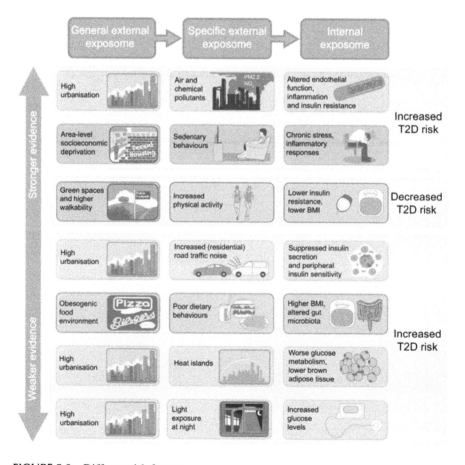

FIGURE 5.9   Different risk factors.

It is essential to be aware of these risk factors and take steps to manage them to reduce the risk of developing diabetes.

5.7 COMPLICATIONS

Diabetes is a chronic condition that can result in various complications, gradually affecting different parts of the body. Poor management of blood sugar levels can lead to long-term complications that are disabling or potentially fatal. Among the complications shown in Figure 5.10, cardiovascular disease is a significant concern and is more prevalent among individuals with diabetes. Nerve damage is another common complication, leading to symptoms such as tingling, numbness, burning or pain in the limbs, as well as digestive issues and erectile dysfunction in men. Damage to blood vessels can cause heart disease, stroke and poor circulation in the legs and feet, increasing the risk of infections and amputations.

Diabetes can also have detrimental effects onthe eyes, resulting in diabetic retinopathy, cataracts and glaucoma, leading to vision loss and potential blindness. Kidney damage can occur, leading to kidney disease or failure. Skin conditions, includingbacterial and fungal infections, can also arise due to diabete-related damage. Moreover, there is an increased risk of hearing loss, depression and Alzheimer's disease, particularly in individuals with type 2 diabetes.

To prevent or delay these complications, effective management of diabetes is crucial. This includes maintaining healthy blood sugar levels, adopting a healthy

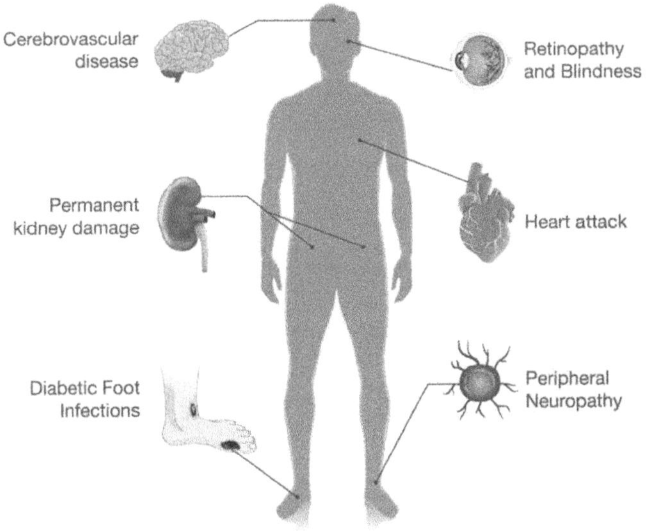

FIGURE 5.10 Complications with diabetes.

lifestyle, adhering to prescribed medications, and seeking regular medical care and check-ups. By actively managing diabetes, individuals can minimize the risk and impact of these long-term complications, thereby maintaining a better quality of life.

5.8   PREGNANCY COMPLICATIONS

5.8.1   Low Sugar Levels

Shortly after birth, newborns of gestational diabetic mothers can experience low blood sugar (hypoglycaemia). This is explained by the fact that they produce a lot of insulin.

5.8.2   Diabetes Type 2

Babies whose mothers have gestational diabetes are more likely to grow up obese and acquire type 2 diabetes.

5.8.3   Death

Uncontrolled gestational diabetes increases the risk of a baby's mortality either during pregnancy or soon after birth.

Gestational diabetes can potentially result in the following maternal complications: preeclampsia, high blood pressure and excessive swelling in the legs and feet. Women are more likely to develop gestational diabetes again if they have already had it during a previous pregnancy, as shown in Figure 5.11.

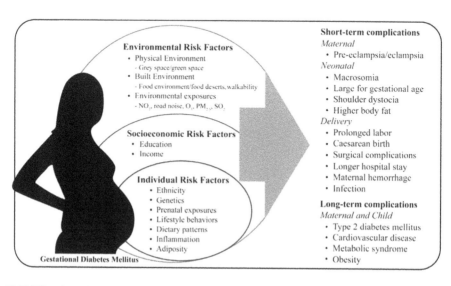

FIGURE 5.11   Gestational diabetes

5.9 PREVENTION

Type 1 diabetes cannot be prevented, but women can take steps to avoid or treat gestational diabetes and prediabetes.

Eating a healthy and nutritious diet is essential in preventing diabetes. It is recommended to choose foods that are high in fibre, lower in calories and fats and rich in whole grains, vegetables and fruits. Eating a variety of foods will help prevent boredom and ensure that you get all the necessary nutrients.

Physical activity plays an important role in preventing diabetes. It is recommended to engage in about 30 minutes of moderate aerobic exercise most days of the week, or at least 150 minutes of moderate aerobic exercise each week. A brisk daily walk can be a suitable example of moderate aerobic exercise, and breaking up a long workout into shorter periods throughout the day can also be effective. However, if a woman is pregnant, it is crucial that they avoid trying to lose weight on their own and that they consult their doctor to determine how much weight gain is safe during pregnancy. It is essential to make long-term changes to food and exercise routines to maintain a healthy weight.

By taking these preventative steps, the risk of developing diabetes can be significantly lowered and health and well-being can be improved.

5.10 CASE STUDY

During the Women in Data Science (WiDS) Datathon 2021, we created a model to predict whether a patient who has previously been diagnosed with DM will be identified as such during the primary 24 hours of being admitted to an Intensive Care Unit (ICU). Knowledge about a patient's medical problems can help clinicians make better judgements in the ICU. Another difficulty arises when a patient is unable to offer such information owing to their medical condition, such as shock or unconsciousness. As a result, it is critical to determine within the first 24 hours after admission whether a patient has a long-lasting illness through the data acquired.

DM is defined by the WHO as follows:

Type 1 diabetes normally disappears after delivery, but the other two kinds of diabetes require long-term treatment. Diabetes affects around 8.5% of the adult population, regardless of gender. Below are some suggestions for the following analysis:

- Examine blood sugar levels, but keep in mind that people who do not have diabetes might also have high blood sugar levels.
- Examine the effects of diabetes on other organs, such as the kidney, but keep in mind that people who do not have diabetes can still have renal dysfunction.
- Ethnicity might be considered since some ethnicities appear to be more prone to diabetes.
- The most intriguing feature categories are demography, vitals, labs and arterial blood gas.

The APACHE scale measures the severity of an illness. However, the APACHE score has inferior calibration, making it difficult to compare between institutions. As a result, the APACHE covariates are unlikely to be as useful in diagnosing diabetes.

5.11   OVERVIEW OF THE DATA

MIT's GOSSIP programme contributed the data. It includes

- 179 characteristics that were selected from two feature categories: identification, demographic.
- 1 DM target

In every machine learning project, the target variable's class imbalance is a difficulty. As a result, it presents an obstacle to the application of diabetes diagnosis. Diabetes was diagnosed in 8.5% of people in 2014, according to the WHO. Diabetes is diagnosed in 22% of the patients in the training data, as shown in Figure 5.12.

5.11.1   IDENTIFIERS FOR DATA CLEANING

In the training data, there are 204 distinct hospital IDs, and 190 in the test data. In the training data, hospital IDs vary from 1 to 204, whereas in the testing data, they

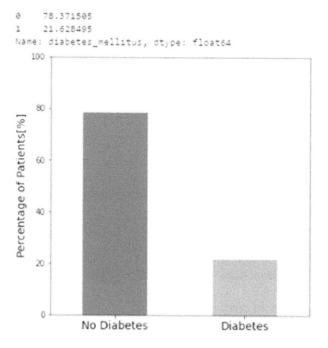

FIGURE 5.12   Percentages of patients

range from 10,001 to 10,199. We could see if hospital ID 1 corresponded to hospital ID 10,001 in the testing data. As a result, the hospital ID should most likely not be included in the final features. However, we shall utilize the hospital ID as an example.

5.11.2 Body Mass Index

BMI is a statistic that shows how a person's weight compares to their height, as shown in Figure 5.13 and the corresponding heatmap in Figure 5.14. We can run a quick sanity check on the BMI statistics because we know the patient's height and weight.

The sanity check revealed that there are differences between the computed and supplied BMI values due to the restricted weight and height measurements. The weight and height can be recreated, but we will skip that step for now.

5.11.3 Probability of Pregnancy

Because diabetes may arise during pregnancy, we will include a feature that will assist the model in determining if a patient is pregnant or not. The mean pregnancy probability is shown in Table 5.1.

The presented graph indicates a higher number of missing values in the measurements obtained within the first hour compared to the data collected over the first 24

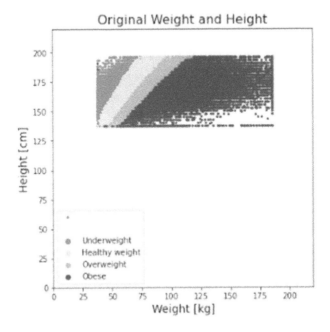

FIGURE 5.13 Body Mass Index (BMI).

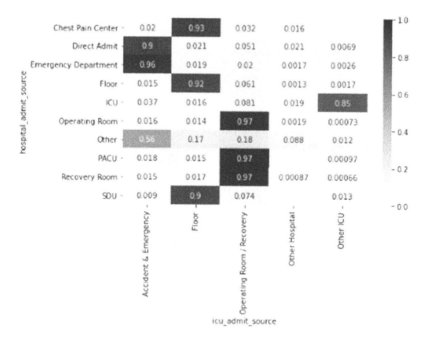

FIGURE 5.14 Heatmap for BMI.

TABLE 5.1
Mean Pregnancy Probability

Mean Pregnancy Probability According to Age and Gender

	Male	Female
<20	0.000000	0.105802
20–30	0.000000	0.180434
30–35	0.000000	0.154916
35–40	0.000000	0.090375
40–45	0.000000	0.019958
>45	0.000000	0.000000

hours. Additional columns with similar names, such as "glucose apache" and "d1 glucose min/d1 glucose max," can be found. According to the provided data dictionary, the "_apache" variables are calculated within a day and yield the highest score. The variables "d1max" and "d1min" represent the patient's concentration throughout their unit stay on day 1, as depicted in Figure 5.15–5.18.

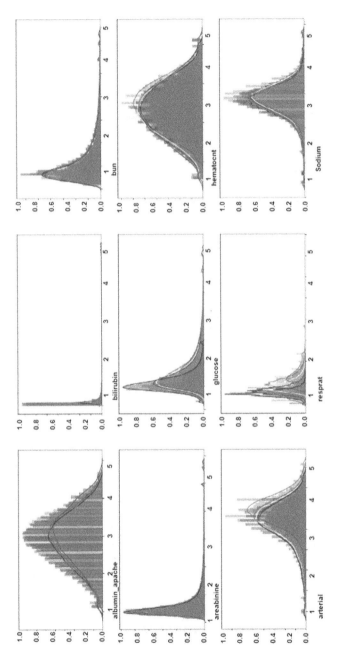

FIGURE 5.15 Patient's (lowest/highest) concentration over the first 24 hours

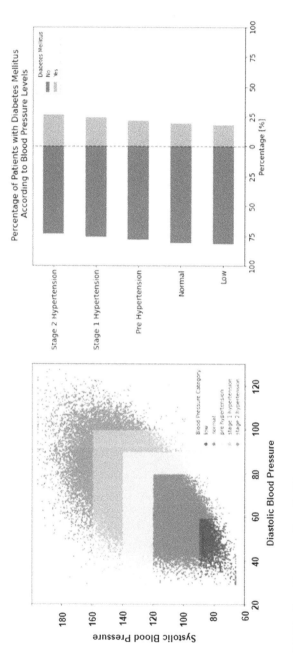

FIGURE 5.16   Systolic versus diastolic BP.

Mean ROC AUC: 0.7078879683340609

F1 Macro Score: 0.7265641042016404

Precision: [0.86801195 0.64566561]
Recall: [0.92577558 0.49000036]

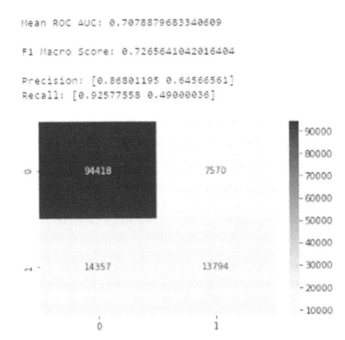

FIGURE 5.17   Confusion matrix parameters

0   85.196404
1   14.803596
dtype: float64

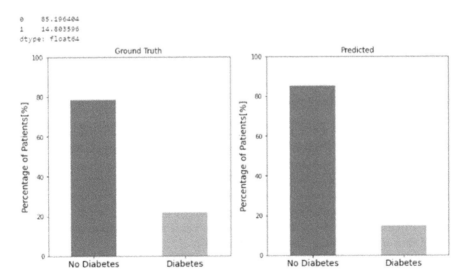

FIGURE 5.18   Result comparison of ground reality and predicted results.

5.12   RESULT AND DISCUSSION

As type 2 diabetes is the most prevalent kind of diabetes, this systematic review concentrated on literature that only addressed type diabetes. To gain a thorough understanding of gender differences in access to type 2 diabetes care as well as the obstacles women encounter, we included both quantitative and qualitative research. Our results show that there are gender variations in type 2 diabetes care access, with women experiencing greater barriers than men.

To access type 2 diabetes care, women struggled with the healthcare system, encountering personal, societal, economic, psychological and geographic challenges. The challenges we found were comparable to those women encounter when trying to get care for other NCDs, including cancer and cardiovascular conditions. The biggest personal hurdles we found were a lack of time caused by caring responsibilities and job commitments. Our research revealed that a lack of social and familial support was the greatest sociocultural challenge. According to the study by AbouZahr, women were unable to access healthcare because of family duties and social norms [AbouZahr, 2018]. Men participating actively in domestic chores and childcare can strengthen family support for women. Launching diabetes awareness campaigns might assist to overcome societal obstacles.

The primary healthcare system challenges that we found were the lack of proper healthcare information and the unsupportive behaviour of healthcare providers. Furthermore, according to Maina [Maina et al., 2011], women had less access to the healthcare system and were less thorough and responsive. It would be easier to overcome hurdles in the healthcare system if healthcare professionals were to offer individually tailored and culturally appropriate healthcare recommendations and were encouraged to adopt a caring and supportive attitude. The primary financial obstacles we found were the price of care, medicine, consultations and testing. Studies on NCDs have also revealed that women lack control of their finances, which prevents them from being able to pay for treatment. We found that women's denial of their condition and its severity was the greatest psychological obstacle. Regarding other NCDs, it has also been shown that women who fear stigmatization sometimes deny having a condition.

An incorporation of a psychologist's services into diabetes care facilities and joining diabetic women's networks would ensure women receive psychological support. The geographical limitations might be solved by consolidating all diabetes care facilities under one roof, implementing telemedicine services, setting up medical camps and implementing home visitation programmes. When developing and implementing diabetes care programmes, a gender-sensitive design will help to minimize gender disparities in access to type 2 diabetes treatment and remove obstacles that women encounter in getting care for their condition.

5.13   CONCLUSION

In conclusion, future research should take into account sex, gender and ethnic disparities. If appropriate, gender differences should be taken into account and used in clinical practice, as well as in approaches to diagnosis and treatment, to enhance care quality and mitigate the burden of the rising prevalence of diabetes. The cost of healthcare will go down significantly as a result. Future T2DM patients may benefit from more gender-sensitive, culturally appropriate preventative initiatives, gender-specific education, lifestyle programmes and medication therapy. There are gender differences in the accessibility of type 2 diabetes care, with women experiencing more barriers than men. When trying to receive treatment for type 2 diabetes, women encounter personal, societal, economic, psychological and geographic challenges and struggle with the healthcare system.

REFERENCES

AbouZahr, C. (2018). Women's limited access to healthcare due to family duties and social norms: The role of men in strengthening family support. *Journal of Health and Gender*, 10(3), pp. 123–145.

Alkali, Y., Routray, I., & Whig, P. (2022). Strategy for reliable, efficient, and secure IoT using artificial intelligence. *IUP Journal of Computer Sciences*, 16(2), 1–9.

Anand, M., Velu, A., & Whig, P. (2022). Prediction of loan behaviour with machine learning models for secure banking. *Journal of Computer Science and Engineering (JCSE)*, 3(1), 1–13.

Araneta, M. R., Kanaya, A. M., Hsu, W. C., Chang, H. K., Grandinetti, A., Boyko, E. J., et al. (2015). Optimum BMI cut points to screen Asian Americans for type 2 diabetes. *Diabetes Care*, 38(5), 814–820. doi:10.2337/dc14-2071

Backholer, K., Peeters, A., Herman, W. H., Shaw, J. E., Liew, D., Ademi, Z., et al. (2013). Diabetes prevention and treatment strategies: Are we doing enough? *Diabetes Care*, 36(9), 2714–2719. doi:10.2337/DC12-2501

Boyle, J. P., Thompson, T. J., Gregg, E. W., Barker, L. E., & Williamson, D. F. (2010). Projection of the year 2050 burden of diabetes in the US adult population: Dynamic modeling of incidence, mortality, and prediabetes prevalence. *Population Health Metrics*, 8, 29. doi:10.1186/1478-7954-8-29

Funk, L. M., Jolles, S., Fischer, L. E., & Voils, C. I. (2015). Patient and referring practitioner characteristics associated with the likelihood of undergoing bariatric surgery: A systematic review. *JAMA Surgery*, 150(10), 999–1005. doi:10.1001/jamasurg.2015.1250

Glechner, A., Harreiter, J., Gartlehner, G., Rohleder, S., Kautzky, A., Tuomilehto, J., et al. (2015). Sex-specific differences in diabetes prevention: A systematic review and meta-analysis. *Diabetologia*, 58(2), 242–254. doi:10.1007/s00125-014-3439-x

International Diabetes Federation. Diabetes: Facts and figures. (2017). Available from: http://www.idf.org/about-diabetes/facts-figures (Accessed: January 9, 2018).

Jupalle, H., Kouser, S., Bhatia, A. B., Alam, N., Nadikattu, R. R., & Whig, P. (2022). Automation of human behaviors and their prediction using machine learning. *Microsystem Technologies*, 28, 1–9.

Kanter, R., & Caballero, B. (2012). Global gender disparities in obesity: A review. *Advances in Nutrition*, 3(4), 491–498. doi:10.3945/an.112.002063

Kautzky-Willer, A., Harreiter, J., & Pacini, G. (2016). Sex and gender differences in risk, pathophysiology, and complications of type 2 diabetes mellitus. *Endocrine Reviews*, 37(3), 278–316. doi:10.1210/er.2015-1137

Khera, Y., Whig, P., & Velu, A. (2021). Efficient effective and secured electronic billing system using AI. *Vivekananda Journal of Research*, 10, 53–60.

Kohl, H. W. III, Craig, C. L., Lambert, E. V., Inoue, S., Alkandari, J. R., Leetongin, G., et al. (2012). The pandemic of physical inactivity: Global action for public health. *Lancet*, 380(9838), 294–305. doi:10.1016/S0140-6736(12)60898-8

Lean, M.E.J., Sattar, N. (2019) Da Qing 30 years on: more reasons to extend diabetes prevention. *Lancet Diabetes Endocrinol*, 7(6), 417-419. doi: 10.1016/S2213-8587(19)30138-X. Epub 2019 Apr 25.

Lovejoy, J. C., Sainsbury, A., & Stock Conference 2008 Working Group. (2009). Sex differences in obesity and the regulation of energy homeostasis. *Obesity Reviews*, 10(2), 154–167. doi:10.1111/j.1467-789X.2008.00529.x

Maina, W.K. *et al.* (2011) Knowledge, attitude and practices related to diabetes among community members in four provinces in Kenya: a cross-sectional study. *Pan Afr Med J 7*, pp. 1–12.doi:10.4314/pamj.v7i1.69095

Madhu, M., & Whig, P. (2022). A survey of machine learning and its applications. *International Journal of Machine Learning for Sustainable Development*, 4(1), 11–20.

Merlotti, C., Morabito, A., & Pontiroli, A. E. (2014). Prevention of type 2 diabetes; a systematic review and meta-analysis of different intervention strategies. *Diabetes, Obesity and Metabolism*, 6(8), 719–727. doi:10.1111/dom.12270

Nadikattu, R. R., Mohammad, S. M., & Whig, P. (2020). Novel economical social distancing smart device for covid-19. *International Journal of Electrical Engineering and Technology (IJEET)*, 15, 1–9.

Perreault, L., Ma, Y., Dagogo-Jack, S., Horton, E., Marrero, D., Crandall, J., et al. (2008). Sex differences in diabetes risk and the effect of intensive lifestyle modification in the Diabetes Prevention Program. *Diabetes Care*, 31(7), 1416–1421. doi:10.2337/dc07-2390

Rockette-Wagner, B., Storti, K. L., Dabelea, D., Edelstein, S., Florez, H., Franks, P. W., et al. (2016). Activity and sedentary time 10 years after a successful lifestyle intervention: The Diabetes Prevention Program. *American Journal of Preventive Medicine*, 52(3), 292–299. doi:10.1016/j.amepre.2016.10.007

Tomar, U., Chakroborty, N., Sharma, H., & Whig, P. (2021). AI-based smart agriculture system. *Transactions on Latest Trends in Artificial Intelligence*, 2(2), 1–8.

Tuomilehto, J., Schwarz, P., & Lindstrom, J. (2011). Long-term benefits from lifestyle interventions for type 2 diabetes prevention: Time to expand the efforts. *Diabetes Care*, 34(Suppl 2), S210–S214. doi:10.2337/dc11-s222

Velu, A., & Whig, P. (2021). Protect personal privacy and wasting time using NLP: A comparative approach using Ai. *Vivekananda Journal of Research*, 10, 42–52.

Velu, A., & Whig, P. (2022). Studying the impact of the COVID vaccination on the world using data analytics. *Vivekananda Journal of Research*, 10(1), 147–160.

Wardle, J., Haase, A. M., Steptoe, A., Nillapun, M., Jonwutiwes, K., & Bellisle, F. (2004). Gender differences in food choice: The contribution of health beliefs and dieting. *Annals of Behavioral Medicine*, 27(2), 107–116. doi:10.1207/s15324796abm2702_5

Whig, P., & Ahmad, S. N. (2014). Simulation of linear dynamic macro model of photocatalytic sensor in SPICE. *COMPEL The International Journal for Computation and Mathematics in Electrical and Electronic Engineering*, 1–22.

Whig, P., Kouser, S., Velu, A., & Nadikattu, R. R. (2022). Fog-IoT-Assisted-Based smart agriculture application. In *Demystifying Federated Learning for Blockchain and Industrial Internet of Things* (pp. 74–93). IGI Global.

Whig, P., Nadikattu, R. R., & Velu, A. (2022). COVID-19 pandemic analysis using the application of AI. In *Healthcare Monitoring and Data Analysis Using IoT: Technologies and Applications*, 1, 1–14.

Whig, P., Velu, A., & Bhatia, A. B. (2022). Protect nature and reduce the carbon footprint with an application of Blockchain for IIIoTIn. In *Demystifying Federated Learning for Blockchain and Industrial Internet of Things* (pp. 123–142). IGI Global.

Whig, P., Velu, A., & Naddikatu, R. R. (2022). The economic impact of AI-Enabled Blockchain in 6G-based industry. In *AI and Blockchain Technology in 6G Wireless Network* (pp. 205–224). Singapore: Springer.

Whig, P., Velu, A., & Nadikattu, R. R. (2022). Blockchain platform to resolve security issues in IoT and smart networks. In *AI-Enabled Agile Internet of Things for Sustainable FinTech Ecosystems* (pp. 46–65). IGI Global.

Whig, P., Velu, A., & Sharma, P. (2022). Demystifying federated learning for Blockchain: A case study. In *Demystifying Federated Learning for Blockchain and Industrial Internet of Things* (pp. 143–165). IGI Global.

6 Prenatal Ultrasound Diagnosis Using Deep Learning Approaches

P. Nagaraja, S. Lakshmanan, P. Shanmugavadivu and M. Mary Shanthi Rani

6.1 INTRODUCTION

One of the most popular and crucial components of medical imaging is ultrasound (US), which is also a diagnostic tool for both qualitative and quantitative disease diagnosis. Two-dimensional US imaging can be used to measure blood flow and the speed of muscle contraction as well as detect the anatomical and morphological features of tissues and organs. In comparison with X-ray, computer tomography (CT) and magnetic resonance imaging (MRI), US imaging has certain unique difficulties, such as increased noise, aberrations and low tissue contrast, that lead to edge ambiguity, extremely subjective diagnosis and reliance on medical professionals' knowledge [1]. The introduction of computer-aided diagnostic (CAD) technologies is to resolve the aforementioned issues. CAD is utilized to enhance clinicians' clinical expertise and knowledge, eventually leading to accurate US diagnosis [2].

Artificial intelligence (AI) is the capacity of a computer to perform any intellectual tasks, like comprehending reasoning and solving problems. Machine learning (ML) is a subset of AI that consists of systems with the ability to gain knowledge from data, which has previously demonstrated the potential to assist humans in a number of medical sectors [3]. Deep learning (DL) is an effective set of models for acquiring real-world semantic information. However, as part of a classification assignment, these are frequently taught indirectly. DL, a subset of ML, has been shown to be effective in medical fields by simulating human thought by stacking numerous simple functions to produce complicated decisions. The machine may learn abstract notions from better ones, thanks to the classification of concepts; some layers of the hierarchy are particularly deep [4].

For prenatal diagnosis, US imaging has evolved into a routine examination technique. It is utilized to observe and quantify many foetal biometric characteristics, including femur and humerus lengths, head and biparietal diameters and crown–rump length. Additionally, the foetal head circumference is calculated to determine information on age, size and weight, as well as to track growth and identify abnormalities in the developing foetus [5]. Despite all of the advantages and common uses

DOI: 10.1201/9781003378556-6

of US imaging, this imaging technique has several flaws, including blurring, speckle noise, missing edges, acoustic shadows and low signal-to-noise ratio. Due to this, it is highly difficult to interpret US images, requiring the employment of trained operators to distinguish between normal and aberrant images.

This chapter compares three convolutional neural network (CNN) models to determine if prenatal images are normal or abnormal and also introduces the dataset augmentation technique to prevent model overfitting. Data augmentation methods can increase the quantity of data in a data set without adding any new data. Data augmentation approaches have been introduced to address unbalanced data. Hyperparameters are more important to train the neural network architectures. This chapter contains some hyperparameters to enhance the functionality of the traditional models. The important parameter is a dropout, which it uses to reduce the features per epoch. It reduces the space complexity and different accuracy based on the size. Dropout value (0.1) is fixed on the regularization method to reduce the overfitting.

Batch size refers to calculating the gradient's loss function, and the weights are updated to the network. It reduces the computation cost and improves the model capacity. A smaller mini-batch size causes noise when calculating the error, which is often more useful to prevent a local minimization in the training process. A fair value of mini-batch size is 32 to get an accurate weight. Epochs are additional crucial hyperparameters. An epoch is utilized for the in-depth learning method that trains the entire data set in a single pass. The learning algorithm's epoch hyperparameter controls how many times it will go through the entire training data set.

The feasibility of classifying prenatal US images as normal or abnormal using CNN-based DL models has been analysed in this chapter. We chose this topic to be the first in a series of investigations by using published reports as the basis of the because foetal central nervous system (CNS) anomalies are among the most prevalent congenital abnormalities. To our knowledge, the transfer learning-based RESNET50, VGG16 and VGG19 models were used in this chapter for analysing the normal/abnormal identification in prenatal US images.

6.2   MEDICAL ULTRASOUND IMAGE PRE-PROCESSING

One of the elements influencing DL's notable success in a range of fields is the support of a large number of labelled training samples to give the neural network a good learning performance. However, it can be challenging to find a lot of labelled data sets for medical image analysis. It is challenging to get DL performance that is suitable for medical image analysis while just using tiny sample data sets. Transfer learning (TL), which is effective in medical image analysis and has been widely employed in diverse tasks, is the approach that is most frequently used to address this issue. Currently, a model transfer is a primary method used by researchers to address the issue of sparsely labelled data in medical pictures [6]. On other data sets, a neural network model is pre-trained before being used for medical image analysis tasks.

Medical US image analysis struggles with a lack of labelled data, but also with the drawbacks of a lot of noise and artefacts. US image preparation becomes especially crucial. DL applications in 3Dprenatal US analysis are on the rise, despite the fact that present medical US assessment still mostly uses 2D US image analysis. The accuracy of medical US image analysis can be significantly increased by using appropriate pre-processing techniques.

6.3 LITERATURE REVIEW

A two-step foetal US image quality assessment (FUIQA) plan was proposed by Wu et al. The first CNN model was utilized to focus on the region of interest (RoI), and categorize the foetal abdominal standard plane based on the RoI. They used a number of data-enhancement techniques, including image cropping and local phase analysis, to boost performance [7]. Similar, Jang et al. used a CNN model specifically created to classify the prenatal US image into different anatomical structures; prenatal measurement was then estimated by an ellipse detection method [8].

Qu et al. developed two primary methods, automatically classifying six typical deep CNNs (DCNNs) planning of the foetus' brain. The first method is based on DCNN, and another method is a CNN-based field TL model. Experimental investigations show that deep CNNs frequently demonstrate their enormous potential and that the tactics offered to create promising results are typically superior to those utilized in other traditional DL systems [9].

A multi-scale, self-attention generator was suggested by Valanarasu et al., who analysed US images from independent segmentation masks. They show that the procedure will produce good-quality US images for each segmentation mark that has been processed. The results show that a sectional method can be made more effective by producing useful US pictures using the current synthesis technology [10].

A newly developed segmentation method using a completely convergent V-Net was introduced by Skeika et al. They developed a novel combination of methods that make use of a 3D V-Net framework, with pre-processing, falling evaluation, batch normalization, activation mechanism and the network's innovative strategy for segmenting 2DUS foetal image used on a V-Net model. According to the results, it was possible to segment foetal skulls correctly up to 97.91% of the time and measure head circumferences more accurately than with existing techniques [11].

Namburete et al. established a model that links brain development to the usage of the illustration technique using MRI images from the US images. The authors proposed a method to accurately estimate the age of infants and children. The computer can estimate prenatal gestational age with an accuracy of up to 6.1 days. The parietooccipital fissure, Sylvian fissure and callosal fissural sulcus are the three age-discriminating brain regions visible in prenatal US scans. Both studies reveal significant variations in gestational times [12].

A study with 23 pregnant women carrying a foetus with congenital brain abnormalities for more than a period of one year with US images was proposed by Hamisa et al., who evaluated the role of MR imaging compared to 2D or 4D US assessments in detection of prenatal brain abnormalities. Foetal MRI is more beneficial in detecting prenatal CNS abnormalities [13].

Lin et al. proposed a multi-task learning framework using a faster regional convolutional neural network (MFRCNN) architecture for prenatal US images. In order to determine whether the US image magnification is appropriate and to assess the US image quality under clinical recommendations, MFRCNN first characterize the fundamental anatomical structure of the foetal brain. According to the experimental results of our own data set, that system can accurately evaluate the quality of an ultrasonic plane in less than half a second [14].

6.4 CONVOLUTIONAL NEURAL NETWORK

CNN is a particular kind of artificial neural network (ANN) that can extract features from local input. Each of the various modules in this is broken down into convolutional and pooling layers in most cases. They come with additional layers, such as batch normalizations and a rectified linear unit, or "ReLU", if necessary. A typical neural multilayer network is formed by totally connected layers in the network's final segment. When it comes to the composition, these modules are often stacked one on top of the other to create a deep model, enabling spatial and layout features to be supplied using 2D or 3D images [15].

For CNN networks to determine the convolutional phase reduction, it is typically critical to determine the hyperparameters in a convolutional layer. These call for the three hyperparameters – deep, padding and transit – in total. Small steps are frequently effective in practice, and the early network will produce a big activation map, which can increase output [16].

An issue with a CNN with multiple convolutional layers is that some regions, especially borders, are wasted during each convolutional process. Padding has many advantages, one of which is that it makes it possible to build deeper networks. Padding also prevents data loss at the input volume's bounds, which improves performance. As a result, trade-offs between various variables must be made while working within the limitations of low measurement costs and time costs for a particular position, namely, network width, number of filters, filter height and step [17].

Traditionally, to reduce a data ratio from the layer below, the outputs of the convolutional layer are sub-sampled through the matching pooling layer. According to the selected pooling techniques, the weight of the convolutional layer will give the CNN some invariant properties, including translational invariance. There are other ways to significantly reduce the number of factors, such as by making the weight number independent of the input image's scale. In a conventional CNN model, a spread among classes is typically achieved by feeding activations into the network's final layer via a softmax activation function.

Many CNN and conventional DL architectures have been improved and expanded to interpret various medical images. This chapter analyses three different CNN models:VGG16, VGG19 and ResNet50.

6.4.1 VGG16 AND VGG19

The 41-layer VGG16 network architecture and the 47-layer VGG19 network architecture were both established by the Visual Geometry Group (VGG) research team with AI as its main area of interest. Each layer's 3×3 filters are created by VGG to streamline the process. The CNN model that was utilized is a component of the ImageNet project contest, which organizes millions of pieces of data into tens of thousands of categories [18]. When compared to AlexNet, VGG can build more complex features with less computing by using uniform and smaller filter sizes. Table 6.1 displays the variation between VGG16 and VGG19models. The architectures of VGG16 and VGG19 are shown in Figure 6.1a and b.

6.4.2   ResNet50

There are other versions of ResNet with different numbers of layers but each layer has the same basic idea. The version that can operate with 50 neural network layers is known as Resnet50. With the 50-layer ResNet, the bottleneck construction block is utilized. A bottleneck residual block, reduces the number of parameters and matrix multiplications by using 11 convolutions. This greatly accelerates the training of each layer. It makes use of three layers as opposed to a stack with two levels. Figure 6.2 depicts the ResNet50 architecture.

TABLE 6.1

The Difference between VGG16 and VGG19

S.No.	Layer	VGG16	VGG19
1	Size of layer	41	47
2	Image input size	224×224 pixel	224×224 pixel
3	Convolutional layer	13	16
4	Filter size	64 and 128	64,128,256 and 512
5	ReLU	5	18
6	Max pooling	5	5
7	FCL	3	3
8	Dropout	0.1	0.1
9	Softmax	1	1

FIGURE 6.1   Architectures of (a) VGG16 and (b) VGG19.

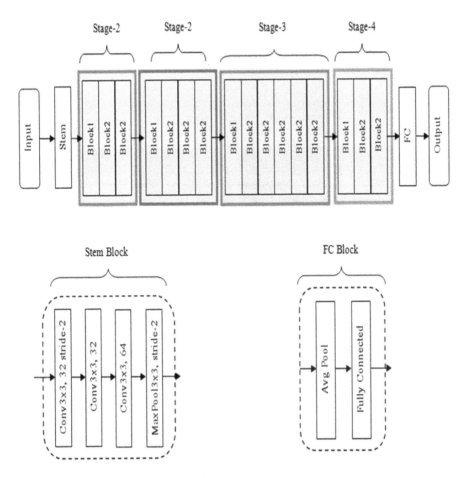

FIGURE 6.2 Architecture of ResNet50.

6.5 METHODOLOGY

6.5.1 TRANSFER LEARNING–BASED PRENATAL CLASSIFICATION USING RESNET50, VGG16 AND VGG19 CNN MODELS

In a neural network, the neurons and synapses link to a mathematical model to simulate the human brain. In essence, DL trains the model using the CNN layer. The identification of normal and abnormal prenatal images experiments with three different types of DL models. The proposed work compares the performance of the three different state-of-art models and is implemented in the following four stages:

Phase I: Data acquisition

Phase II: Data augmentation

Phase III: Training the three different types of models (RESNET50, VGG16 and VGG19) with transfer learning using prenatal data set

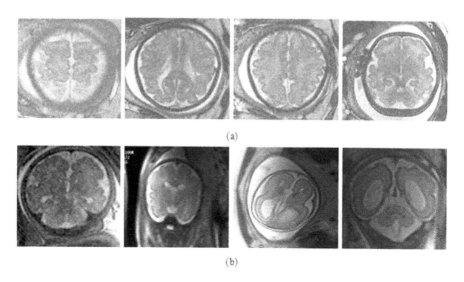

(a)

(b)

FIGURE 6.3   (a) Normal prenatal images. (b) Abnormal prenatal images.

Phase IV: Test and predict normal or abnormal images
Phase V: Compare the performance of the three models with standard metrics

6.5.1.1   PHASE I: DATA ACQUISITION

The dataset in DL is crucial for training the model, and for reliable results, it should be large enough to include every potential pattern. The most popular prenatal brain identification dataset, which includes both normal and abnormal images, is taken from Kaggle. Generally, datasets are divided into two disjoint sets in the ratio 80:20 for the training set and testing set, respectively. Figure 6.3 represents the normal and abnormal prenatal images.

6.5.1.2   PHASE II: DATA AUGMENTATION

The essential element of data classification and the most significant aspect of ML and DL models is feature extraction. Features describe many patterns relating to various diseases. These characteristics are taught to DL/ML models during the training phase to determine the class labels of data samples. Therefore, for precise prediction, the training dataset should contain a substantial number of data sets describing both normal and abnormal prenatal detection.

The size of the prenatal dataset, which has 105 normal images and 104 abnormal images, is increased by the data augmentation process. In particular, data augmentation is done to avoid overfitting conditions. For all experiments, traditional data augmentation consisted of applying rescaling (1./255), zoom range(0.2), shear range (0.2), validation split (0.2) and horizontal flip (True).The implementation of

TABLE 6.2
Augmented Data Set Details

Type	Original	Augmented Data	Training DataSet 80%	Testing DataSet 20%
Prenatal normal	105	525	420	105
Prenatal abnormal	104	520	516	104
Total	**209**	**1045**	**936**	**209**

data augmentation is to increase the models' performance level for both the training and testing dataset, respectively. Table 6.2 presents the augmented dataset details.

6.5.1.3 PHASE III: TRAINING THE THREE DIFFERENT TYPES OF MODELS (RESNET50, VGG16 AND VGG19) WITH TRANSFER LEARNING

This phase trains the conventional models, namely RESNET50, VGG16 and VGG19, with TL and an average pooling layer. An activation function is the powerhouse of a neural network. So we used two activation functions such as ReLu in the convolution layer and sigmoid activation functions in the fully connected layers. The last layer is the dense layer to flatten into a single vector, which is also referred to as the fully connected layer. Dropout (0.1) is used in the fully connected layer to r regularize the network. Adam optimizer is used during the compilation of the developed model.

6.5.1.4 PHASE IV: TEST AND PREDICT NORMAL OR ABNORMAL IMAGES

Once our model is trained, the model was tested to predict the normal and abnormal prenatal images using the test dataset. The above three conventional methods were tested; the VGG16 method almost reached the highest prediction when compared with all other methods,.

6.5.1.5 PHASE V: PERFORMANCE ANALYSIS

The experimental results of the three models were analysed and compared using standard performance metrics.

6.6 RESULTS AND DISCUSSION

The experiments were run on Google Collaboratory (Colab) using Lenovo with 4 GB of RAM. Colab notebook is based on the Jupyter Notebook, and it works on the Google Docs objects. The notebooks were configured with the necessary DL and ML library files such as Tensorflow, Keras, Matplotliband NumPy. The model's efficiency was also experimented with by fine-tuning the hyperparameters suitable for normal and abnormal detection in prenatal images.

In this chapter, the standardized accuracy calculation criteria can be defined as follows:

$$Accuracy = \frac{TN + TP}{TN + FN + TP + FP} \quad (6.1)$$

where *TP*, *FN*, *TN*, *FP* stand for true positive, false negative, true negative and false positive, respectively.

The dataset was split into training data with 936 images and testing data with 209 images. The unique work was to train the data with augmented images and non-augmented images with better accuracy. Table 6.3 presents the hyperparameters used in conventional work.

The comparative analyses of three models experimented with test data set of each class and the testing accuracy is listed in Table 6.4.

TABLE 6.3

Hyperparameter Values Used in the Proposed Work

Hyperparameter	Value
Epoch	100, 200, 500
Batch size	32
Dropout value	01
Learning rate	0.001
Training set	936
Testing set	209
Activation function	Softmax

TABLE 6.4

Accuracy of Transfer Learning–based Models

S.No	Epoch	Model	Accuracy
1	100	ResNet50	0.6257
2		VGG19	0.7244
3		VGG16	0.8134
4	200	ResNet50	0.6728
5		VGG19	0.7842
6		VGG16	0.8853
7	500	ResNet50	**0.7115**
8		VGG19	**0.8462**
9		VGG16	**0.9432**

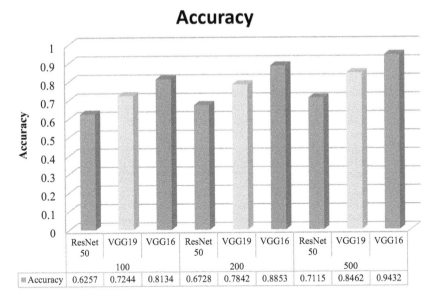

Accuracy	ResNet 50	VGG19	VGG16	ResNet 50	VGG19	VGG16	ResNet 50	VGG19	VGG16
		100			200			500	
Accuracy	0.6257	0.7244	0.8134	0.6728	0.7842	0.8853	0.7115	0.8462	0.9432

FIGURE 6.4 Accuracy measurement graph for the three different models.

For the entire three models, the TL-based VGG16 model reached the highest accuracy when compared with all other models. TL-based VGG16 predicted the normal or abnormal prenatal images correctly and reached 0.9432 of accuracy. It is worth noting that the proposed TL-based VGG16 model achieved better results for both normal and abnormal prenatal images.

The graph represents the quantitative results of the accuracy of the proposed methods with bar representation. In Figure 6.4, x-axis shows three different models with different epoch values (100, 200 and 500) and y-axis represents the accuracy values of the proposed methods. TL-based VGG16 model gave good results for prenatal images.

6.7   CONCLUSION

Using deep-CNN collaboration, a model for identifying normal or abnormal prenatal classification was created. To get over the overfitting issue and enhance performance, a deep learning technique with transformation and augmentation was applied. The scope of this study could be expanded on by minimizing the training period by adjusting the parameters in the future. This chapter presents a thorough analysis of three different CNN transfer learning application models– ResNet50, VGG16 and VGG19 –for detecting normal or abnormal foetal development. We found that the VGG16 model, which is based on transfer learning, is the best model for identifying normal or abnormal pregnancies.

REFERENCES

1. L. Wu, Y. Xin, S. Li, T. Wang, P.-A. Heng, and D. Ni, "Cascaded fully convolutional networks for automatic prenatal ultrasound image segmentation," in *Proc. IEEE 14th Int. Symp. Biomed. Imag. (ISBI)*, Apr. 2017, pp. 663–666.
2. D. Shen, G. Wu, and H.-I. Suk, "Deep learning in medical image analysis," *Annual Review of Biomedical Engineering*, vol. 19, pp. 221–248, 2017.
3. X. Liu, J. Shi, and Q. Zhang, "Tumor classification by deep polynomial network and multiple kernel learning on small ultrasound image dataset," in *Proc. Int. Workshop Mach. Learn. Med. Imag.*, Munich, Germany: Springer, 2015, pp. 313–320.
4. D. Q. Zeebaree, H. Haron, A. M. Abdulazeez, and D. A. Zebari, "Machine learning and region growing for breast cancer segmentation," in *2019 International Conference on Advanced Science and Engineering (ICOASE)*, 2019, pp. 88–93.
5. P. Loughna, L. Chitty, T. Evans, and T. Chudleigh, "Fetal size and dating: Charts recommended for clinical obstetric practice," *Ultrasound*, vol. 17, no. 3, pp. 160–166, 2009.
6. D. S. Kermany et al., "Identifying medical diagnoses and treatable diseases by image-based deep learning," *Cell*, vol. 172, no. 5, pp. 11221131, 2018.
7. L. Wu, J. Z. Cheng, S. Li, B. Lei, T. Wang, and D. Ni, "FUIQA: Fetal ultrasound image quality assessment with deep convolutional networks," *IEEE Transactions on Cybernetics*, May, vol. 47, no. 5, pp. 1336–1349, 2017.
8. J. Jang, J. Y. Kwon, B. Kim, S. M. Lee, Y. Park, and J. K. Seo, "CNN-based estimation of abdominal circumference from ultrasound images," arXiv: 1702.02741.
9. R. Qu, G. Xu, C. Ding, W. Jia, and M. Sun, "Deep learning-based methodology for recognition of fetal brain standard scan planes in 2D ultrasound images," *IEEE Access*, vol. 8, pp. 44443–44451, 2019.
10. J. M. J. Valanarasu, R. Yasarla, P. Wang, I. Hacihaliloglu, and V. M. Patel, "Learning to segment brain anatomy from 2D ultrasound with less data," *IEEE Journal of Selected Topics in Signal Processing*, vol. 14, pp. 1221–1234, 2020.
11. E. L. Skeika, M. R. Da Luz, B. J. T. Fernandes, H. V. Siqueira, and M. L. S. C. De Andrade, "Convolutional neural network to detect and measure fetal skull circumference in ultrasound imaging," *IEEE Access*, vol. 8, pp. 191519–191529, 2020.
12. A. I. Namburete, R. V. Stebbing, B. Kemp, M. Yaqub, A. T. Papageorghiou, and J. A. Noble, "Learning based prediction of gestational age from ultrasound images of the fetal brain," *Medical Image Analysis*, vol. 21, pp. 72–86, 2015.
13. M. Hamisa, N. Dabees, W. M. Ataalla, and D. H. Ziada, "Magnetic resonance imaging versus Ultrasound examination in detection of prenatal fetal brain anomalies," *The Egyptian Journal of Radiology and Nuclear Medicine*, vol. 44, pp. 665–672, 2013.
14. Z. Lin, S. Li, D. Ni, Y. Liao, H. Wen, J. Du, et al., "Multi-task learning for quality assessment of fetal head ultrasound images," *Medical Image Analysis*, vol. 58, p. 101548, 2019.
15. A. S. Issa and A. M. A. Brifcani, "Intrusion detection and attack classifier based on three techniques: A comparative study," *Engineering and Technology Journal*, vol. 29, pp. 386–412, 2011.
16. K. He and J. Sun, "Convolutional neural networks at constrained time cost," in *Proceedings of the IEEE Conference on Computer Vision and Pattern Recognition*, 2015, pp. 5353–5360.
17. P. Sharma, Y. P. S. Berwal, and W. Ghai, "Performance analysis of deep learning CNN models for disease detection in plants using image segmentation," *Information Processing in Agriculture*, vol. 7, pp. 566–574, 2020.
18. P. Shanmugavadivu, M. Mary Shanthi Rani, P. Chitra, S. Lakshmanan, P. Nagaraja, and U. Vignesh, "Bio-optimization of deep learning network architectures," *Security and Communication Networks*, vol. 2022, pp. 1–11, 2022.

7 Deep Convolutional Neural Network for the Prediction of Ovarian Cancer

S. Lakshmanan, P. Nagaraja, M. Mary Shanthi Rani and P. Shanmugavadivu

7.1 INTRODUCTION

The most frequent cause of mortality from other gynaecological malignancies is ovarian cancer (OC) [1]. The early symptoms of OC are bloating, pelvic pain, weight gain and an enlarged belly. which are often ignored by women [2]. However, as the illness migrates to other tissues in the body, it becomes very challenging to cure. Over time, women's ovaries' reproductive capacity experiences considerable functional and structural changes. Women who are menopausal and those who have OC in their families are more likely to get the disorder. Several imaging techniques and serum markers have been utilized in the research [3–5] to boost the likelihood of early OC diagnosis.

Although OC biomarkers have shown considerable potential, they have many limitations, including missed detections, which are time consuming and call for highly qualified medical professionals. Among the most commonly used indicators for detecting OC is the serum carbohydrate antigen 125 (CA125). In the initial stages of OC, some patients may have higher blood CA-125 concentrations than normal, and in the later stages, more than 80% of female cases with elevated CA125 levels have ovarian cancer [6]. The identification and characterization of OC tumours in women involve the use of imaging techniques such as positron emission tomography, magnetic resonance imaging and ultrasound imaging. For classification accuracy, machine learning (ML) techniques like the random forest, support vector machine (SVM), logistic regression or boosting and ensemble SVM [7] do not look promising. However, by combining a biomarker with a machine learning (ML) algorithm, OC may be detected earlier [7, 8].

In the past, supervised ML algorithms were used to categorize images as either cancerous or non-cancerous groups using a sequence that was not automatically retrieved. To identify thyroid nodules, Chen et al.'s [9] work included pathological and textural information to an SVM. Chang et al. [10] applied an SVM to identify Graves' disease in ultrasound images. Jose Martínez-Más et al.'s [11] objective was to assess popular ML techniques' ability to carry out automatic classification of OCs from ultrasound images, including KNN (K-Nearest Neighbors), LD (Linear Discriminant), SVM (Support Vector Machine) and ELM (Extreme Learning Machine). Lu et al. implement ML methods like logistic regression to predict OC [12].

The human construction of computationally complex procedures is a key component of traditional feature extraction approaches, which leads to high dimensionality, demanding workloads, low capacity and subpar classification rates [11, 12]. Additionally, a detailed grasp of characteristics is necessary during data collection to extract the most pertinent aspects. Deep learning can be used to process enormous volumes of data and help ML surpass its limitations [12]. Deep learning algorithms can automatically recognize features in raw data.

Akizur Rahman et al. classified OCs in Ref. [13] using the 15-neuron ANN model. Numerous researchers have been inspired by the potential of deep learning algorithms for medical image analysis. Recent developments in deep learning algorithms can be used for a variety of medical applications, such as cancer prediction, tumour cell segmentation and disease identification [14].

7.2　RELATED WORK

Roth et al. [15] suggested a DCNN technique to detect lymph nodes. The features extracted from images using DCNN, and it can help identify, recognize and retrieval. These deep learning techniques use a non-linear network to build a multilayer neural network. These low- and high-level elements should be used for a detailed representation of data received and should quickly identify the salient properties of the data set. Based on pathological images, OC has been classified using a DCNN-based technique established by Spanhol et al. [16]. Li et al. [17] categorized pulmonary modules using the DCNN method.

The research demonstrated that, despite traditional AI algorithms being crucial in the detection of OC, they are still unable to match the criteria of a pathologist's assessment. Recently, deep learning methods have excelled at analysing medical images, such as those of breast cancer, thyroid nodules, lung cancer and other conditions. Even though there are not currently many research papers utilizing deep learning to classify OC, as technology advances, more research could be done in this area. The AlexNet model pre-trained for OC diagnosis from histopathological images was unable to achieve an accuracy of more than 78%, according to the findings of Wu et al. [7].

The training data set for cutting-edge models like AlexNet and VGG-Net contains 14 million images over 1,000 classes in ImageNet. In addition to AlexNet, which debuted in 2012, VGG-Net and GoogleNet made their debut in 2014, followed by Res Net in 2015, and finally MobileNet and DenseNet in 2017. These provide the foundation of the majority of CNN designs. The research described in this article introduces a completely new architecture for deep learning–based

OC prediction from histopathology images. Our algorithms are trained exclusively using histology images. Comparing this design to the other ones examined in the literature study, it has a higher area under the curve–receiver operating characteristics (AUC-ROC).

When analysing medical images, such as for cancer detection, epilepsy forecasting, Alzheimer's diagnosis and other purposes, CNN and RNN deep learning algorithms are crucial [31]. There are numerous technologies used in deep learning, including Torch, Tensorflow, Caffle, Theano and Keras [14]. Even though computer vision experts do not have medical knowledge and possess only rudimentary deep learning capabilities, the knowledge gap should be rapidly closed to deliver satisfactory outcomes in terms of accuracy as well as sensitivity when working with biological images [7]. This knowledge gap poses a significant challenge to deep learning and medical image processing researchers [25]. Instead of manually calculating, training or categorizing the characteristics, ML relies on data representation [25]. Instead of using created features from images, the deep learning method directly employs image pixel values to make it simpler and more effective [25].

Xu et al. claim that the classification, segmentation and visualization of tissues in histopathology images may be accomplished using the DCNN technique. Teramoto et al. [31] classified microscopic images into different subtypes of lung cancer using the DCNN technique. Masood et al. developed a deep learning–based computer-assisted decision support system to identify lung cancer that provided more precise outcomes. DCNN has seen increasing the success and adoption of medical imaging [7]. Recognition, identification and retrieval are just a few applications for DCNN characteristics gleaned from images [7–14]. To build a deep learning architecture, a non-linear network reads and extracts data from a multilayer neural network [7] [14]. The representation of received data produced by these deep learning techniques, which mix low- and high-level features, is deeper than the sum of its parts. As a result, feature extraction techniques, which are frequently computationally demanding in ML algorithms, can be streamlined. Deep learning methods are, therefore, advantageous for diagnostic systems. In terms of resilience, deep learning algorithms do better than feature extraction methods [19–24], [31–32]. In this research, OC subgroups are automatically identified from a small number of histopathological pictures using DCNNs.

7.3 MATERIALS AND METHODS

7.3.1 Data Set

7.3.1.1 Image Data Set

The National Cancer Institute's Genomic Data Commons (GDC) data portal, TCGA-OV repository, provided 500 labelled histopathological images, including 80 clear-cell, 60 endometroid, 100 mucinous, 175 serous and 85 non-cancerous images. These images were utilized for training, predicting and additional analysis in this research. Researchers and bioinformaticians can quickly locate and download cancer-related information using the GDC Data Portal for additional research. The

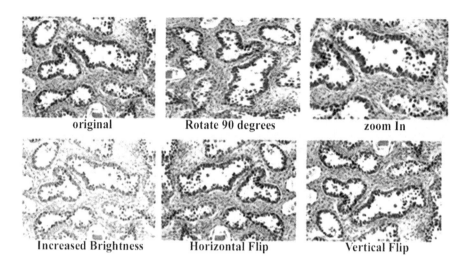

FIGURE 7.1   Augmented histopathological images.

authors have also posted OC and subtypes data set histopathology on the Mendeley Data website [29].

7.3.1.2   Data Augmentation

The incorporation of new data is a crucial deep-learning process. When employing DCNN, data augmentation is required since a large amount of data is required; an enormous quantity of images is not always obtained. All things considered, it contributes to increasing the size and uncertainty of the database. Insufficient training data may also contribute to overfitting [7, 13]. Some of the techniques utilized to carry out this image augmentation or alteration include zooming, tilting and accentuating particular qualities. The shots were zoomed in to capture greater details, rotated 90 degrees from their original position, flipped horizontally and vertically and brightened. After the images were improved, a total of 24,742 new shots were acquired, which is roughly 50 times the size of the initial data set. All RGB images were converted to JPG files with a 227 × 227 pixel resolution and scaled to the same size. Various improved techniques for increasing the amount of training data are shown in Figure 7.1. The enlarged picture data set, which was about 50 times larger than the initial data set, was the focus of one model creation while the original data set served as the basis for the other. The data augmentation code created by the authors is accessible on GitHub [30].

7.4   PROPOSED DCNN ARCHITECTURE (TL-NET)

According to our review of the literature, there are numerous pre-trained DCNN architectures for classifying images, including the ResNet [28], MobileNet [29], DenseNet [30], AlexNet [14], VGG-Net [26], and GoogleNet [27]. We developed

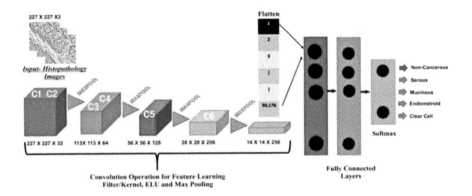

FIGURE 7.2   Architecture of TL-Net.

and applied an upgraded DCNN architecture including six convolutional layers, four max-pooling layers and an exponential linear unit (ELU) as the activation function in response to these pre-trained models. The architecture of the proposed TL-Net is shown in Figure 7.2. Using the data set that was supplemented in the previous step, we trained this model. Feature map, kernel size, stride and activation function are the main variables taken into account when constructing the TL-Net architecture.

- The convolutional, fully connected and max-pooling layers are all included in the proposed method, which is built layer by layer sequentially.
- The first two layers have convolutional layers with 32 filters of kernel size of 3 × 3. As a result, the first layer requires an input image with the dimensions 227 × 227 × 3.
- All layers except the final output layer use the activation function known as the ELU.
- The maximum value in the 2 × 2 window is taken into account by the max-pooling layer 1, which reduces dimension. Max-pooling layer 1 output measures 113 × 113 × 32.
- Both the third and fourth convolutional layers feature 64 filters and a kernel size of 3 × 3 with a window size of 2 × 2 for the max-pooling layer 2. The output size of the second max-pooling layer is 56 × 56 × 64.
- With each layer, the quantity of filters in the convolutional layer increases. Deeper layers learn more sophisticated characteristics, while the first layers with fewer filters learn simpler features from the input images.
- The third max-pooling layer with a window size of 2 × 2 follows the fifth convolutional layer, which has a filter size of 128 and is largely used for feature mapping. The output of max-pooling layer 3 is 28 × 28 × 128.
- To further reduce overfitting, max-pooling layer 4 of a 2 × 2 window size is applied after the sixth and final convolutional layer. The output of max-pooling layer 4 is 14 × 14 × 256.

TABLE 7.1
Hyperparameters of TL-Net

Parameter	Value
Learning rate	0.001
Cost function	Mean squared error (MSE)
Optimizer	Adam
Epoch number	10
Batch size	32
Dropout (dense layer)	0.4
Dropout (convolution layer)	0.2
Activation function	ELU

- From a 3D feature map to a 1D feature vector, the result of the max-pooling layers is flattened. The flattened layer's output is coupled with other fully connected layers. The neuron sizes in the three completely connected layers are 32, 16 and 5, respectively. The number of neurons in layer 3, the final completely connected layer, is equal to the number of classes. Since there are five classes in the current situation, SoftMax is set to 5.

The proposed TL-Net, which has 2,043,877 (2 million) parameters reached an accuracy of 91%. Table 7.1 lists the hyperparameters chosen for the TL-Net architecture.

7.4.1 Performance Evaluation Metrics

This section discusses in great depth the performance measurements. The models that are provided are assessed using a variety of metrics, including accuracy, precision, recall and F1 score. These performance requirements in Ref. [18] are constructed using the confusion matrix's four values. This confusion matrix can be used to comprehend a deep learning technique that produces different forms of output which are discussed below:

A. *Accuracy:* It is a metric based on the ratio of correctly predicted occurrences to all other predictions. It is computed mathematically as follows:

$$Accuracy = \frac{True\,Positive + True\,Negative}{True\,Positive + True\,Negative + False\,Positive + Flase\,Negative} \quad (7.1)$$

B. *Recall:* It evaluates the extent to which each positive classification can be predictably expected:

$$Recall = \frac{True\,Positive}{True\,Positive + Flase\,Negative} \quad (7.2)$$

C. *Precision:* It measures how many predictions were accurate compared to all other predictions:

$$Precision = \frac{True\,Positive}{True\,Positive + False\,Positive} \tag{7.3}$$

D. *F1 score:* This is calculated using recall and precision as given in Equation 7.4.

$$F1 - Score = 2 * \frac{Recall * Precision}{Recall + Precision} \tag{7.4}$$

The AUC-ROC may be utilized as a performance metric at various thresholds. ROC represents the probability curve, whereas AUC shows the degree of potential class separation. Thus, this test evaluates the model's capacity to distinguish between the classes. The model performs better at predicting when AUC values are higher.

7.5 RESULTS AND DISCUSSION

A DCNN needs to be trained on a large data set and generalized well to produce the best results. By applying brightness, zooming, reversing the horizontal and vertical axes, rotation and other effects, the original image collection was multiplied by 50. The proposed TL-Net is trained and evaluated using the original and modified data set. The effectiveness of its categorization was evaluated using tenfold cross-validation. The classwise distribution of images in the original and augmented data sets is shown in Table 7.2. After augmentation, each class has about 5,000 images in total.

The training accuracy, training loss and testing accuracy of the classification model are depicted in Table 7.3.

Figure 7.3 demonstrates the change in training accuracy and loss as well as validation accuracy and loss with an increase in the number of epochs.

Figure 7.4 compares the classification accuracies of TL-Net for the original and augmented images.

Instead of using conventional image recognition techniques, DCNN models were employed to predict OC and its four variants using histopathological images.

TABLE 7.2
Number of Images of Each Class

Class	Original Images	Augmented Images
Clear cell	80	5,000
Mucinous	100	5,220
Endometroid	60	4,350
Non-cancerous	85	4,530
Serous	175	5,640
Total	500	24,740

TABLE 7.3

Performance Metrics of TL-Net

Class	Precision	Recall	F1 Score	Testing Images
Clear cell	0.87	0.93	0.90	100
Mucinous	0.88	0.93	0.90	100
Endometroid	0.94	0.94	0.94	98
Non-cancerous	0.89	0.85	0.87	100
Serous	0.95	0.93	0.94	100

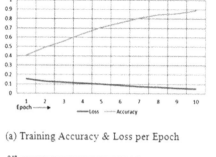

(a) Training Accuracy & Loss per Epoch

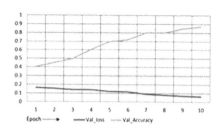

(b) Validation Accuracy & Loss per Epoch

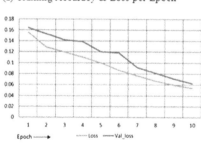

(c) Training & Validation Loss per Epoch

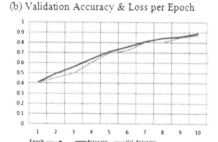

(d) Training & Validation Accuracy per Epoch

FIGURE 7.3　Various graphs of training and validation accuracy and loss versus epoch.

This can be seen in Figure 7.3a, where the training accuracy and loss per epoch demonstrate a rise in training accuracy and a decline in the loss. We were able to finish training at the highest performance at epoch 10, even if the accuracy started to deteriorate after ten epochs. After epoch 8, as shown in Figure 7.3b, the validation accuracy started to decline; as a result, a checkpoint is formed and the CNN model is generated in h5 format.

Figure 7.3c illustrates the training and validation losses, which are predicted to get smaller as more model learning occurs. Zero loss is ideal, but the model needs a lot of data to get there. For both the training and validation data sets, it was still

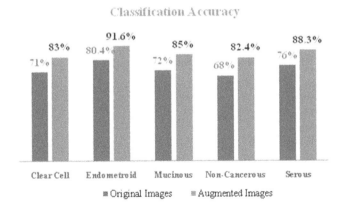

FIGURE 7.4   Comparison of the original and augmented images classification accuracy.

viable to get close to zero losses at 0.05. The model's training and validation accuracy follow the same route, as illustrated in Figure 7.3d, demonstrating that it is capable of generalization.

The classification accuracy of the proposed TL-Net model improved from 75% to 91% for the five classes when applying the extended data set, as shown in Table 7.4 and Figure 7.3. With a supplemental data set, Wu M. et al. had achieved 78.2% in Ref. [7], and we increased it by 12.8%.

The relationship between training accuracy and training loss is seen in Figure 7.3, and this graph needs to be linear for the model to be successfully generalized. Additionally, when the training and testing accuracy increased, the risk of inaccurate classifications in the data decreased.

Precision is crucial when the cost of false positives is high. A non-cancerous image cannot be classified as malignant given the issue statement in place. The recall measure becomes more significant when false negatives are expensive. The F1 score is used as a counterweight to the accuracy and recall measurements in the TL-Net results, which are above 80% for all classes.

Clear cell classification accuracy has increased by 12%; endometroid, mucinous and serious classification accuracy has increased respectively by 11%, 13% and 14%; and non-cancerous classification accuracy has increased by 12%, according to Figure 7.4. The main cause of misclassification is the challenge of learning the morphological characteristics of cells. Some images are blurry or have unclear, occasionally overlapping cell membranes, while others have multiple types of carcinomas in one image, which can lead to errors. To retrain the upcoming research model, we would like to gather a greater number of samples with subpar cell morphology.

Additionally, we contrasted our data set with cutting-edge methods currently being used, including pre-trained architectures-based AlexNet, GoogleNet, VGG-16 and VGG-19. Table 7.4 lists the findings that were attained using these techniques and finally predicted images by TL-Net shown in Figure 7.5.

TABLE 7.4

Performance Comparison of the Proposed Method with DCNN Methods

Methods	Ovarian Cancer Subtype	Precision (%)	Recall (%)	F1 Score (%)	Accuracy (%)	AUC (%)
AlexNet	Clear cell	52	76	62	72	75
	Endometroid	63	62	62		
	Mucinous	74	58	65		
	Benign	77	52	62		
	Serous	67	89	76		
VGG-16	Clear cell	76	81	78	84	85
	Endometroid	82	84	83		
	Mucinous	78	71	74		
	Benign	80	64	71		
	Serous	61	83	70		
VGG-19	Clear cell	85	89	87	90	93
	Endometroid	90	88	89		
	Mucinous	82	87	84		
	Benign	83	79	81		
	Serous	85	88	86		
Google-Net	Clear cell	49	71	58	70	72
	Endometroid	61	64	62		
	Mucinous	62	61	62		
	Benign	72	53	61		
	Serous	70	61	65		
TL-Net proposed	Clear cell	87	93	90	91	95
	Endometroid	94	94	94		
	Mucinous	88	93	90		
	Benign	89	85	87		
	Serous	95	93	94		

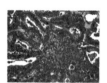

Predicted – Endometroid
Ground Truth - Endometroid

Predicted – Serous
Ground Truth - Serous

Predicted – Mucinous
Ground Truth - Mucinous

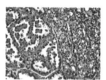

Predicted – Clear Cell
Ground Truth – Clear Cell

FIGURE 7.5　Predicted images by TL-Net.

7.6 CONCLUSION

This new research is the first to use a unique DCNN, TL-Net, to diagnose OC and classify its four subtypes from histopathology images. With enhanced images, our model's accuracy improved from 72% to 93%, which is much better than what Ref. [7] accomplished. Getting in-depth may not always be beneficial, and fine-tuning the hyperparameters according to DCNN can solve a variety of problems. The problem statement determines how important the other performance measures are; accuracy is not the only metric. TL-Net, which has only been trained in the cancer domain, thus delivers the best outcomes for multiclass OC prediction.

REFERENCES

1. World Health Organization. (2019). Cancer [OTLine]. Available from https://www.who.int/news-room/fact-sheets/detail/cancer. Accessed on 11th November.
2. Cancer Facts & Figures 2021. (2021). Cancer.org [OTLine]. Available from https://www.cancer.org/content/dam/ cancer-org/research/cancer-facts-and-statistics/annual-cancer-facts-and-figures/2021/cancer-facts-and-figures-2021.pdf.
3. Torre, L. A., Trabert, B., DeSantis, C. E., Miller, K. D., Samimi, G., Runowicz, C. D., ... Siegel, R. L. (2018). Ovarian cancer statistics, 2018. *CA: A Cancer Journal for Clinicians, 68*(4), 284–296.
4. Chornokur, G., Amankwah, E. K., Schildkraut, J. M., & Phelan, C. M. (2013). Global ovarian cancer health disparities. *Gynecologic Oncology, 129*(1), 258–264.
5. El-Bendary, N., & Belal, N. A. (2018). Epithelial ovarian cancer stage subtype classification using clinical and gene expression integrative approach. *Procedia Computer Science, 131*, 23–30.
6. Zhang, L., Huang, J., & Liu, L. (2019). Improved deep learning network based in combination with cost-sensitive learning for early detection of ovarian cancer in color ultrasound detecting system. *Journal of Medical Systems, 43*(8), 1–9.
7. Wu, M., Yan, C., Liu, H., & Liu, Q. (2018). Automatic classification of ovarian cancer types from cytological images using deep convolutional neural networks. *Bioscience Reports, 38*(3), 1–7.
8. Shibusawa, M., Nakayama, R., Okanami, Y., Kashikura, Y., Imai, N., Nakamura, T., ... Ogawa, T. (2016). The usefulness of a computer-aided diagnosis scheme for improving the performance of clinicians to diagnose non-mass lesions on breast ultrasonographic images. *Journal of Medical Ultrasonics, 43*(3), 387–394.
9. Chen, S. J., Chang, C. Y., Chang, K. Y., Tzeng, J. E., Chen, Y. T., Lin, C. W., ... Wei, C. K. (2010). Classification of the thyroid nodules based on characteristic sonographic textural feature and correlated histopathology using hierarchical support vector machines. *Ultrasound in Medicine & Biology, 36*(12), 2018–2026.
10. Chang, C. Y., Liu, H. Y., Tseng, C. H., & Shih, S. R. (2010). Computer-aided diagnosis for thyroid Graves' disease in ultrasound images. *Biomedical Engineering: Applications, Basis and Communications, 22*(2), 91–99.
11. Martínez-Más, J., Bueno-Crespo, A., Khazendar, S., Remezal-Solano, M., Martínez-Cendán, J. P., Jassim, S., ... Timmerman, D. (2019). Evaluation of machine learning methods with Fourier Transform features for classifying ovarian tumors based on ultrasound images. *Plos One, 14*(7), e0219388.

12. Lu, M., Fan, Z., Xu, B., Chen, L., Zheng, X., Li, J., ... Jiang, J. (2020). Using machine learning to predict ovarian cancer. *International Journal of Medical Informatics, 141,* 104195.

13. Rahman, M. A., Muniyandi, R. C., Islam, K. T., & Rahman, M. M. (2019, October). Ovarian cancer classification accuracy analysis using 15-neuron artificial neural networks model. In *2019 IEEE Student Conference on Research and Development (SCOReD)* (pp. 33–38). IEEE.

14. Krizhevsky, A., Sutskever, I., & Hinton, G. E. (2017). Imagenet classification with deep convolutional neural networks. *Communications of the ACM, 60*(6), 84–90.

15. Roth, H. R., Lu, L., Seff, A., Cherry, K. M., Hoffman, J., Wang, S., ... Summers, R. M. (2014, September). A new 2.5 D representation for lymph node detection using random sets of deep convolutional neural network observations. In *International Conference on Medical Image Computing and Computer-Assisted Intervention* (pp. 520–527). Springer, Cham.

16. Spanhol, F. A., Oliveira, L. S., Petitjean, C., & Heutte, L. (2016, July). Breast cancer histopathological image classification using convolutional neural networks. In *2016 International Joint Conference on Neural Networks (IJCNN)* (pp. 2560–2567). IEEE.

17. Li, W., Cao, P., Zhao, D., & Wang, J. (2016). Pulmonary nodule classification with deep convolutional neural networks on computed tomography images. *Computational and Mathematical Methods in Medicine, 2016,* 1–7.

18. Simonyan, K., & Zisserman, A. (2014). Very deep convolutional networks for large-scale image recognition. arXiv preprint arXiv:1409.1556.

19. Szegedy, C., Liu, W., Jia, Y., Sermanet, P., Reed, S., Anguelov, D., ... Rabinovich, A. (2015). Going deeper with convolutions. In *Proceedings of the IEEE Conference on Computer Vision and Pattern Recognition* (pp. 1–9).

20. He, K., Zhang, X., Ren, S., & Sun, J. (2016). Deep residual learning for image recognition. In *Proceedings of the IEEE Conference on Computer Vision and Pattern Recognition* (pp. 770–778).

21. Howard, A. G., Zhu, M., Chen, B., Kalenichenko, D., Wang, W., Weyand, T., ... Adam, H. (2017). Mobilenets: Efficient convolutional neural networks for mobile vision applications. arXiv preprint arXiv:1704.04861.

22. Huang, G., Liu, Z., Van Der Maaten, L., & Weinberger, K. Q. (2017). Densely connected convolutional networks. In *Proceedings of the IEEE Conference on Computer Vision and Pattern Recognition* (pp. 4700–4708).

23. Jung, K. H., Park, H., & Hwang, W. (2017). Deep learning for medical image analysis: Applications to computed tomography and magnetic resonance imaging. *Hanyang Medical Reviews, 37*(2), 61–70.

24. Haque, I. R. I., & Neubert, J. (2020). Deep learning approaches to biomedical image segmentation. *Informatics in Medicine UTLocked, 18,* 100297.

25. Guo, L. Y., Wu, A. H., Wang, Y. X., Zhang, L. P., Chai, H., & Liang, X. F. (2020). Deep learning-based ovarian cancer subtypes identification using multi-omics data. *BioData Mining, 13*(1), 1–12.

26. Ghoniem, R. M., Algarni, A. D., Refky, B., & Ewees, A. A. (2021). Multi-modal evolutionary deep learning model for ovarian cancer diagnosis. *Symmetry, 13*(4), 643.

27. Sone, K., Toyohara, Y., Taguchi, A., Miyamoto, Y., Tanikawa, M., Uchino-Mori, M., ... Osuga, Y. (2021). Application of artificial intelligence in gynecologic malignancies: A review. *Journal of Obstetrics and Gynaecology Research, 47*(8), 2577–2585.

28. Genomic Data Commons Data Portal. Cancer.gov [OTLine]. Available www.portal.gdc .cancer.gov.

29. Kasture, K. (2021). Ovarian cancer & subtypes dataset histopathology. Mendeley.

30. Kasture, K. (2021). Kokilakasture/ovarian cancer prediction [OTLine]. Available www .github.com/kokilakasture/OvarianCancerPrediction.

31. Shanmugavadivu, P., Mary Shanthi Rani, M., Chitra, P., Lakshmanan, S., Nagaraja, P., & Vignesh, U. (2022). Bio-optimization of deep learning network architectures. *Security and Communication Networks*, *2022*, 3718340. https://doi.org/10.1155/2022 /3718340

32. Mary Shanthi Rani, M., Chitra, P., Lakshmanan, S., Kalpana Devi, M., Sangeetha, R., & Nithya, S. (2022). DeepCompNet: A novel neural net model compression architecture. *Computational Intelligence and Neuroscience*, *2022*, 1–13.

8 Risk Prediction and Diagnosis of Breast Cancer Using ML Algorithms

Neeru Saxena, Rashmi Vaishnav,
Surya Saxena and Umesh Kumar

8.1 INTRODUCTION

Women nowadays are more involved in balancing their family and professional obligations. They are overburdened with handling daily activities and do not have time for themselves. Because of managing these responsibilities, women do not get time to eat proper food regularly. They do not even have the time to care for themselves. Due to improper diet and lifestyle, women are facing many health issues like type-2 diabetes, high cholesterol leading to untimely heart attacks and various kinds of cancer, including breast cancer, etc. Artificial intelligence (AI) is the technique which helps in the early diagnosis of breast cancer by analysing an image and detecting the masses of the breast, density of the breast, assessment of cancer risk and segmentation of the breast. Breast cancer is the second most deadly illness in women, after lung cancer, and, of all cancers, it occurs quite frequently. Although various kinds of breast cancer are categorized, the two main types of breast cancer are (1) invasive ductal carcinoma (IDC) and (2) ductal carcinoma in situ (DCIS) [1].

DCIS evolves gradually and does not have a negative effect on the daily life of patients, whereas IDC surrounds the entire breast tissue and is more dangerous and harmful. In 2018, approximately 18% of cancerous cases were of breast cancer as per the graph in Figure 8.1, which has increased in 2020 to approximately 2.3 million women identified with breast cancer and approximately 685,000 deaths identified globally as per World Health Organization (WHO) data. As per the data from the International Agency for Research on Cancer, 37.2% of women died due to breast cancer in India. Two types of cancer can be seen: (1) benign cancer which is non-cancerous and does not spread to other body parts; (2) malignant which is a cancerous tumour that affects other parts of the body and is uncontrollable. Biopsies are

DOI: 10.1201/9781003378556-8

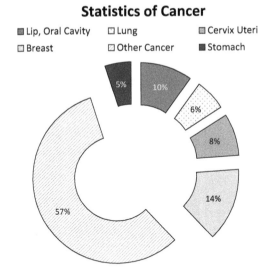

FIGURE 8.1 Cancer statistics [2].

the technique used by doctors for tumour detection. To save the life of a patient, the cancer-affected portion of the body is removed. The patient's life may be saved if the condition is detected early.

Breast cells start dividing abnormally, leading to the development of breast cancer. It can originate from various portions of the breast. Ductal carcinoma is the most prevalent kind of breast cancer which originates in the tube-like duct that carries milk to the nipple. Lobular carcinoma is another type of breast cancer. Lobular are the glands that are responsible for producing milk. Lobular carcinoma develops in the lobular gland and gradually multiplies to neighbouring tissues. The spread of cells of cancer from the breast to other areas of the body via blood and lymph vessels is referred to as metastasis.

If breast cancer is discovered early on, it can be efficiently treated. Various imaging methods can be used for screening to find this illness, with mammography, thermography and ultrasound being the most popular options. Mammography is the best method for early detection of breast cancer.

8.2 BREAST CANCER

The key sites for the beginning of breast cancer are the lobules or ducts. The ducts are the tubes that convey milk from the lobules to the mammilla, whereas lobules are milk-producing glands. Cancer cells can evolve uncontrollably and can penetrate healthy breast tissue and lymph nodes in the arms. The lymphatic nodes are in charge of transporting the tumour cells to other areas of the body. Breast cancer physical symptoms include swelling, breast pain, nipple discharge which is not breast milk, an inverted nipple, a change in breast size, soreness or a blister under the arm. Age,

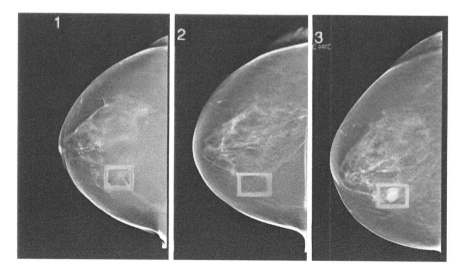

FIGURE 8.2   Mammogram of breast cancer.

obesity, inactivity, excessive alcohol use, thick breasts, genes, early menstruation and advanced maternal age are all potential risk factors for breast cancer [2].

8.3   MAMMOGRAMS

The best technique to identify cancer at an early stage before it becomes large enough to be felt or produce symptoms is with a mammogram, as shown in Figure 8.2 similar to the type of breast X-ray. Regular mammograms can reduce the risk of reaching the acute stage. At present, AI and machine learning (ML) are the techniques that provide improved technological systems to resolve complex tasks with reduced human intervention. There are two types of mammograms shown in Figure 8.3: (a) screening mammograms; (b) diagnostic mammograms. These two types of mammograms are further classified as (a) digital mammography in 2D and (b) digital mammography in 3D.

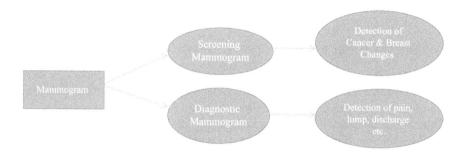

FIGURE 8.3   Types of mammograms

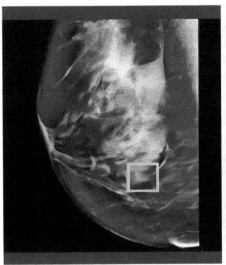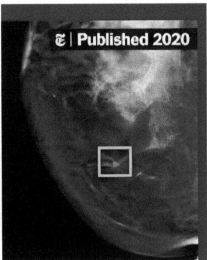

FIGURE 8.4 AI reading mammograms

To detect breast cancer, various screening techniques are available. Mammography can be seen in Figure 8.4 is one of the techniques that are essential to the precise initial identification and diagnosis of breast cancer. Although radiologists might utilize mammography to check for breast cancer in women, how well they do so depends on their knowledge of the subject. If efforts are made to improve accuracy and lessen uneven change, mammography may become more successful at identifying early breast cancers.

Full-field digital mammography (FFDM) is stored on a computer as images: a device designed for mammography that can only see breast tissue. In comparison to standard X-beams, the machine uses lower dosages of X-rays. Because of the ineffectiveness of these x-beams in separating tissue, the machine comprises two plates that pack or straighten out the breast in order to blowout the tissue apart.

The following are reasons why getting a mammogram is advised:

- Detection of breast abnormalities
- Follow-up after a mammography that was previously abnormal
- Keeping an eye on the growth of lumps or other irregularities

8.3.1 Screening Mammograms

Women can receive screening mammograms to look for signs of breast cancer even if they have no symptoms or problems with their breasts. Each breast is imaged with an X-ray from two separate perspectives. Screening mammography is a minimal X-ray inspection of a woman's breasts used to recognize cancer when a malignancy is too minor to be noticed as a lump. By identifying early-stage, undiagnosed breast cancer, screening mammography seeks to lower the death rate from breast cancer. Finding breast cancer at its early stage is the goal. The chance of cancer being effectively treated increases with early discovery, which also frequently opens up more therapy options. It has been demonstrated that screening mammography lowers the mortality rate from breast cancer.

8.3.2   Diagnostic Mammograms

If any symptom of breast cancer is seen in screening mammograms, then diagnostic mammograms are a technique to diagnose breast cancer. In this technique, additional views or pictures of the breast are taken that were not taken in the screening mammograms.

Mammograms have the potential to reveal breast abnormalities. While not all abnormalities are cancerous, they might aid in the decision-making process for further tests like breast biopsies. The following alterations can be seen on mammograms: (a) calcification; (b) masses; (c) asymmetries; (d) distortions.

8.3.3   Digital Mammography in 2D

Both the mammography procedures listed above employ X-rays to create a picture of the breast. The distinction is that in traditional mammography, the picture is immediately preserved on film, but with digital mammography, the electronic image is kept as a computer file. With the use of digital mammography, healthcare practitioners may store the file electronically, which can then be conveniently analysed and shared.

8.3.4   3D Mammograms

A more recent form of mammogram known as 3D mammography, or digital breast tomosynthesis (DBT), compresses each breast just once while taking a series of low-dose X-rays while the machine moves in an arc. The computer then keeps all the photos together, enabling medical professionals to see the breast tissues more clearly in three dimensions.

8.4   PROCESS OF CLASSIFICATION

Classification is used to classify cancer into normal and abnormal (benign/malignant) categories, which are derived from the images of a mammogram. The classification phases are represented in Figure 8.5 [3].

8.4.1   Pre-processing

With the mammography approach, which also covers pectoral muscles and markers, less X-ray radiation is required to acquire pictures. By eliminating the undesirable noise with the aid of the appropriate filtering techniques, the effectiveness

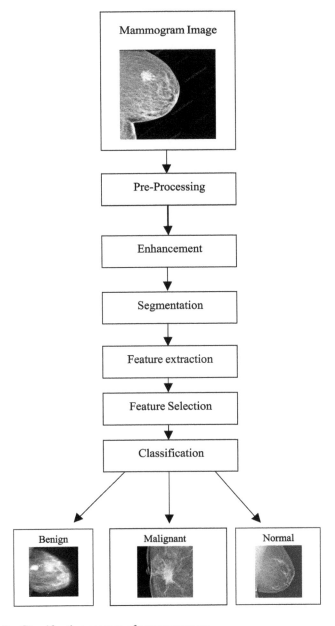

FIGURE 8.5   Classification process of mammograms

of any CAD system may be boosted. Any database of mammography pictures has impulse noise that may have been present during the acquisition of the data.. The high-intensity, triangular-shaped area on the upper direction of the acquired mammography that is opposing the direction of the nipple is referred to as the pectoral muscle in mammograms. These pectoral muscle areas must be eliminated for avoiding misclassifications. The deletion of pectoral muscle is important and can be removed by using a global thresholding technique [4].

8.4.2 ENHANCEMENT

This method is highly beneficial for the operation of medical images since contrast is a key factor in the subjective evaluation of image quality. Contrast is the variation in visuals effects that distinguishes one thing from another thing and its background. Contrast is determined by the item's variation in colours and brightness in relation to other items. Unlike the entire picture, contrast limited adaptive histogram equalization (CLAHE) only functions in discrete areas of images called tiles. The gap of each tile is enhanced, with the objective that the localized histogram of the findings appears to be almost equal to the possible spread. Enhancement using deep learning improves the visual contrast by working pixel by pixel on the entire image. Enhancement can be done through an already pre-trained model of convolution neural network (CNN) [5].

8.4.3 SEGMENTATION

One of the most important steps in the automated identification of mammography pictures for the early diagnosis of breast cancer is the segmentation of the region of interest (RoI). Each pixel in the data set image could be classified as either an RoI of the breast area or a background during segmentation. This phase's inputs are the mammography pictures as the input of this phase, and its output is the RoI (breast regions) pictures. The RoI pictures are then combined with the original mammography images to create the RoI images that will be used as an input in the classifier step. Using a modified U-Net model, mammography picture segmentation is carried out. The modified U-Net segmentation is made up of encoder and decoder networks. The conventional CNN is referred to as the encoder section because it contains more semantic information than spatial information. For the segmentation of semantic information, spatial information is equally important. The specific data from the decoder component is supplied into the U-Net, where semantic data is extracted from the network's bottom layer. High-resolution features are transferred from the encoder component to the decoder, skipping the linkage and offering fine segment structures [6].

8.4.4 FEATURE EXTRACTION

Feature extraction is used to isolate the important data as compactable features from any mammogram input. Feature extraction is the quickest and easiest way to make use of the representational skills of pre-trained deep networks. A network that has previously been stored and trained on a sizeable data set, often on important image classification tasks, is referred to as a pre-trained network. If the trained original data set is broad and sizeable enough, the spatial feature hierarchy learnt using the pre-trained model can serve as an effective generic network of our visual surroundings. So, even though these new tasks may provide wholly distinct output classes from the original one, their properties have been shown to be beneficial for a variety of classification issues [4].

8.4.5 FEATURE SELECTION

Feature selection significantly contributes to minimizing the dimensionality of the classifier's inputs while preserving accuracy by lowering the likelihood of overfitting and the complexity of the classifier. There are two methods for selecting features: supervised and unsupervised. A supervised classifier serves as the foundation for the majority of supervised feature selection approaches. One of the unsupervised feature selection techniques used to reduce the dimensionality of the data is principal component analysis (PCA). The approach known as correlation-based high distinction feature selection (CHDFS) chooses the most important characteristics from the input [7].

8.4.6 CLASSIFICATION

The classification phase is the final stage of the CAD system. The classification's purpose is to distinguish between healthy and unhealthy, benign and cancerous breast tissues [7]. The stages of a CAD system that uses ML are as follows:

As shown in Table 8.1, number of ML algorithms exist for the diagnosis and prediction of breast cancer. Some of them are as follows:

- support vector machine (SVM)
- logistic regression (LR)
- random forest (RF)
- k-nearest neighbours (KNN)
- decision tree (DT)

8.5 MACHINE LEARNING ALGORITHMS

ML algorithms that assist in the study of breast cancer are as follows.

8.5.1 SUPPORT VECTOR MACHINE

A well-known classification method in the realm of cancer diagnosis is SVM. The SVM, a classifier, splits the data sets into classes with the largest margin in order to determine a maximum marginal hyperplane (MMH) using the nearby data points [2]. This approach aims to catch the hyperplane in N-dimensions that classify the input points.

This method determines the plane with the greatest margins. The number of features separates N-dimensions. If two features are compared, the result could be better against the multiple features for classification. Margin maximization could provide more accurate results. Support vector visualization is denoted in Figure 8.6 [8].

TABLE 8.1
Classifier Comparison

Classifier	Procedure	Advantage	Disadvantage
SVM	Algorithm for supervised learning that may be applied to both regression and classification. Statistical approach can be used by this algorithm to find the best line which separate the different classes present in the data	• Operating in a high-dimensional environment • When the number of samples is smaller than the number of measurements, it is effective [3] • Memory efficient algorithm	• Efficiency is not that good where the data has more noise [3] • When the number of samples is fewer than the number of features, control is crucial [3]
KNN	When a series of samples is unknown, KNN calculates the distance between each one and selects the K samples that are closest to it as the foundation for categorization [10]. KNN is a non-parametric algorithm	• Easy to understand and implement • Best for non-linear data as there is no assumption about primary data • Handle multiclass cases	• All training data is stored, so associative computation cost is high • High memory storage required • Value of K need to be determined • In the case of a high value of N, prediction is slow
Decision Tree	A supervised learning technique where the data set's characteristics are represented by internal nodes, the decision-making process is represented by branches and the results are represented by each leaf node. Possible solution to a problem can be obtained through graphical representation	• Non-parametric does not require significant assumption to be fulfilled • Highly versatile and can exhibit multiple roles apart from the standard prediction • Can be able to solve non-linear problems also	• Time-consuming in training phases • In case of imbalanced class data sets, model can be biased towards the majority class
Naive Bayes	Algorithm for probabilistic classifiers. Based on a probability model with high independence assumptions that have no bearing on reality and are regarded as naive	• Work quickly and saves lots of time • Helpful in solving multiclass prediction problems	• In reality, naive Bayes presupposes that all predictors are independent, which is not the case • The estimation of this algorithm is wrong in many cases

(Continued)

TABLE 8.1 (CONTINUED)
Classifier Comparison

Classifier	Procedure	Advantage	Disadvantage
Logistic regression	An algorithm is used to calculate the likelihood of an event's success or failure. This algorithm is used when dependent variable is binary. Using the given data set, it learns linear relationships and introduces non-linearity in the form of Sigmoid function	• Easy to implement and understand • Very efficient to work on data set • Make no assumptions about distribution of classes in feature space • Very fast in classification of unknown records	• This algorithm cannot be used at a place where the number of observation is lesser than the number of features otherwise lead to overfitting • Build linear boundary • Assumption of linearity between dependent and independent variables • Non-linear problems cannot be solved

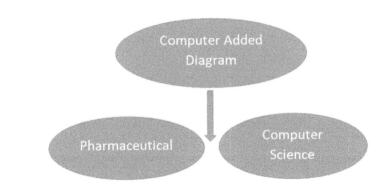

FIGURE 8.6 CAD system [2].

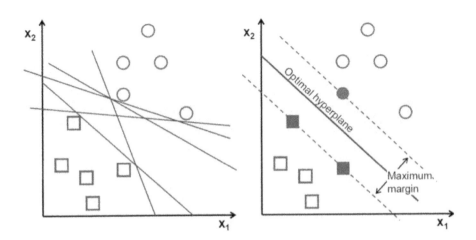

FIGURE 8.6.1 Support vector visualization.

8.5.2 RANDOM FOREST

SVMs and trees remain the foundation of the RF classifier. One or more DTs are integrated, and the output for the classification task is a mode class. It is also recognized as the random decision forest collaborative technique for regression, classification and further tasks because it works by creating a large number of DTs during training time and providing the yield of the class, which is the method of the classes referred to as classification or mean prediction referred to as regression of the distinct trees. The random choice forest is best suited for DTs that tend to overfit their training set [2]. Random forest algorithms extract the best feature out of the random subset of features rather than extracting the most prominent feature at the time of splitting nodes [8].

8.5.3 K-NEAREST NEIGHBOURS

Before making predictions, the supervised classification algorithm gathers a cluster of labelled points and uses them to study how to label more points. It takes into account the surrounding or adjacent neighbours of the location to be labelled and

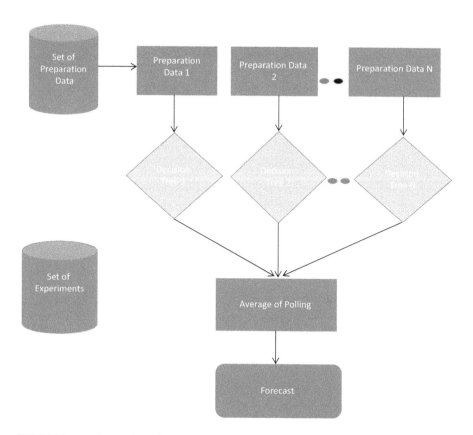

FIGURE 8.6.2   Integration of decision tree within the process of random forest for prediction.

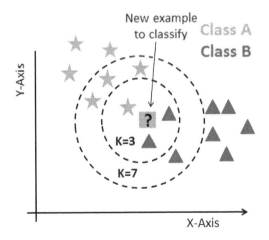

FIGURE 8.6.3   KNN representation of non-parametric supervised learning classifier.

solicits their input before changing the label [2]. It had two uses: (a) clustering; (b) regression. This algorithm is used to classify instances in a more comprehensive manner. Regression can also be performed with it by giving each neighbour a weight. Predictions using the KNN algorithm are based on Euclidean distance to the KNN and do not require any training. Because the prediction of breast cancer data set already includes labels for malignant and benign tumours, this method may be used with it. KNN is represented in Figure 8.4 [8].

8.5.4   LOGISTIC REGRESSION

LR is used to determine if a risk factor is involved in the emergence of a disease or condition that affects one's strength (and covariates). It is a well-liked simple classifier model that shows how dependent and independent variables are related. The relationship between one or more independent variables (Xi), also known as exposure or predictor variables, and a dichotomous dependent variable (Y), also known

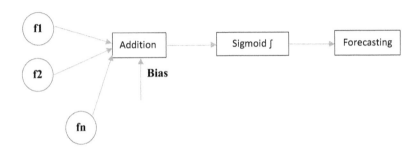

FIGURE 8.6.4   Logistic regression.

TABLE 8.2
Comparison of Various ML Algorithms

Authors	Data Set	Result Analysis	Accuracy (%)	Challenges
M.A. Naji, S. El Filali [11]	569 instances	SVM was considered to be the most efficient algorithm	97.2	The database used was WBCD which was considered to be a limiting factor. Larger data set will be used with new parameters to get more accurate results
S.A. Alanazi et al. [1]	275,000 instances	CNN is the most appropriate	87	Secondary data set was used. Future research should be based on primary data for conclusions that are more accurate
Muhammet Fatih[9]	202,932 patient's data set	LR gave better accuracy results	98.1	Before running algorithm, the data set must be pre-processed, as it does not deal with massive values
M. Razu Ahmed [12]	699 instances	SVM gives highest classification accuracy	97.07	Larger data set is required in case of high income or mass population countries
Sajib Kabiraj [13]	275 instances	RF provides more accuracy	74.73	Less sample size is used. Need to use large sample size and more efficient methods for training and pre-processing data set
Tanishk Thomas Nitesh Pradhan [9]	699 instances	ANN gives better prediction	97.85	Accuracy may be changed due to enhancement in data set
M. Milon Islam [14]	712 instances	ANN obtained highest accuracy	98.57	May vary with large data set
Yolanda D. Austria [15]	116 instances	The most accurate classifier in predicting breast cancer is the gradient boosting (GB) machine learning algorithm	74.14	Multiple ML algorithms can be used to increase accuracy for futuristic study

as the outcome or response variable, is examined using both basic and sophisticated LR. Use this method to forecast dependent variables that are binary or have several classes [2].

8.5.5 DECISION TREE

DT ML algorithms are used for regression as well as for classification. DT forms a tree-like structure, which has an internal node, representing the test condition for the vector to travel further, and a terminal node, the prediction value to be predicted or a class. Several fields, including game theory, cognitive science, AI, diagnosis, data mining and engineering, can improve from the use of DT. DT works well when there are only a few class labels to classify, but does not produce accurate results when there are numerous classes and few training observations. This algorithm is expensive to train computationally [9].

8.6 CLASSIFIERS COMPARISONS

8.6.1 LITERATURE REVIEW

In reference to Table 8.2, the comparison between the accuracy of various ML algorithms as per the graph analysis shown in Figure 8.7. SVM, LR and ANN are the best algorithms in terms of accuracy, but we cannot conclude that these are the best algorithms in terms of other parameters. Various parameters like the size of data set, time taken to execute the result etc. will also affect while considering accuracy.

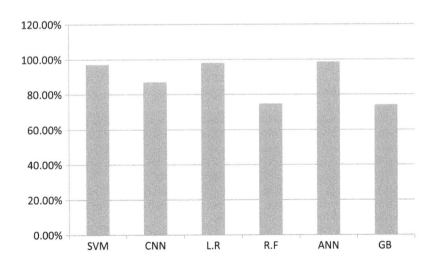

FIGURE 8.7 Comparison among various ML algorithm accuracy.

8.7 CONCLUSION

Several academics have reviewed and compared the results using different classification techniques, including LR, SVM, DT, RF and CNN. It has been observed that the accuracy of any algorithm on breast cancer detection depends upon mammogram features. Extracted features are used as an input for prediction by experts. Observation shows that the application of ML algorithms requires a large amount of data for accuracy, which was the biggest challenge for the ML algorithm application. CNN is used for processing automated feature selection through mammography images. We can conclude that ANN can be used for prediction but because of the limited number of neurons and the number of layers, the best accurate results cannot be produced. The accuracy of the ML algorithms can be improved through CNN image classifier models like ResNet50, VGG10, VGG16, VGG19, inception V3 or deep learning algorithms.

REFERENCES

1. S. A. Alanazi *et al.*, "Boosting breast cancer detection using convolutional neural network," *Journal of Healthcare Engineering*, vol. 2021, 2021, doi: 10.1155/2021/5528622.
2. G. Chugh, S. Kumar, and N. Singh, "Survey on machine learning and deep learning applications in breast cancer diagnosis," *Cognitive Computation*, vol. 13, no. 6, pp. 1451–1470, 2021, doi: 10.1007/s12559-020-09813-6.
3. G. Meenalochini and S. Ramkumar, "Materials today: Proceedings survey of machine learning algorithms for breast cancer detection using mammogram images," *Materials Today: Proceedings*, no. xxxx, 2020, doi: 10.1016/j.matpr.2020.08.543.
4. S. R. Sannasi Chakravarthy and H. Rajaguru, "Automatic detection and classification of mammograms using improved extreme learning machine with deep learning," *Irbm*, vol. 43, no. 1, pp. 49–61, 2022, doi: 10.1016/j.irbm.2020.12.004.
5. C. Singla, P. Kumar, A. Kumar, and P. Kumar, "Materials today: Proceedings deep learning enhancement on mammogram images for breast cancer detection," *Materials Today: Proceedings*, no. xxxx, 2020, doi: 10.1016/j.matpr.2020.10.951.
6. W. M. Salama and M. H. Aly, "Deep learning in mammography images segmentation and classification: Automated CNN approach," *Alexandria Engineering Journal*, vol. 60, no. 5, pp. 4701–4709, 2021, doi: 10.1016/j.aej.2021.03.048.
7. A. Andreica and C. Chira, "Towards feature selection for digital mammogram classification," *Procedia Computer Science*, vol. 192, pp. 632–641, 2021, doi: 10.1016/j.procs.2021.08.065.
8. T. Thomas, "Comparative analysis to predict breast cancer using machine learning algorithms: A survey," IEEE Xplore Part Number:CFP20F70-ART, pp. 192–196, 2020.
9. Muhammet Fatih Ak, "A comparative analysis of breast cancer detection and diagnosis using data visualization and machine learning applications," *Healthcare*, vol. 8, no. 2, pp. 111, 2020. https://doi.org/10.3390/healthcare8020111
10. P. Apelgren *et al.*, "Novel drug delivering conduit for peripheral nerve regeneration," *Materials Today: Proceedings*, vol. 27, no. xxxx, pp. 0–31, 2019, [Online]. Available: https://doi.org/10.1016/j.slast.2023.03.006.
11. M. A. Naji, S. El Filali, K. Aarika, E. H. Benlahmar, R. A. Abdelouhahid, and O. Debauche, "Machine learning algorithms for breast cancer prediction and diagnosis," *Procedia Computer Science*, vol. 191, pp. 487–492, 2021, doi: 10.1016/j.procs.2021.07.062.

12. S. Ahmed and N. Ahmed, "Breast cancer risk prediction based on six machine learning algorithms," IEEE Asia-Pacific Conference on Computer Science and Data Engineering (CSDE). pp. 2–6. doi 10.1109/CSDE50874.2020.9411572

13. S. Kabiraj *et al.*, "Breast cancer risk prediction using XGBoost and random forest algorithm," in *2020 11th International Conference on Computing, Communication and Networking Technologies, ICCCNT 2020*, pp. 1–4, 2020, doi: 10.1109/ICCCNT49239.2020.9225451.

14. M. Islam, R. Haque, H. Iqbal, M. Hasan, M. Hasan, and M. N. Kabir, "Breast cancer prediction: A comparative study using machine learning techniques," *SN Computer Science*, pp. 1–14, 2020, doi: 10.1007/s42979-020-00305-w.

15. J. P. Lalata, L. B. S. Maria, J. E. E. Goh, M. L. I. Goh, and H. N. Vicente, "Comparison of machine learning algorithms in breast cancer prediction using the Coimbra dataset," pp. 1–8, doi: 10.5013/IJSSST.a.20.S2.23.

9 Comparative Analysis of Machine Learning Algorithms to Diagnose Polycystic Ovary Syndrome

Arpit Raj, Poonam Joshi, Sarika Devi and Sapna Rawat

9.1 INTRODUCTION

Polycystic ovary syndrome (PCOS) is the most common type of disease among young women of child-bearing age; these women mostly lie within the age group of 15–44 years. PCOS is considered an alarming disease and thus it is the most challenging task for medical practitioners to diagnose it at a very early stage [1]. This alarming disease when converted to the most drastic case is called polycystic ovarian disorder [2]. This disease mainly occurs due to an imbalance in the normal hormonal levels of a woman or it may be due to certain changes in the normal lifestyle of females caused by diabetic conditions or certain environmental changes which directly or indirectly enter the body and affect the normal physiology of the reproductive organ which interferes with the normally healthy ovum in the female body [3]. In several studies, much research has been done to provide a better way of diagnosing PCOS at an early stage. This process is ongoing and medical practitioners have found better diagnostic procedures and novel approaches to improve the treatment of this disease by only detecting the hormonal level – the androgenic level in the normal female body, known as "hyperandrogenic anovulation" (HA) – or by examining blood samples of ill patients that are affected by PCOS [4]. In most studies, it was seen that a combination of the following diseases can result in PCOC: abnormal growth of the hair on the face of a normal female known as "Hirsutism", abnormal fat deposition on the female body known as "obesity", irregularity in the menstrual cycles of normal females, known as "amenorrhea" [5]. The problem of early diagnosis of PCOS is overcome by the introduction of the latest technology using artificial intelligence, which is helpful not only in the early diagnosis of PCOS but also in assisting emerging medical practitioners to provide better treatment for

DOI: 10.1201/9781003378556-9

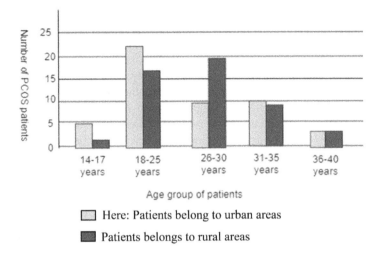

FIGURE 9.1   Number of PCOS patients versus age group of patients.

PCOS, as proved by several recent studies. Researchers and many emerging technical teams in the field of medicine as well as pharmaceutical companies aim to not only provide better treatment to patients but also to foster increased awareness about diseases from which people are suffering [6]. The latest technology works based on detecting the main causes of PCOS like determining each layer of the developing follicle and determining immature follicles by evaluating images with the help of three-dimensional ultrasound. It also works effectively in determining problems at the genetic level by identifying PCOS at some stages when left untreated. With the help of the latest artificially designed algorithms, emerging medical practitioners are able to effectively examine the receptors which allow effective proteins to bind to receptors through which the hormonal changes can be easily determined, which is the prime cause of PCOS [7]. With the help of the latest ultrasonic technology, the better resolution of the cysts can be determined easily by emerging medical practitioners who can assist the patients to be protective, which was difficult earlier. By counting the number of cysts in the follicles and through the latest technology, it was estimated that PCOS develops due to environmental changes [8]. Here,

Figure 9.1 depicts PCOS awareness among patients of different age groups and this statistical data also shows the number of medical practitioners using the latest technologies to detect PCOS, as can be seen through the comparative records of the number of patients in rural areas in comparison to urban areas [9].

9.2   DETECTION TECHNIQUES

There are a number of techniques for detecting PCOS, although they differ in their efficacy and in their precise results at appropriate time intervals. These techniques are listed below.

- *Biochemical test:* This is the most preliminary test of any common disease. It is used to examine the hormonal levels of the body, which are a primary cause of PCOS. Through this test, many intracellular fluids can be examined like Luteinizing hormones and follicle-stimulating hormones, tracing the levels of male hormones in the female body, i.e. androgen, whose level must be maintained. Through this test, many other tests can be determined, like testing the level of thyroid, serum prolactin, blood sugar level and many associated tests which can help determine PCOS at its primary stages [10].
- *Radiological test:* This is another important test for examining the intracellular structures of the body through rays that pass through specific equipment on a specific organ. This test helps determine any deformities in the organ system. This test was popularly known as the computerized tomography test, which is commonly named a CT scan. The most commonly used technique is the ultrasound scanning technique which works by scanning a particular organ and then giving a result. Magnetic resonance imaging is one such technique which works based on the latest technology. It is used to examine not only the anatomy of the specific organ but also its biological process, which is helpful for medical practitioners to effectively examine problems related to PCOS [11].
- *Histological test:* This is a unique test to effectively determine the layer of the uterus by making a small cut on the layers of the uterine and examining its condition under the microscope with full precautions inside the laboratory. This test is popularly known as the endometrial biopsy [12].
- *GIST-MDR (gastrointestinal stromal tumour–multifactor dimensionality reduction):* This is a unique technique of determining the number of cysts in the ovary under high resolution with the help of the latest designed filter under the category of the low-pass filter named the Gaussian pass filter. Specifically, Gaussian low-pass filters have a better capability of determining the threshold at multilevel image segmentations that provide better ways for emerging medical practitioners to easily classify PCOS forming cysts and diseases that affect the normal ovary [13].
- *Support vector machine (SVM):* This is the latest technology that effectively works in diagnosing PCOS at an early stage. SVM determines biological effects which can be examined by their metabolic effects, in combination with the latest machine-based techniques. This newly designed machine helps obtain high-resolution images of the cysts by applying newly designed filters that can effectively allow only those intensities of light which are useful rather than emitting huge amounts of rays which can affect the normal tissues. Through this latest technology, not only the cyst's structure but also the hormonal level can be determined, which is a major cause of PCOS. Due to the numerous advantageous features of this machine, its performance shows its accuracy of about 91.6% [14].
- *Endocrine-disrupting chemicals test:* This is the most advanced technique for detecting PCOS, which it achieves by determining the surrounding conditions. According to recent studies, environmental pollution plays a key

role in spreading PCOS among young women either directly or indirectly. Environmental pollution enters the body and affects the reproductive organ as well as alters the normal physiology of endocrine glands in the female body which results in the adverse situation named PCOS. So, by detecting the plasma concentration or by determining hormonal changes, it is possible through the latest technology to predict the presence of PCOS at an early stage in the female body [15].

- *ANN model (artificial neural network models):* This is the most advanced technique for the early detection of PCOS, which it achieves by determining other associated causes of PCOS like imbalances in the glucose level which may lead to diabetes, especially type II diabetes. Disturbance in normal sleeping patterns may also lead to improper release of the ovum and many associated problems, which gives rise to drastic conditions, including PCOS. The latest technology helps medical practitioners to provide better advice to patients. The introduction of these innovative techniques of detection is not only helpful to emerging medical practitioners but it also reduces the time of diagnosis and it is cost-effective as well. Due to its wide advantages in the field of medical technology, its accuracy rate is about 99% [16].

- *PCONet:* This is the latest technology which works using a specially designed algorithm that allows for the examination of images of the cysts under high resolution. This is helpful for medical practitioners in the early diagnoses of PCOS. This technology is more effective than earlier technology which worked using Inception V3 techniques that examine only 45 distinct layers of the cyst and only had an accuracy of about 96.56%. However, examining the whole distinct layer of images of the cysts under high resolution is more effective with accuracy levels of about 98% and it is much more helpful to medical practitioners [17].

- *D-PD (Three-dimensional Power Doppler):* This is the most advanced technique for determining the scan images of the cysts under high resolution with the help of the advanced Doppler effects. Three-dimensional power Doppler effects effectively enhance the images of the cysts in comparison to two-dimensional images in which the cyst is not clear. Recent research displays the usefulness of three-dimensional pictures in relation to examining the internal female body, which comes beneath the gynaecology branch of science. They are most effective in correctly figuring out abdominal organ placement, particularly trans region of the rectal, through ultrasound strategies on the women who are suffering from PCOS. Its vast advantages in the field of diagnosis have created the most advantageous ways for emerging medical practitioners to effectively count the number of cysts [18].

- *FSH–MIP sensor (follicle stimulating hormone–molecularly imprinted polymers sensors):* This is a novel approach that is based on specially designed artificial intelligence which works in determining the FSH levels in the female body. In recent studies, it was seen that the unique hormone which plays a major role in ovulation is somatostatin (SOM), which is known as a universal type of endocrine hormone as well as peptide hormone, that acts on the central nervous system. If there is a disturbance in their levels, it affects the follicular growth which may lead to PCOS. This unique chemical hormone inside the female body is effectively determined by the novel approach called MIP (molecularly imprinted polymer) porous sensor, which works based on polymerization techniques, especially the electronic-based detection of MAA (methacrylic acid) and EDMA (ethylene glycol dimethacrylate), which detect the $Ni_2Co_2O_4/rGO$ (graphene oxide) and is known as a nanocomposite – a modified form of indium tin oxides (ITO) [19, 20].

- *OvulaRing Sensor:* This is a unique approach to detecting PCOS by figuring out the temperature of the abdominal vicinity which includes the vagina. This technique uses a specially designed biosensor which is applied to the vagina. This technique is mainly used with female patients who are suffering from irregular menstrual cycles. To avoid continuous checkups, the temperature of the vagina can be checked at regular intervals and compared with standard high temperatures by determining the Ovula Ring. Its introduction is not only helpful in determining abnormal temperatures of the vagina during the POCS but also effective in determining infertility which arises in the case of PCOS and also it is a less time consuming and cost-effective process for the early detection of PCOS [21, 22].

- *T-lymphocyte biosensors:* These are considered to be the most advanced techniques of evaluation as well as discriminating the two similar aetiological diseases like congenital androgenic hormone–related problems which are caused by changes in the level of the androgen. This symptom is also seen in the case of PCOS with the level of androgens being the key factor of PCOS. This novel technology uses artificial intelligence and is used to determine the binding capacity of T-lymphocyte cell proteins to particular receptors and shows the suitable expression patterns of the conditions of the disease [23].

- *DCNN (Deep Convolutional Neural Network):* This is a specially designed algorithm which is based on the Python machine learning program, which works by storing all the data sets of PCOS and has a better capability of enhancing images recorded during ultrasound by determining its concentration in all the changes occurred in intracellular fluids during PCOS that can be helpful in assisting emerging medical practitioners to detect the images of cysts at their primary stages. As this innovation is also helpful in removing the unsuitable noise that occurs during detections of the images such as speckle noises which affect the resolution of the images during the ultrasound [24, 25].

- *AS–qPCR (Allele-specific–qpolymerase chain reaction):* This is the latest technology-based polymerization reaction of the suitable chain of the sequence of the different genes which proves to help determine the main cause of the genetic problems that are responsible for PCOS in the next generation of a particular individual. This introduction in the field of medical science proves to be most beneficiary for emerging medical practitioners who believe that genes are also the main cause of PCOS as seen in many cases with Sri Lankan women. These innovative techniques have a better capability of diagnosing the multi-gene sequencing at one time and give accurate results with reduced time periods and help in the early detection of PCOS [26].

- *CDD (Cangfu Daotan Decoction):* This is the latest technology which works on the networking system in the field of medical science, creating changes in recognising the pharmacology effects on networking platforms. Usually, this works on TCM-based systems which are novel approaches for effective analysis of the pharmacological effects and improve results in detecting PCOS. Its active components detect the gene based for PCOS that are isolated from the OMIM as well as the specially designed Gene Cards that have high potency to establish the best interactions between protein -protein in the specific DNA sequence that are commonly termed as STRING then with the help of the GO latest analysing techniques. As it provide best routes for the effectively analysis that are based on specially designed studio- named as R studios which is bioconductor data sets for the PCOS detection [27].

- *Raman spectroscopy with machine learning:* This is considered to be the most advanced technique in the field of medical chemistry. Combining spectroscopy with the latest technology effectively works on specially designed machine learning programs which have a better capability of detecting PCOS by only determining the intracellular fluids that are associated with follicular developments rather than its plasma concentrations. Its effective detection process is also helpful for emerging medical practitioners to distinctly separate the PCOS patient from those patients who are not affected by PCOS but have similar symptoms [28].

- *Otsu methods (operational test support units methods):* These are novel approaches based on equipment systems that are used to obtain cyst images with high resolutions. This proved to be difficult with previous systems that prompted noise on the ultrasonic images, making it far more difficult to correctly examine the cysts captured. Using the state-of-the-art technology, which goes on particularly designed algorithms that dispose of the greater rays, noises and lots of altering dealers that can have an effect on the actual images of the cysts, specially concentrated on the main organ and generating the photos that help medical practitioners to provide better remedy to the patients [29].

- *CNN (convolutional neural network):* This important technique is based on the novel approaches of detecting PCOS. It is highly effective and accurate in determining the number of cysts as well as obtaining effective images of the cysts through ultrasonic graphic techniques, as these novel approaches are based on specially programmed machine learning. Its obtained images exclude the irrelevant data and allows the medical practitioners to extract only important data sets related to POCS that can provide the better and effective results obtained from the diagnosed patients. Through the obtained images it is easy for the emerging medical practitioners to discriminate the PCOS-affected patients from the non-affected patients by determining their ovaries' conditions. It obtains effective and accurate results as it works on a specially designed model, popularly called "VGGNet 16", which itself is a pre-trained model and works on the CNN techniques. It is attached with the latest techniques which enhances the obtained results named as "XGBoost" model, which has a better capability to separate the obtained images with high accuracy of about 99.89% [30].

- *KNN model (k-nearest neighbour):* This is the latest technology used to effectively obtain the image of the cysts with their appropriate segment layers, areas and by excluding the irrelevant data from the obtained images. These usually work by initially adding the images through which the data is extracted and then processing the images under high resolution and then finally extracting the important information related to the diagnosed PCOS. Like its affected areas, its geometric areas, counting the actual number of deformed follicles found in the ovaries with a high accuracy of more than 97% [31].

- *Bayesian classifiers:* These are the latest technology that works on the better identification of PCOS as it works by determining the blood concentration or intracellular fluids and cholesterol levels to effectively detect the presence of the PCOS conditions at an early stage and also it clearly distinguishes the PCOS and non-PCOS conditions as it works on logistic regression techniques which show better results [32].

9.3   ADVANCED METHODOLOGY USED FOR DETECTING PCOS

- *ANN model:* This is a recently developed novel technology used for the early detection of PCOS through the proper examination of sonographic results and extracting specific information regarding PCOS. This new approach helps to categorise PCOS through the help of sonography. This is considered to be the most effective way for all emerging medical practitioners to diagnose PCOS early, that provide better treatment to affected patients as these work on the latest artificial intelligence which is based on programming languages that work on the data set of the particular tasks. It includes the record sets, the different classes of PCOS, are inserted that may efficaciously produces the consequences with the aid of comparing the neuronal impulses that are taken into consideration as the most vital enter indicators for the detection of PCOS and then the statistics came out by means of extracting the output signal in most effective methods such as through the sound acquired from the sonographic strategies after which through this modern-day strategies all the relevant records regarding PCOS is extracted out via converting it into suitable output indicators which could assist the clinical practitioners to evaluate PCOS [33].

9.4 METHODOLOGY

The unique procedures were performed using ANN models for the early detection of PCOS. This is an interlinking technology process which links two different biological active systems and technical system together in order to obtain effective results. It also produces high accuracy rates in the detection of PCOS. The procedures involved in this novel technology are performed in the unique pattern shown in Figure 9.2.

- Inserting the highly effective tasks for the detection of PCOS by assigning all the information regarding different types of PCOS.

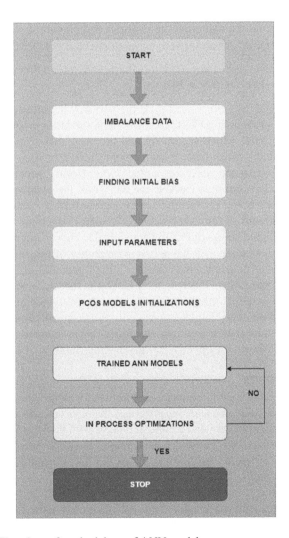

FIGURE 9.2   Flowchart of methodology of ANN models.

- Assisting the machines by giving proper information on weight variability of the patients which is the key factor for the variation of diseases.
- Classifies the ANN models on the basis of different strata which can distinctly differentiate PCOS into its distinct layers.
- Input the relevant data sets of neuronal signals related to PCOS onto the first strata repeatedly in order to activate the signals for the next network strata.
- Then, the machine will interpret the input signals and effectively classify them accordingly.
- The investigator checks whether the neuronal signals that are to be evaluated are matched with the response of the networks provided.
- After obtaining the results, the networks determine the powerful networks of dedication which is tested by evaluating the frequency at which it can remove all the inappropriate statistics and reap most effective results required for PCOS detection with an accuracy of about 99%[26].

9.4.1　Flow Charts for ANN Model

- *CNN Model:* This is considered to be the best way of performing the novel technology for detecting PCOS as it works on the latest programming language techniques, which accurately and precisely differentiate images of PCOS-affected ovaries from those of non-affected ovaries with the help of specially designed software called "VGGNet16" which works with "XGBoost". This not only extracts the data from the obtained images, but also provides a better platform for emerging medical practitioners to analyse the conditions of the ovary at its early stages which are considered to be the most initial stages of PCOS detection. This novel approach to detecting PCOS is effective as it has a better capability of discriminating large input images of different kinds and has a high potential of converting the required information on the data in the software, that extracts the important images such as in this case, the data input is related to obtaining the images of the disturbed ovary which convert only those specific images into suitable formats and then it has high capability of the interpreting the results detected and shows the effective results in short duration of time [27].

9.4.1.1　Methodology

This is the latest technology for determining ultrasonographic images with the help of specially designed machine learning programs. It creates an effective link between the obtained biological images and technical images with the help of software-based procedures, which make this technique very unique and effective compared to other machines learning programs, as shown in Figure 9.3. The procedures to follow when applying the CNN method are outlined below:

- Applying the obtained images from the ultrasonographic techniques for both PCOS ovaries and non-PCOS ovaries as the input data for the machine.

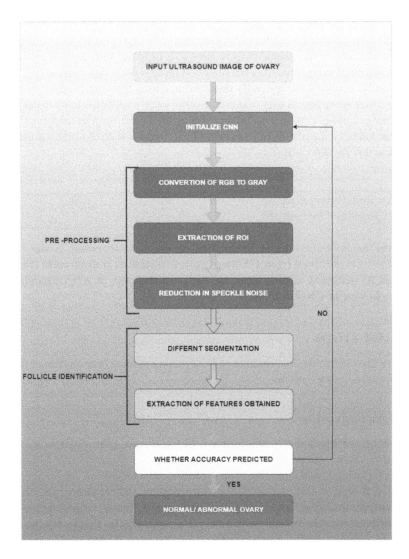

FIGURE 9.3   Flowchart of methodology of CNN models.

- Machine converted all the input images into the suitable format like in the specially designed colour space named greyscale colour space which works on OpenCV Python function "COLOR_BGR2GRAY" and resized the images into distinct dimensions, i.e., 224 × 224 size.
- By using advanced techniques, it is able to effectively discriminate the PCOS images from the non-PCOS images by omitting all the relevant errors that can affect the actual image quality.

- Interprets the obtained images by comparing them with the actual sample and then obtains the correct data sets related to PCOS by making some of the changes in the geometric structure like flipping, shifting and rotating which helps with enhancing the obtained images with high accuracy.
- Finally, applying the specially designed machine learning program based on DNN (deep neural network) architecture helps to effectively interpret the obtained images by decreasing the errors with the help of a trained machine that helps to classify PCOS and non-PCOS ovaries with the high accuracy of about 99.89% [24].

Here:
RGB = Red, Green, Blue.
ROI = Region of Interest.

On the basis of the studies performed on machine learning, it was shown that the results obtained from CNN are quite effective as compared to the ANN model as its accuracy rate is high, i.e. 99% (in the case of ANN models) and 99.89% (in case of CNN models).

9.5   CASE STUDY

Objective: To determine the presence of PCOS using the machine learning convolutional neural network models.

9.5.1   METHODOLOGY

In this study, we selected different forms of PCOS images from different locations, i.e. from medical centres and several registered diagnostic centres; a few images were also collected from a registered specialist of radiography.

This technique mainly involves the extraction of information from obtained images using ultrasonographic techniques based on the latest technology software which differentiates the images of PCOS in distinct layers by examining the image at different strata in the following manner.

- *Fine-tuning layer:* This is an important stratum for the detection of PCOS which is considered to be a challenging task for machine learning to specifically target the main process for transferring the data sets into the suitable formats with the help of the pre-trained models, including VGGNet16 models, Inception V3 models, Xception model and MobileNet model, which enhance the transformation of important data sets for PCOS into suitable formats that could provide better results in examining PCOS [34, 35].
- *Convolution layer:* This is the fundamental layer after fine-tuning in detecting PCOS as it works by applying suitable filters on the obtained images. In the case of PCOS, this includes two distinct layers. The first is considered

as the input layer which is named the padding. The second layer acts as the outer signal, called the striding, which helps in obtaining images under the defined parameters and shows better effects when compared with the actual images under the defined kernel size of 7 × 7.

- *Pooling layer:* This is the crucial layer in the CNN-based model which effectively obtains the images by reducing the dimension of the images up to 4 × 4 and it also excludes the irrelevant data obtained during the counting of the effective number of cysts. To enhance the techniques, specially designed pooling techniques were also introduced called "Max Pooling" operations. Max Pooling helps to enhance the obtained images of each patch that were found in the PCOS cases.

- *Dropout layer:* This is considered the first layer in CNN models as it works by reducing the irrelevant problems that arise during predicting the results after sonography. It basically works by converting the input signals into distinctly designed output values of 0 at regular intervals during the training process.

- *Flatten layer:* This is considered to be the most important layer in the CNN model as it works by converting all the images obtained from the previous layers that were found to be multilayer as per the data obtained but at this layer, the obtained multilayered images were converted into a single-dimension image layer, which is better able to classify the input neuronal layers from which the network expand into each distinct neurons, which is considered as important features for the PCOS detection through this novel approach.

- *Fully connected layer:* This is considered to be the last layer in the CNN model as this is the stage where all the neurons come together from the previous adjoining layers of the CNN model and finalized images are obtained from the latest software. It classifies the images according to their performance and produces effective results after passing each screening layer of the CNN model and the investigators investigate the images and provide better treatment to the patients affected by PCOS [36–38].

- *Observation records:* Table 9.1 shows the observation record of deep learning model.

- *Graphical presentations*: See Figure 9.4.

9.5.2 RESULTS

Thus, it is found that the novel approach which is based on machine learning is quite effective compared to previous methods for determining images of cysts. Figure 9.4 shows a comparison between accuracy and machine learning models.

It is estimated that this CNN model which works using the VGGNet16 software provides the best results as compared to the other process.

It shows the feature extraction segmentations of PCOS with a high accuracy of about 99.89% [24].

TABLE 9.1

Observation Record of Deep Learning Model

No.	Deep Learning Models	Accuracy	Precision	Recall	Specificity	F1 Score	Time (seconds)
1	CNN without transfer learning	0.7438	0.75	0.77	0.73	0.75	46.0
2	CNN with VGG Net 16	0.9782	0.97	0.95	0.96	0.97	82.8
3	CNN with Xception	0.9187	0.93	0.91	0.93	0.91	96.7
4	CNN with Inception V3	0.7555	0.76	0.75	0.76	0.76	55.6
5	CNN with MobileNet	0.9162	0.91	0.92	0.90	0.90	70.8

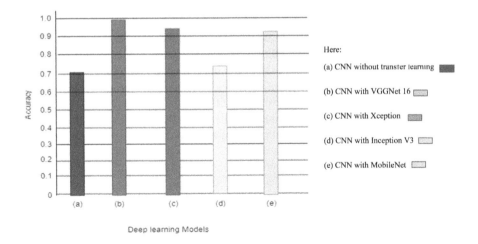

FIGURE 9.4   Comparison between accuracy and machine learning models.

9.6   FUTURE DIRECTIONS

The creation of synthetic intelligence within the discipline of scientific techno-logical know-how has created a large increase in the number of uses for today's designed machines that aren't handiest helpful in extracting critical data either from the sound-based diagnostic procedure as it's far executed inside the case of the ANN fashions or from the pix obtained from the ultrasonographic tech-niques [28]. By using the latest technology, it was found that the obtained result through this technique is not only helpful in producing images with high accuracy rates but also in making it easier for emerging medical practitioners to differen-tiate PCOS conditions from non-PCOS conditions. As it can be estimated from the above evaluations of images through latest technology, the inbuilt linking of neural networks with novel software technology to diagnose each segment of the PCOS at its different strata is seen in CNN models. There are also certain enhancements done in this emerging field of medical science with the help of machines learning programs. As it has great potential to produce the effective solutions of the effective results, especially in the cases of PCOS by combin-ing the two different pathways of detecting together, i.e. previously performed machine learning techniques with novel deep neural detectors, that works by combining both distinct layers such as finetuning layer with appropriate transfer-ring techniques that altogether improve the detecting process of PCOS conditions in females at its early stages [29]. Thus, it can be estimated that in future the emerging researchers are trying to develop much more AI–related machines that are not only effective in producing accurate results but also assist in diagnosing other related problems that cause PCOS, which is major challenge for medical practitioners and researchers [30, 35].

9.6   CONCLUSION

Ovarian syndrome is considered to be the most common disease worldwide, especially in young females. Recent studies show that every ten women in the locality is directly or indirectly affected by PCOS which may be either due to not having proper awareness or having other associated diseases likes type II diabetes and excessive obesity. The lack of a proper diagnosis of PCOS can also sometimes lead to cancerous conditions. Therefore, it is a major challenge for emerging medical practitioners and researchers and they need better diagnostic procedures so that the affected patients can obtain early diagnosis of PCOS. To resolve this problem, a number of novel technologies were developed that support the early diagnosis of PCOS by detecting the ultrasonographic images or by determining the fluids concentrations of the ovary, whose imbalance is the major cause of PCOS. So many new technologies have been developed based on artificial intelligence that enhances the image quality by minimizing the noise problems that often come during the production of ultrasound images using OTSU techniques. ANN models resolve these noise problems and thus obtain effective images of the cysts. Latest models of the CNN which work in association with pre-trained machine learning programs like VGG Net16, which is considered to be the most effective machine learning program, have the ability to discriminate the PCOS conditions from the non-PCOS conditions, but it also enhances the deformed cyst images quickly with accuracy rates of about 99.89%. By determining the different layers of PCOS by its own specially designed machines which discriminate each layer through different neuronal attachment it obtains the results in much more effectives ways. So, to conclude, the introduction of artificial intelligence is not only helpful in detecting PCOS but it also creates many other opportunities for medical practitioners to diagnose all the associated problems that lead to PCOS.

REFERENCES

1. Morang, M.D., Chasta, P. and Chandrul, M.K. (2019) "A review on 'polycystic ovary syndrome PCOS,'" *International Journal of Trend in Scientific Research and Development*, 3(4), pp. 60–66. Available at: https://doi.org/10.31142/ijtsrd23542.
2. Theisler, C. (2022) "Polycystic ovarian syndrome (PCOS)," *Adjuvant Medical Care*, pp. 282–282. Available at: https://doi.org/10.1201/b22898-281.
3. Kumar, R. *et al.* (2022) "Role of genetic, environmental, and hormonal factors in the progression of PCOS: A review," *Journal of Reproductive Healthcare and Medicine*, 3, p. 3. Available at: https://doi.org/10.25259/jrhm_16_2021.
4. Shah, N.S. *et al.* (2022) "Picomolar or beyond limit of detection using molecularly imprinted polymer-based electrochemical sensors: A review," *Biosensors*, 12(12), p. 1107. Available at: https://doi.org/10.3390/bios12121107.
5. Sumathi, M. *et al.* (2021) "Study and detection of PCOS related diseases using CNN," *IOP Conference Series: Materials Science and Engineering*, 1070, p. 012062. Available at: https://doi.org/10.1088/1757-899x/1070/1/012062.
6. Kulshrestha, S. and Goel, A. (2022) "Role of artificial intelligence in revolutionizing cancer detection and treatment: A review," *Proceedings of International Conference on*

Communication and Artificial Intelligence, pp. 615–621. Available at: https://doi.org/10.1007/978-981-19-0976-4_51.

7. Jiang, N.-X. and Li, X.-L. (2021) "The disorders of endometrial receptivity in PCOS and its mechanisms," *Reproductive Sciences*, 29(9), pp. 2465–2476. Available at: https://doi.org/10.1007/s43032-021-00629-9.

8. Goeckenjan, M., Schiwek, E. and Wimberger, P. (2020) "Continuous body temperature monitoring to improve the diagnosis of female infertility," *Geburtshilfe und Frauenheilkunde*, 80(7), pp. 702–712. Available at: https://doi.org/10.1055/a-1191-7888.

9. BM, R. (2019) "Exploration and comparison of ovarian hormones with anti - mullerian hormone amongst women with polycystic ovarian syndrome," *Open Access Journal of Gynecology*, 4(2), pp. 1–8. Available at: https://doi.org/10.23880/oajg-16000179.

10. Hawley, J.M. *et al.* (2022) "The biochemical investigation of PCOS: A UK wide survey of laboratory practice," *Endocrine Abstracts* [Preprint]. Available at: https://doi.org/10.1530/endoabs.81.p698.

11. Kumar, N. and Agarwal, H. (2022) "Early clinical, biochemical and radiological features in obese and non-obese young women with polycystic ovarian syndrome: A comparative study," *Hormone and Metabolic Research*, 54(9), pp. 620–624. Available at: https://doi.org/10.1055/a-1880-1264.

12. Peng, F. *et al.* (2022) "Apigenin exerts protective effect and restores ovarian function in dehydroepiandrosterone induced polycystic ovary syndrome rats: A biochemical and histological analysis," *Annals of Medicine*, 54(1), pp. 578–587. Available at: https://doi.org/10.1080/07853890.2022.2034933.

13. Gopalakrishnan, C. and Iyapparaja, M. (2021) "Multilevel thresholding based follicle detection and classification of polycystic ovary syndrome from the ultrasound images using machine learning," *International Journal of System Assurance Engineering and Management* [Preprint]. Available at: https://doi.org/10.1007/s13198-021-01203-x.

14. Abu Adla, Y.A. *et al.* (2021) "Automated detection of polycystic ovary syndrome using machine learning techniques," *2021 Sixth International Conference on Advances in Biomedical Engineering (ICABME)* [Preprint]. Available at: https://doi.org/10.1109/icabme53305.2021.9604905.

15. Jala, A. *et al.* (2022) "Implications of endocrine-disrupting chemicals on polycystic ovarian syndrome: A comprehensive review," *Environmental Science and Pollution Research*, 29(39), pp. 58484–58513. Available at: https://doi.org/10.1007/s11356-022-21612-0.

16. Boomidevi, R. and Usha, S. (2021) "Performance analysis of Polycystic ovary syndrome (PCOS) detection system USING neural network approach," *Data Engineering and Communication Technology*, pp. 449–459. Available at: https://doi.org/10.1007/978-981-16-0081-4_47.

17. Salman Hosain, A.K.M., Mehedi, M.H. and Kabir, I.E. (2022) "PCONet: A convolutional neural network architecture to detect polycystic ovary syndrome (PCOS) from ovarian ultrasound images," *2022 International Conference on Engineering and Emerging Technologies (ICEET)* [Preprint]. Available at: https://doi.org/10.1109/iceet56468.2022.10007353.

18. Ziogas, A., Xydias, E. and Tsakos, E. (2022) "Novel methods in the diagnosis of PCOS: The role of 3D ultrasonographic modalities," *Polycystic Ovary Syndrome – Functional Investigation and Clinical Application* [Preprint]. Available at: https://doi.org/10.5772/intechopen.101995.

19. Zhao, Y. *et al.* (2022) "Biosensors for single-cell proteomic characterization," *Biosensors for Single-Cell Analysis*, pp. 7–36. Available at: https://doi.org/10.1016/b978-0-323-89841-6.00004-9.

20. Branavan, U. *et al.* (2021) "Genotyping Sri Lankan women with polycystic ovary syndrome (PCOS): Towards A novel screening tool," *Ceylon Medical Journal*, 66(3), p. 129. Available at: https://doi.org/10.4038/cmj.v66i3.9491.

21. Xu, W. *et al.* (2020) "Identification of the active constituents and significant pathways of Cangfu Daotan decoction for the treatment of PCOS based on Network Pharmacology," *Evidence-Based Complementary and Alternative Medicine*, 2020, pp. 1–15. Available at: https://doi.org/10.1155/2020/4086864.

22. Zhang, X. *et al.* (2021) "Raman spectroscopy of follicular fluid and plasma with machine-learning algorithms for polycystic ovary syndrome screening," *Molecular and Cellular Endocrinology*, 523, p. 111139. Available at: https://doi.org/10.1016/j.mce.2020.111139.

23. Gopalakrishnan, C. and Iyapparaja, M. (2019) "Active contour with modified OTSU method for automatic detection of polycystic ovary syndrome from ultrasound image of ovary," *Multimedia Tools and Applications*, 79(23–24), pp. 17169–17192. Available at: https://doi.org/10.1007/s11042-019-07762-3.

24. Suha, S.A. and Islam, M.N. (2022) "An extended machine learning technique for polycystic ovary syndrome detection using ovary ultrasound image," *Scientific Reports*, 12(1). Available at: https://doi.org/10.1038/s41598-022-21724-0.

25. Rachana, B. *et al.* (2021) "Detection of polycystic ovarian syndrome using follicle recognition technique," *Global Transitions Proceedings*, 2(2), pp. 304–308. Available at: https://doi.org/10.1016/j.gltp.2021.08.010.

26. Thomas, Neetha and Kavitha, A. (2020) "Prediction of polycystic ovarian syndrome with clinical dataset using a novel hybrid data mining classification technique," *International Journal of Advanced Research in Engineering and Technology*, 11(11), pp. 1872–1881. Available at: http://iaeme.com/Home/issue/IJARET?Volume=11&Issue=11.

27. Priya, N. and Jeevitha, S. (2022) "Classification of ovarian cyst using regularized convolution neural network with data augmentation techniques," *Lecture Notes in Networks and Systems*, pp. 199–209. Available at: https://doi.org/10.1007/978-981-16-7657-4_17.

28. Mostafa, S. and Wu, F.-X. (2021) "Diagnosis of autism spectrum disorder with convolutional autoencoder and structural MRI images," *Neural Engineering Techniques for Autism Spectrum Disorder*, pp. 23–38. Available at: https://doi.org/10.1016/b978-0-12-822822-7.00003-x.

29. Sudha, R. *et al.* (2023) "Computerized diagnosis of polycystic ovary syndrome using machine learning and swarm intelligence techniques." Available at: https://doi.org/10.21203/rs.3.rs-2027767/v2.

30. Wang, W. *et al.* (2022) "Machine learning prediction models for diagnosing polycystic ovary syndrome based on data of tongue and pulse," *SSRN Electronic Journal* [Preprint]. Available at: https://doi.org/10.2139/ssrn.4095191.

31. Yedulapuram, S.H., Gunda, M., Moola, N.R. and Kadarla, R.K. (2019) "An overview on polycystic ovarian syndrome," *Asian Journal of Pharmaceutical Research and Development*, 7(4), pp. 72–80.

32. Radhakrishnan, S.A. (2012) "Polycystic Ovarian Syndrome (PCOS) in adolescence," *Asian Journal of Nursing Education and Research*, 2(2), pp. 55–64.

33. Mukerjee, N. (2020) "Polycystic Ovary Syndrome (PCOS) symptoms, causes & treatments-a review," *International Journal of Science and Research*, 9(7), pp. 1949–1957.

34. Choudhary, K., Singh, R., Garg, A., Verma, N., Purohit, A. and Deora, D. (2019) "An updated overview of polycystic ovary syndrome," *International Journal of Biological Sciences*, 7(3), pp. 1–13.

35. Barbosa, G., de Sá, L.B.P.C., Rocha, D.R.T.W. and Arbex, A.K. (2016) "Polycystic ovary syndrome (PCOS) and fertility," *Open Journal of Endocrine and Metabolic Diseases*, 6(1), pp. 58–65.
36. Kaur, R., Kumar, R. and Gupta, M. (2022) "Food image-based nutritional management system to overcome polycystic ovary syndrome using Deep learning: A systematic review," *International Journal of Image and Graphics*, vol. 22, no. 4 p. 2350043.
37. Kaur, R., Kumar, R. and Gupta, M. (2022) "Predicting risk of obesity and meal planning to reduce the obese in adulthood using artificial intelligence," *Endocrine*, 78(3), pp. 458–469.
38. Kaur, R., Kumar, R. and Gupta, M. (2022) "Food image-based diet recommendation framework to overcome PCOS problem in women using deep convolutional neural network," *Computers and Electrical Engineering*, 103, p. 108298.

10 A Comparative Analysis of Machine Learning Approaches in Endometrial Cancer

*Chaitanya Pandey, Nitya Nagpal,
Rahul Khurana and Preeti Nagrath*

10.1 INTRODUCTION

In this chapter, the relevance of machine learning (ML) approaches for the detection, prognosis, prevention and screening of patients suffering from endometrial cancer (EC) is discussed, drawing attention to the advantages and limitations of utilizing ML-based modalities to solve computational biology-related issues. The chapter has been structured as follows: Section 10.2 acts as an entry point to what EC and ML exactly are and how advancements in ML have benefited EC prognosis. In Section 10.3, we offer a thorough examination of the benefits and drawbacks of the ML methods used in the study of EC. In section 10.4 the content should be:

we studied the different evaluation metrics to analyze the performance of different classifiers. Section 10.5 offers a comprehensive look into the different methodologies integrating ML to solve a diverse range of EC-related clinical issues. In Section 10.6, we list the limitations associated with using ML-based algorithms with an emphasis on EC-specific cases.

10.2 ENDOMETRIAL CANCER

The uterus, a hollow, pear-shaped pelvic structure that is in charge of embryonic growth, is where EC first manifests itself. EC develops in the layer of cells that make up the uterine lining (endometrium). Endometrial carcinoma is another name for EC. It is a form of uterine cancer, the other variety is uterine sarcoma, which is less frequent and more difficult to cure. Figure 10.1 gives the biological depiction of the different stages of uterine cancer.

Late menopause, obesity, early menarche, unopposed oestrogen and even our eating choices, all contribute to the development of EC. According to a study, tamoxifen increases the risk of EC-related oestrogen and unbalanced hormone replacement

 DOI: 10.1201/9781003378556-10

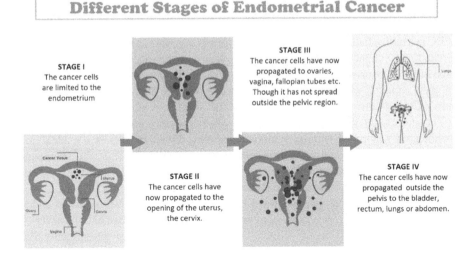

Different Stages of Endometrial Cancer

STAGE I
The cancer cells are limited to the endometrium

STAGE II
The cancer cells have now propagated to the opening of the uterus, the cervix.

STAGE III
The cancer cells have now propagated to ovaries, vagina, fallopian tubes etc. Though it has not spread outside the pelvic region.

STAGE IV
The cancer cells have now propagated outside the pelvis to the bladder, rectum, lungs or abdomen.

FIGURE 10.1 Biological depiction of different stages of uterine cancer. A four-stage depiction of how endometrial cancer spreads. The figure of each stage is accompanied with a brief textual depiction describing the spread of cancer cells from the endometrium in stage 1 to the pelvis and abdomen, including rectum, lungs and bladder, in stage 4.

therapy. Menopausal vaginal haemorrhage, bleeding in between periods and pelvic pain are possible warning signs of EC.

EC is classified into two types: endometrioid and non-endometrioid. Both exist in the uterine lining, although they appear differently under a microscope.

a. Endometrioid tumours are more frequent (they account for 75–80% of uterine malignancies), are generally discovered at an early stage and may lead to a positive prognosis, according to the National Cancer Institute (NCI). Because of the little myometrium invasion, this EC type has a positive result.

b. Non-endometrioid tumours (which include serous, clear cell and other, more rare kinds of EC) are frequently more aggressive and have a bad prognosis.

10.2.1 Significance of Research in Endometrial Cancer

In developed nations, EC is a common type of uterine cancer and is becoming more common. Although 20–25% of ECs are diagnosed before menopause [1], it is more common in postmenopausal women. Death rates for malignancies of the uterine corpus are growing, and cancer is now one of the primary causes of death in the states, owing to extraordinarily substantial decreases in death from heart disease. Given the present trend of rising EC prevalence and mortality, by 2030, it is expected that there will be an extra 3,700 new instances reported annually and 850 more people will pass away from the disease [2]. According to the NCI, the number of new instances of EC has climbed modestly each year since the mid-2000s. EC fatalities increased by roughly 2% every year between 2009 and 2018.

EC is usually found early, and with early diagnosis comes early medical intervention and more chances of survival. The five-year mortality rate for individuals with stage I EC has been shown to be higher than 95%, making it the highest of all gynaecological cancers, whereas it lies in the range of 47–58% and 15–17% for stages III and IV EC patients, respectively, lowering their chances of medical recovery.

The traditional therapy for EC involves hysterectomy and bilateral salpingo-oophorectomy with or without lymphadenectomy; however, this is not ideal for young women of reproductive age who plan on having children. Thus, the procedure of EC diagnosis and treatment is time-consuming and invasive, and still may not guarantee full recovery. There is no standard routine for EC diagnosis.

We need a system that analyses the different biomarkers and techniques of endometrial diagnosis [2–5]. A system that can predict the risk, the stage and the severity (like lymph node involvement) of EC so that we can avoid invasive treatments like hysterectomy [6–7] can add value to the existing medical science.

10.3 INTRODUCTION TO MACHINE LEARNING

Giving a computer any task nowadays necessitates a set of particular instructions or the execution of an algorithm that describes the rules that must be followed. The modern computer system lacks the ability to learn from previous experiences and hence cannot easily improve on the basis of past failures. So, in order to tell a computer to accomplish a task, one must first describe a comprehensive and proper algorithm for the task and then programme the said algorithm.

Artificial intelligence (AI) is becoming increasingly important in modern technology, particularly in the medical industry. AI uses technology and computer programmes to simulate the human mind's decision-making and problem-solving skills. Machine learning and deep learning can be used to create AI in medical imaging. A subset of AI known as machine learning could indeed understand data without having to be expressly coded. Deep learning is a subcategory of ML wherein input and output are connected by a large number of concealed layers. Several factors are used for determining the existence of endometriosis. They include MRI pictures, soft markers and laparoscopic images, among other things.

Recently, the burgeoning trend involving the use of ML methods for cancer prediction has opened the gate to a wide assortment of techniques benefiting biomedical engineers, molecular biologists, oncologists and bioinformaticians across the globe, ultimately raising the consistency of predicting EC vulnerability and identifying its severity.

Algorithms for ML are mathematical models that convert a set of variables that can easily be observed, commonly referred to as "predictors" or "features", through a sample or data point into a set of outcome variables, referred to as "targets" or "labels" [8]. In the "training" phase, the algorithms have been honed to be capable of anticipating labels by examining data points. Currently, three popular approaches

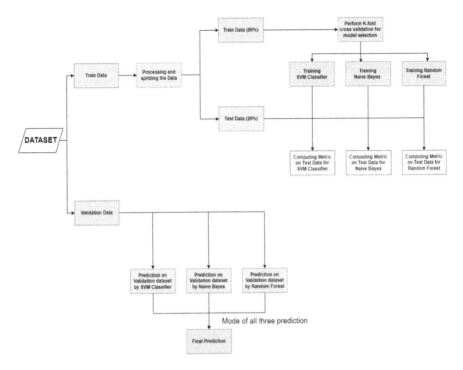

FIGURE 10.2 General workflow of disease prediction using ML. A flowchart showcasing the prediction methodology for machine learning models. Here the data set is divided into training and validation data. The training data is trained on classifiers and tested using evaluation metrics. The obtained results are validated on the validation data.

for training ML algorithms are used: supervised, unsupervised and reinforcement learning. Figure 10.2 gives the general workflow of disease prediction using ML.

10.3.1 Evolution of Machine Learning in the Medical Sphere

ML, a significant concept of AI, uses data mining software to create completely automated analytical models. It is founded on the idea that machines can extend the use of data, from analysing trends to generating outcomes with minimum intervention. The essential ingredients necessary to construct a strategy for the implementation of ML algorithms are contained in data samples. ML is a thriving medical discipline that uses technologies to connect medical difficulties with the aid of computer science and mathematical models. In medicine, ML might lead to more precise diagnosis algorithms and individualized treatment of patients.

ML methods date back to 1959 when the expression "machine learning" was first introduced by Arthur Samuel, completely changing the scope of the industry, giving us self-driving vehicles and AI-based helpers. In the medical sector technology has blended the lines separating computer science and medical challenges. The versatility and scalability of ML make it possible for solving a diverse range of use cases from classifying diseases to predicting survival rates. It has given us a civilization of self-driving cars, functional voice comprehension, sophisticated web search and a substantially improved comprehension of the human genome.

Because each data is connected to a huge number of categorization values, understanding the specific type of data that will be utilized in the future permits the correct repertoire of approaches and algorithms to implement for assessment. Another feature of ML algorithms is their capacity to mix several types of data (for example, demographic data, experimental results and imaging data) to discover patterns that may be used to efficiently categorize the data [9].

ML has increased in prominence to the point that it is now one of the preferred methodologies for academics when dealing with a variety of biological difficulties. The availability of increasing computational power has facilitated a surge in algorithms built around improving pattern recognition [10] and has enhanced image processing software. These developments have resulted in the evolution of computers, designed to perform difficult tasks in tandem with humans in fields like bioinformatics and medical imaging. Despite these advantages, the use of ML in healthcare confronts unique hurdles, such as data preparation and designing trials customized to an individual's clinical situation.

Head and neck cancer, oesophageal cancer, osteosarcoma, thoracic cancer, breast cancer and prostate cancer have all been successfully treated using ML algorithms. The past has shown us that an increase in the number of variables leads to more sophisticated cancer forecasting. ML provides the chance to examine past parameters to learn from cases with identical outcomes. Implementing ML techniques for EC prediction and prognosis could be useful in segregating patients into different phases and building prioritization mechanisms.

10.3.2 Machine Learning and Endometrial Cancer

Given the importance of personalized medication and the expanding use of ML in predicting cancer, a critical analysis of ML usefulness in EC may give motivation for future EC research and aid in collaboration with other domains. This chapter begins with an overview of EC and diagnosis methods before delving deeply into ML methods for EC prognosis.

However, before discussing the various methodologies used while studying EC it is imperative to highlight the significance of the data set creation process, which is possible due to data mining. Data mining is the process of extracting useful information from enormous data sets by employing modern data analysis tools to detect previously unknown, valid patterns and correlations, hence simplifying the discovery of knowledge linkages between medical parameters connected to EC.

In the categorization of EC risk in 100 women, Hart et al. [11] contrasted the findings of ML models (random forest and neural network) with a public opinion classification of 15 gynaecology specialists and primary care clinicians. Their models outperformed real physicians in identifying high-risk above-average-risk females, demonstrating the relevance of a risk prediction approach that can aid in making clinical decisions. This opens up a whole new discussion about the benefits of using ML approaches over human-driven detection, having its own advantages and disadvantages, which we look to cover in this chapter.

ML techniques have emerged to improve the prediction of cancer recurrence [12]. Rather than a simple presentation of symptoms, frequent screening, timely detection and predicting the chances of recrudescence or survival may improve EC patient survival rates.

10.3.3 Machine Learning Algorithms

Table 10.1 shows commonly used ML algorithms, along with their advantages and disadvantages. In the "training" phase, an algorithm is trained to be capable of anticipating an outcome by examining data and its corresponding label. The ML algorithms were trained using reinforcement, unsupervised and supervised learning. The algorithms listed have been used in a wide range of sub-domains, each contributing equivalently to the early prognosis of EC in patients, as discussed in Section 10.5.

10.4 EVALUATION METRIC

Evaluation metrics forecast model's performance. Using these measurements, we may compare the performance of different models in a variety of ways, depending on the evaluation metric used. The following measures were discovered to be employed in this study.

10.4.1 Error Rate

The error rate, as the term suggests, is the percentage difference between something's precise value (or actual value) and its estimated (or observed) value. It is used to highlight the variation between observed and actual values in scientific investigations. It is expressed as a percentage of the actual value. The mathematical representation of the error rate is shown in Equation (10.1).

$$\text{Error rate} = \left(\frac{|\text{Observe value} - \text{Actual value}|}{\text{Actual value}} \right) \times 100 \qquad (10.1)$$

10.4.2 Accuracy

It is the fraction of correct forecasts out of the total number of predictions. The accuracy formula aids in determining the inaccuracies in value measurement. If the measured value equals the real value, the system is considered to be very accurate and error-free. It can be mathematically formulated as shown in Equation (10.2).

$$\text{Accuracy} = 100 - \text{Error rate} \qquad (10.2)$$

TABLE 10.1
Machine Learning Algorithms

Approach	Advantage	Disadvantage
K-nearest neighbour	• Non-linear classification algorithm • KNN is resistant to new or trivial features	• Considers that all attributes are significant in equal measure • Cannot handle a large number of attributes; becomes computationally demanding with an increased number of attributes
Support vector machine	• Class boundaries modelled as non-linear are less likely to face overfitting • It has quadratic complexity of computation; therefore, it is more optimized than other classifiers	• When the training data cannot be separated linearly, it becomes hard to search for optimum settings • Requires longer training time
Genetic algorithm	Utilized for feature categorization and selection	It is not an ideal approach to finding some optima as it focuses more on local optima than global optima
Random forest classifier	• It works well with numerical and categorical data • It does not necessitate the transformation or scaling of variables	Can be computationally intensive for large data sets
3D convolutional neural network (UNet3D)	• Calculates a pixel-wise output (apart from the validity margins of the convolutions) • It tackles segmentation tasks here, without modifications	• In deeper models, learning might slow down in the intermediate layers • There is some risk that the network might learn to ignore the layers that represent abstract features
Artificial neural networks	Can handle more than one task at the same time	They need processors that support parallel processing, so the ANNs are dependent on the hardware
YOLOv3	• High detection speed and accuracy • Frame processing rates vary from 45 fps to 150 fps (for larger and smaller networks, respectively) which is quite better than real time	• Struggles to detect small objects • Low recall and more localization error as compared to faster R-CNN

(Continued)

TABLE 10.1 (CONTINUED)
Machine Learning Algorithms

Approach	Advantage	Disadvantage
Logistic regression	• It offers a natural probabilistic view of class predictions and can be extended to multiple classes (multinomial regression) • Less inclined to overfitting	• The presumption that the dependent and independent variables are linearly related is one of its limitations • It is a good predictor for discrete functions only. Thus, it has a limited spectrum of usage
VGGNet-16	High detection speed and accuracy	• VGGNet-16 is very slow to train • It occupies a lot of disk space and bandwidth which makes it inefficient • Exploding gradients problem arises due to 138 million parameters
Decision tree	• The sequencing of training occurrences has little effect on training • Pruning minimizes the complexity of the classifier and increases predicted accuracy by reducing overfitting	• The sequence of arrangement of the parameters in the algorithm determines the final decision tree • Discrepancies in the training set may result in unnecessarily complex decision trees
Naive Bayes	• Based on statistical modelling • Training method that is easy to understand and effective	Its limitation is that it assumes numeric characteristics to show normal distribution

10.4.3 PRECISION

Mathematically, precision can be calculated by taking the total number of true positives (TP) and dividing it by the sum of TP and false positives (FP), as presented in Equation (10.3). Precision gives us the measure of FP predicted by our model. If there are no FP, the model has 100% accuracy as well as 100% precision. Precision can be easily found with the help of a confusion matrix, as illustrated in Figure 10.3.

$$\text{Precision} = \frac{TP}{TP + FP} \tag{10.3}$$

10.4.4 SPECIFICITY AND SENSITIVITY

The sensitivity and specificity of a test are measures of its capacity to correctly detect whether or not an individual has a condition. In a medical subtext,

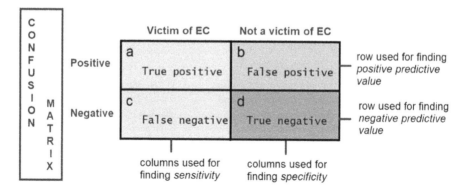

FIGURE 10.3   Confusion matrix. A diagram of a confusion matrix. A 2•2 matrix where the four quadrants are defined as true negative (TN), true positive (TP), false positive (FP) and false negative (FN).

sensitivity is a test's ability to detect a diseased individual as positive. The number of cases of illness that go unnoticed decreases with highly sensitive tests, due to fewer false negative (FN) results. A test is said to be specific if it is capable of designating someone not having an ailment as negative. A highly precise test yields fewer FP results. A poor specificity test may not be appropriate for screening since people who do not have the ailment may test positive, resulting in the prescription of unnecessary diagnostic treatments. Mathematical representations of both sensitivity and specificity are formulated in Equations (10.4) and (10.5), respectively.

$$\text{Sensitivity} = \left(\frac{\text{TP}}{\text{TP} + \text{FN}} \right) \times 100 \qquad (10.4)$$

$$\text{Specificity} = \left(\frac{\text{TN}}{\text{FP} + \text{TN}} \right) \times 100 \qquad (10.5)$$

10.4.5   AUC (Area under the ROC Curve)

The AUC–ROC curve leverages variable threshold values as a performance metric for classification tasks. The AUC measures separability, whereas the ROC represents a probability curve. It assesses the ability of a model to discriminate between different classes. The greater AUC indicates that the model predicts 1 as 1 and 0 as 0 more accurately. Similarly, a higher AUC indicates a better prediction capability of the model. This prediction model can then be used to perform a diagnosis of a given medical condition.

The ROC curve in Figure 10.4 is displayed using TPR versus FPR, with FPR on the x-axis and TPR on the y-axis.

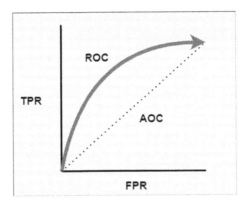

FIGURE 10.4   AUC-ROC curve. Diagram of an AUC-ROC curve. In a ROC curve, the two parameters, true positive and false positive rate, show the performance of a graph and AUC measures the two-dimensional area under the ROC curve.

10.4.6   CONCORDANCE INDEX (C-INDEX)

The concordance index, often known as the C-index, is an extension of the area under the ROC curve (AUC) that may account for censored data. The C-index, which represents statistically predictive accuracy, may be estimated in the Cox proportional hazard model. A higher C-index indicates better survival forecast accuracy. Refer to Equation (10.6) for the mathematical representation of the C-index.

$$\text{C-index} = \frac{\sum_{ij} 1_{T_j < T_i} \cdot 1_{\eta_j < \eta_i} \cdot \delta_j}{\sum_{ij} 1_{T_j < T_i} \cdot \delta_j} \tag{10.6}$$

where

- η_i is the risk score of unit i;
- $1_{T_j < T_i} = 1$, if $T_j < T_i$, else 0;
- $1_{\eta_j < \eta_i} = 1$, if $\eta_j < \eta_i$, else 0.

10.5   SPECIFIC USE CASES OF MACHINE LEARNING FOR EC

In this section, previous approaches used to solve a diverse range of clinical issues associated with EC have been grouped together on the basis of similar approaches, with the goal of offering a comprehensive comparison of each subsection paying due diligence to establish a through-line while listing out their advantages and disadvantages.

10.5.1 Applications of Machine Learning in EC Prediction, Prognosis and Diagnosis

The advanced stage of diagnosis, along with restricted treatment choices, severely limits the prediction of EC patients. Various studies (as shown in Table 10.2) in the past have demonstrated that screening, early identification and monitoring of EC might improve patients' prognoses dramatically. Advancements in the sector of AI and ML have introduced several novel techniques to identify and predict malignancies. ML has recently had a considerable influence on developing prospective algorithms for grading and predicting cancer patients in order to enhance the chances of a patient's survival [13]. Thus, ML tools incorporating AI [14] can be applied to EC diagnosis and prognosis to attain enhanced sensitivity and specificity of prediction. Constantinou et al. [15] presented a hysteroscopy imaging computer-aided system (CAD) for detecting EC which used the SVM algorithm (accuracy: 79.4%) for the classification.

Yamamoto et al. [16] used deep autoencoders to predict the BCR (biochemical recurrence) of prostate cancer with the goal of demonstrating that deep learning algorithms outperform people in the prognostic prediction of prostate cancer recurrence, leading to the automated extraction of explainable features from diagnostic annotation-free histopathology images.

Ofra et al. [17] tried to highlight the effect of eating habits and regimes on the reappearance of symptoms and survival of EC patients with the help of a random survival forest (RSF) technique.

10.5.2 Applications of Machine Learning in Pattern and Image Recognition

Pattern recognition is an automated technique using which regularities and patterns in data are identified, recognized and segmented using ML techniques. It makes use of analytics, statistical models and information drawn from pattern recognition to differentiate data. In supervised pattern identification, data is taught using specific labels. Each input data is used to produce an output based on patterns as a label. In the absence of labelled data, unsupervised pattern recognition applies different computer approaches, such as clustering or principal component analysis, to uncover unknown patterns. IP is a sort of computer technology that enables the processing, analysis and extraction of data from images. Table 10.3 compares the existing research done in pattern and image recognition in EC using ML.

The tumour appearance and volume of EC patients' tumours were precisely determined by Hodneland et al. [18] using a 3D convolutional neural network (UNet3D). Tumour texture traits, tumour volume predictions and tumour segmentation precision were all obtained. The study proved that current ML algorithms can accurately segment tumours in EC at a level comparable to a human practitioner. Tumour volume, tumour borders and volumetric tumour images are all provided by the model. This study demonstrates that this self-developed technique for primary EC tumour fragmentation is capable of achieving near-real-time whole-volume radiomic tumour

TABLE 10.2

Applications of Machine Learning in EC Prediction, Prognosis and Diagnosis

Paper Title	Year	Method	Result	Limitation
An integrated CAD system facilitating the endometrial cancer diagnosis	2009	C4.5 (a decision tree classifier) and SVM (support vector machine)	The SVM classifier achieved the best accuracy, i.e. 79.4% for the YCrCb colour scheme utilizing the SF+SGLDS texture feature sets	(a) The data set was small. A total of 404 subjects (202 normal + 202 abnormal ROI of the endometrium) were used for prediction (b) There is a need to validate the model with additional cases and users
Automated acquisition of explainable knowledge from unannotated histopathology images	2019	Deep autoencoders-generated features on which prediction of BCR (biochemical recurrence) of prostate cancer was done using SVM, Ridge and Lasso	AUC (SVM + Gleason score calculated by pathologist) came out to be 84.2%	
Artificial intelligence as the next step towards precision pathology	2020	CNN + segmentation (using QDA, LDA, SVM)	AUC of all the models was above 70%	(a) Setup expenses (maintenance contracts, digital slide scanners, IT support systems, image storage, image analysis software etc.) are high (b) The AI model must be validated in a pathology department over consecutive cases recorded over a set duration of time (c) The minimum level of performance that AI models must reach in order for pathologists to approve their use has not yet been addressed

(Continued)

TABLE 10.2 (CONTINUED)
Applications of Machine Learning in EC Prediction, Prognosis and Diagnosis

Paper Title	Year	Method	Result	Limitation
Dietary habits and daily routines as prognostic factors in endometrial cancer: a machine learning approach	2022	Random survival forest (RSF)	Only three variables (consumption of sugar-sweetened drinks, fried potatoes and decreased physical activity) increased EC risk out of 186 variables	There was no conclusion on how abstaining from alcohol affected patients with EC because the distribution was unequal
Using machine learning to create prognostic systems for endometrial cancer	2020	Modified ensemble algorithm for clustering cancer data (m-EACCD)	Using given attributes (TNM: tumour [T], nodes [N], metastases [M], grade, stage and three age groups), 11 prognostic groups were found with a C-index of value 0.8380	(a) The database used information on key clinical factors like lymphovascular space invasion that may be predictive of the outcome (b) To provide appropriate data on outcomes for the algorithm, it is necessary to have 100 patients or an event in a specific group at the minimum (c) The study only looks at cancer-specific survival. Other causes of death could have been wrongly classified

TABLE 10.3

Applications of Machine Learning in Pattern and Image Recognition

Paper Title	Year	Method	Result	Limitation
Automated segmentation of endometrial cancer on MR images using deep learning	2021	3D convolutional neural network (UNet3D)	AUC (for single image sets 0.88–0.95 and for combined image sets 0.87–0.93)	(a) A very small cohort (i.e. MRI images of 139 endometrial cancer patients formed the data set, out of which 34 were used for training) (b) It is a quite time-consuming task to manually identify tumours in 3D image data with good accuracy
The efficacy of deep learning models in the diagnosis of endometrial cancer using MRI: a comparison with radiologists	2022	Xception model		Small data set, 388 (204 non-cancerous + 184 cancerous) for training and 97 (51 non-cancerous + 46 cancerous) for testing
Using deep learning with convolutional neural network approach to identify the invasion depth of endometrial cancer in myometrium using MR images: a pilot study	2020	UNet	Prediction accuracy percentages were obtained as follows: contrast-enhanced T1w (79.2%), T2w (70.8%) and radiologists (77.8%)	(a) The data sets were not large enough and diverse as they were built based on cases from a single organization (b) The MRI and pathology diagnosis was based on one's own skill and experience, which might reveal individual disparities (c) The impact of ethnic differences was not taken into concern

(Continued)

TABLE 10.3 (CONTINUED)
Applications of Machine Learning in Pattern and Image Recognition

Paper Title	Year	Method	Result	Limitation
Deep learning for the determination of myometrial invasion depth and automatic lesion identification in endometrial cancer by MR imaging: a preliminary study in a single institution	2020	YOLOV3	The mean precision percentage was obtained as follows: sagittal images (77.14%) and coronal images (86.67%)	The proposed model might not be able to completely employ the volume information and capture the spatial information as it includes two-dimensional lesion patches (paired patch images) as its input
Multiplanar MRI-based predictive model for preoperative assessment of lymph node metastasis in endometrial cancer	2019	Logistic regression	Accuracy: (a) Normal sized (<0.3 cm) – 84.9% model CR1 and model C (b) Normal sized (0.3–0.8 cm) – 84.6% model CR1 (c) Enlarged (>0.8 cm) – 85.7% model CR1	(a) No external validation (b) Information and diagnosis using genetics have not been integrated into the model
Deep myometrial infiltration of endometrial cancer on MRI: a radiomics-powered machine learning pilot study	2020	J48 decision trees	Accuracy of 86%	(a) This research has a small data set due to few patients (b) The statistical capacity of "McNemar testing" to evaluate shifts in performance is restricted
Image analysis and multilayer perceptron artificial neural networks for the discrimination between benign and malignant endometrial lesions	2017	ANN model	The accuracy percentage for endometrial nuclei classification is 81.33%	Higher time complexity

profiling, including tumour volume and texture properties, which could be useful for EC diagnosis and developing more personalized treatment strategies. This study also found out the utility of deep muscle invasion, which could be a valuable predictor for EC. Urushibara et al. [19] compared the accuracy of the diagnosis of deep learning models using CNNs with that of radiologists. The comparison was done using CNN and Xception models. Arnaldo et al. [20] proposed an MRI radiomics-powered ML model for the detection of Deep Myometrial Invasion (DMI) in EC patients. For feature extraction in this model, "T2-weighted pictures" were employed, and an ensemble classification technique known as "J48 Decision Trees" was modified to achieve a classifier accuracy of 86%.

Dong et al. [21] built a deep muscle invasion (DL) model based on 4896 MR images from 72 uterine cancer patients and compared it to radiologist readings, obtaining an accuracy percentage of 75%; however, the variation was not scientifically notable. Chen et al. [22] conducted a similar study on 530 MR images and got accuracy, sensitivity and specificity of 84%, 66.7% and 87.5%, respectively. One of the strongest predictors of EC is lymph node metastasis (LNM) [23]. Xu et al. [24] devised a prediction model for LNM of normal size using MRI (magnetic resonance imaging) scans and CA125 protein data from around 200 EC victims.

The outcome was around 85% accurate. Endometrial cytology has recently been found as a feasible diagnostic method with good sensitivity and specificity for identifying EC [25–26]. Markis et al. did a study in which they sought to build an automated diagnosis system utilizing deep learning to analyse liquid endometrial cytology images of 416 patients and discovered that this model had 90% accuracy [27]. These figures revealed that ML has made major strides in EC therapy.

10.5.3 Application of Machine Learning in Classifying Endometrial Lesions

Endometrial hysteroscopy is one of the gold standards for examining the endometrium. Hysteroscopy is utilized to differentiate uterine body cancers such as endometrial polyps and EC, although the hysteroscopy skills are required. It has several limitations, such as being dependent on the physician's overall expertise and comprehension of the target disease, lesion size, lesion penetration depth, skills and competency, equipment and resource availability and evaluation of patients' comorbidities [28].

ML-assisted techniques of EC examination not only improve accuracy but also give a less intrusive and inexpensive tool for appropriately diagnosing EC, as mentioned in Table 10.4. Zhang et al. created a diagnostic hysteroscopy picture categorization system using the VGGNet-16 model [29]. Zhang et al. tested the VGGNet-16 CNN model efficacy for categorizing endometrial lesions using 1,851 hysteroscopic pictures of patients. The total accuracy was 80.8%, indicating that the CNN model may be utilized to diagnose EC.

The authors used GLMNet to perform prefiltering on data from a cohort of 422 patients. Their findings revealed that radiomic models based on ML algorithms can

TABLE 10.4

Application of ML in Classifying Endometrial Lesions

Paper Title	Year	Method	Result	Limitation
Deep learning model for classifying endometrial lesions	2021	VGGNet-16	Accuracies of 80.8% (five-category) and 90.8% (five-category) tasks of predicting EC lesions	(a) Only top five endometrial lesions were included. Lesions with lower occurrence were excluded (b) Images lacked diversity (c) This study did not include any prospective validation
Image analysis and multilayer perceptron artificial neural networks for the discrimination between benign and malignant endometrial lesions	2017	In cytological specimens, an ANN-MLP (artificial neural network based on multi-layer perceptron) was employed to distinguish between benign and malignant endometrial nuclei and lesions	Accuracy: 81.33%, specificity: 88.84%, sensitivity: 69.38%	Small data set ($n = 416$) with less diversity

be used as a repeatable diagnosis for clinical trial enrolment and therapy. Makris et al. [27] investigated the efficacy of ANN using multi-layer perceptrons to distinguish between harmless and harmful endometrial nuclei and lesions in cytological specimens. Based on the sample size of 416 histologically confirmed liquid-based cytological smears collected from a diverse range of patients, ANN was shown to perform with sufficient sensitivity and specificity on the classification task of endometrial nuclei and lesions.

10.5.4 ML ALGORITHMS IN EC PROGNOSIS

A model for the predictive prognostic EEA is of great clinical significance. Gao et al. [30] studied the behaviours, pathways and networks of EC-related hub proteins by critically examining the expression of EC and its corresponding genes. The EC gene information was acquired from the database PubMed (MEDLINE) with text mining, a subset of natural language processing (NLP), with the goal of revealing the mechanisms of EC development at a molecular level and implicating targeted therapy for EC. Yin et al. [31–32] used RF to construct a predictive model for endometrioid endometrial adenocarcinoma (EEA) that integrates gene expression and conventional characteristics. Three models were created: (a) using stage and grade, (b) using 11 genes and (c) using both (a) and (b) (11 genes along with stage and grade), thus alleviating the issue of poor prognosis for EEA, associated with late surgical stage, a high tumour grade and LVSI (lymphovascular space invasion). This ensures that a combination of both the random forest model and clinical criteria may assist in predicting EC.

Akazawa et al. used several clinical factors such as age, body mass index, stage, histological type, grade, surgical content and adjuvant chemotherapy on EC patients using five ML algorithms to predict recurrence based on signs of stage one and two EC, despite showing a good prognosis: RF, logistic regression (LR), decision tree (DT), support vector machine (SVM) and boosted tree. The area under the curve (AUC) and accuracy was used as the evaluation metrics to corroborate the efficiency of obtained results. SVM had the highest accuracy, followed by LR, while boosted trees had the lowest. LR had the highest AUC, and RF had the lowest. As a result, they identified linear regression as the best-performing classification approach for the research. Through the current study, they established the viability of AI in determining patients having EC and indicated that the application of ML classifiers may boost the speed and accuracy of predicting the recurrence and treatment response of EC at an early stage [33].

LNI can prognostically predict a variety of malignancies, including EC. However, there is currently no established approach for properly predicting LNI in EC. Günakan et al. studied the application of the naive Bayes (NB) algorithm [34] for the prediction of LNI in patients, by observing the presence of lymphovascular space invasion (LVSI), grade, cervical glandular, tumour diameter, tubal or ovarian involvement, pelvic LNI, stromal invasion and depth of myometrial invasion. According to the study, the algorithm predicted the LNI utilizing histopathological criteria with great accuracy. Subsequent research combining sentinel lymph nodes (SLNs) and imaging with ML algorithms or biochemical data could help with the management of EC [35]. Reijnen et al. conducted another study with the goal of constructing and externally testing a preoperative Bayesian network (BN) to predict LNM and disease-specific survival (DSS) in EC patients [36]. The research comprised 763 individuals who had had surgical treatment for EC. An externally validated ENDORISK-BN [37] incorporating numerous molecular, histological and clinical indicators was constructed using score-based ML for EC patients. Both findings demonstrated excellent calibration and discriminative performance. With an FN rate of 1.6%, ENDORISK was able to identify more than 55% of individuals at 5% risk for LNM. This study showed how, by using easily accessible and multimodal biomarkers, BN can customize treatment decision-making in cancer [36–38].

Praiss et al. [39] employed an unsupervised ML technique called ensemble algorithm for clustering cancer data (EACCD) to identify patients based on TNM (tumour [T], nodes [N], metastases [M]), grade and age in research. EACCD is a clustering approach that constantly applies criteria-based clustering to determine dissimilarity between two combinations, then integrates the learned dissimilarity estimate with a hierarchical clustering strategy to find final clusters of combinations. This novel ML technique enhanced EC prognostic prediction [40]. Chen and colleagues created the ESTIMATE (Estimation of STromal and Immune cells in MAlignant Tumours), which analyses gene expression data to estimate tumour content and the degree of infiltrating stromal/immune cells from tumour tissues and used it to calculate immune and stromal scores in tumours such as breast cancer, glioblastoma, prostate cancer, colon cancer and cutaneous melanoma. ESTIMATE total scores were shown to be strongly related to tumour purity in clinical tumour samples and tumour cell line samples, and they provided a straightforward and effective way for assessing the number of tumour cells in samples. Qi et al. built on this work by examining various aspects of EACCD using a large breast cancer patient data set. They investigated the influence of different parameters of the classifier on the output of EACCD and their related survival curves. They also compared EACCD to various clustering techniques.

10.5.5 SCREENING, CLASSIFICATION AND RISK PREDICTION OF EC USING MACHINE LEARNING MODELS

Table 10.5 gives a comparative analysis of existing studies which have used ML for EC risk prediction, screening and classification. Knific et al. [5] evaluated the diagnostic and prognostic strength of preoperative serum CA-125 and HE4 levels in patients suffering from EC by performing a controlled study on 133 females who underwent surgical treatment using logistic regression and analysed the importance of CA-125 and HE4 levels and body mass index, in a diagnostic model to obtain an AUC of 0.804. Downing et al. [41] developed a new categorization method for classifying EC-infected tissues as "Benign normal (NL), premalignant (EIN) and malignant endometrial (EMCA)" using ML classifiers. Random forest classification was used to classify the test cases into three different EC tissues. Chao et al. [42] used Cox proportional hazard regression to conclude that if the age-stratified cut-off level for CA125 is in the range of 35 U/ml in patients older than 49 years old and 105 U/ml in patients having age ≤49 years old, then it has the potential to enhance the predictive stratification of patients with EC.

Hart et al. [12] employed ML to classify patients based on risk by comparing the performance of the model with physicians' judgement on a categorization task broken into three tiers and discovered promising findings. EC models could benefit from early screening as they provide a cost-efficient way of locating high-risk populations without being invasive. By performing a statistical biopsy of personal health data, they devised a novel and efficient approach for timely cancer diagnosis and preventative treatments for individuals. Seven distinct models (random forest,

TABLE 10.5

Screening, Classification and Risk Prediction of EC Using Machine Learning Models

Paper Title	Year	Method	Result	Limitation
The utility of artificial neural networks and classification and regression trees for the prediction of endometrial cancer in postmenopausal women	2018	ANN (artificial neural network), logistic regression, CART (classification and regression tree)	Best performance by ANN (sensitivity: 86.6%, specificity: 83.3%, overall accuracy [OA]: 85.4%)	(a) Small data set (b) The "black box" aspect of ANNs may not correlate the variables in a pathophysiologically stable manner (c) Overfitting might have caused due to excessive training resulting in an overconfident outcome
Identifying high-risk women for endometrial cancer prevention strategies: proposal of an endometrial cancer risk prediction model	2017	A pragmatic risk prediction model is proposed to categorize all the biological females into three risk categories for EC	The proposed model: (a) Include measures such as level of reproductive hormones, obesity, insulin resistance and family medical history for prediction (b) Use random decision forests and unconditional logistic regression for classification (c) Validate the model in an independent group of individuals sharing a common trait	(a) This might not safeguard females having undiagnosed Lynch syndrome, who are more likely to develop uterine cancer at a fairly young age (b) This approach is completely theoretical and needs to be validated against a large and diversified data set of asymptomatic females collected over a long period of time

(Continued)

TABLE 10.5 (CONTINUED)
Screening, Classification and Risk Prediction of EC Using Machine Learning Models

Paper Title	Year	Method	Result	Limitation
The potential of an age-stratified CA125 cut-off value to improve the prognostic classification of patients with endometrial cancer	2013	Cox proportional hazard regression	It implies that a CA125 cut-off level based on age (35 U/ml in patients >49 years old and 105 U/ml in patients ≤49 years old) might enhance prognostic stratification in endometrial cancer patients	The data set used was small ($n = 923$) and limited to a single population (of Taiwan)
Novel algorithm, including CA-125, HE4 and Body Mass Index in the diagnosis of endometrial cancer	2017	Logistic regression and Cox proportional hazards regression model	Using CA-125, HE4 and BMI as parameters, AUC: 80.4%, sensitivity: 66.7%, specificity: 84.6%	(a) Small data set ($n = 133$) (b) Lack of diverse validation data set, including cases with different histological types, grades, stages, depths of myometrial invasion etc.
A New classification of benign, premalignant and malignant endometrial tissues using machine learning applied to 1,413 candidate variables	2020	With the help of image processing and random forest (RF) classifier, endometrial tissues can be categorized as follows: Benign normal (NL), premalignant (EIN) and malignant endometrial (EMCA) cancer tissues	3-class error rates of (NL, EIN, EMCA) training: 0.04; validation: 0.058 2-class error (NL versus EIN + EMCA) training: 0.016; validation: 0	(a) This model's diagnostic range is limited to normal EIN-cancer endometrial tissues (b) Pathologists routinely employ biopsy; however, it was not included in this model

neural network, decision tree, NB, SVM and LDA) were developed based on publicly available personal health records to assess the likelihood of a female having EC in five years. [43]. In terms of AUC, the other six models were outperformed by the RF model, followed by NN. The two models were used to categorize the population into low, medium and high. Despite not assisting in determining the ideal preventive measure based on effectiveness (e.g., diet and exercise, progestin or antioestrogen therapy and insulin-lowering therapy), it has significant potential for aiding in the timely identification of EC since it gives high-accuracy predictions by leveraging personal health information prior to the start of the illness, without costly procedures like TVUS or endometrial biopsy [12]. A risk prediction model that categorizes individuals into several risk groups may be useful in developing tailored cancer preventive measures for individuals [44]. Models that make use of this categorization can help clinicians identify high-risk individuals and propose appropriate EC-prevention treatments like as dietary and exercise changes [17], progestin or antioestrogen medication, insulin-lowering therapy and planned endometrial biopsies.

Hutt et al. [45] used a statistical meta-analysis approach to determine the order of risk variables by rank and provided a detailed overview of the percent and collective risk for each constituent, before constructing a mathematical model that used neural networks to forecast whether a patient's total cancer incident rate will rise or decline. The results were intended to provide a detailed evaluation of a patient and offer advice for preventive measures. To quantify relative risk, a meta-analysis of available data was conducted, proceeded by the development and execution of a risk stratification computer model based on the NN algorithm.

The National Cancer Institute (NCI) was able to establish the risk factors for EC in a sequential order based on rank using a statistical meta-analysis approach, which was then utilized to construct a pooled risk along with risk percentage for every component. They developed a predictive algorithm to determine the rise or fall in percentages of cancer risk and diagnosis for particular patients and achieved an accuracy of 98.6% using an NN-based system. The study's findings substantially limit the amount of unneeded invasive tests performed on EC patients. This could be a useful tool for clinicians to use in conjunction with other signs to determine if individuals need further preventive measures prior to the development of EC [45].

10.5.6 ML MODELS TO UNDERSTAND TREATMENT DECISIONS OF EC

Table 10.6 provides a comparative study of proposed ML models for taking treatment decisions for EC. In one of the studies, ML models were constructed to predict whether EC patients require a hysterectomy and to assist gynaecologists in determining the likelihood of fertility-preserving therapy in EC patients. This study gathered information from 1534 EC and EAH (endometrial atypical hyperplasia) patients in West China. The borderline SMOTE algorithm was used along with Adaptive Boosting (AdaBoost) technique. The suggested model was compared to many basic models; the suggested model outperformed basic ML approaches with 0.904 accuracies in the majority class and 0.905 accuracies in the minority class (with data augmentation).

TABLE 10.6

ML Models to Understand Treatment Decisions of EC

Paper Title	Year	Method	Result	Limitation
Fertility-sparing treatments decision in patients with endometrial cancer based on machine learning	2022	Ensemble learning	90.4% accuracy in majority class and 90.5% accuracy in minority class with data augmentation	
A novel prediction method for lymph node involvement in endometrial cancer: machine learning	2019	Naive Bayes	Accuracy percentage obtained is as follows: 84.2–88.9% (LNI) and 85.0–97.6% for PaLNI (para-aortic LNI)	(a) Backdated design (b) Lack of power analysis (c) These outcomes are observed with the least number of variables

Another study used the NB ML technique for LNI (lymph node involvement) prediction to enhance medical decision-making support systems in developing a predictive classifier for EC patients. The accuracy rate for LNI was reported to be 84.2–88.9% for LNI and 85.0–97.6% for PaLNI in the study of 762 individuals with EC (Para-aortic LNI).

10.5.7 ML Models to Find Proteomic and Metabolomic Biomarkers for EC Detection

EC is among the most common gynaecological tumours in developed countries, yet there are currently no screening biomarkers available. Because the proteome highly resembles the dynamic state of cells, tissues and organisms, it has a high probability of delivering medically significant biological indicators for cancer detection. The current state of EC diagnostic biomarker discovery with the help of proteomics is presented in this study. Protein biomarkers were grouped using the STRING database (Search Tool for the Retrieval of Interacting Genes/Proteins) and the Markov cluster algorithm (MCL). Proteomic analysis of blood, tissue samples and urine was performed, and the accuracy of various proteins was discovered. Several blood and tissue-based biomarker candidates for EC detection have been identified, though they are still to be incorporated on a widespread basis [46].

This work used nuclear magnetic resonance (NMR) spectroscopy to detect and assess metabolomic biomarkers in cervicovaginal fluid (CVF) for identifying EC. Asparagine, phosphocholine and malate from cervicovaginal fluid were recognized using ML algorithms and were discovered to be potential metabolomic biomarkers for detecting EC using NMR spectroscopy [47]. A comparative analysis of existing research in identifying biomarkers for EC using ML is presented in Table 10.7.

TABLE 10.7

ML Models to Find Proteomic and Metabolomic Biomarkers for EC Detection

Paper Title	Year	Method	Result	Limitation
Proteomic biomarkers for the detection of endometrial cancer	2019	Clustering of the protein biomarkers was done with MCL algorithm with the help of STRING database	Protein biomarkers (in blood, tissue samples and urine) were discovered to closely mirror the dynamic state of cells, suggesting that they have significant promise as a biomarker for cancer diagnosis	(a) Small sample size (b) Variability in storage duration of case and control specimens (c) Defective outcomes about a biomarker might have arose due to chance or due to lack of assay generalizability or bias
Metabolomic biomarkers in cervicovaginal fluid for detecting endometrial cancer through nuclear magnetic resonance spectroscopy	2019	Classifiers used were partial least squares discriminant analysis (PLS-DA), support vector machine (SVM), logistic regression (LR) and random forest (RF)	From 29 identified metabolites: phosphocholine, malate and asparagine were chosen for the prediction model. AUC obtained for training data set (SVM, PLS-DA, RF and LR methods): 88% and 92%. For testing data set, highest accuracy obtained was 78% (SVM and RF methods)	(a) Small data set (NMR data set) and low sensitivity (b) The records of patients with medical conditions such as bacterial vaginosis, ovulation, cervicovaginal swab contamination, pregnancy and unclear histological results were removed from the study, resulting in a roughly 50% difference between those screened and those finally chosen

10.5.8   Application of ML for Categorizing DNA Mismatch Repair–Deficient ECs

MMR-deficient (MMR-D) cancers account for around 3% of ECs caused by germ-line mutations in MMR genes (namely MLH1/2, MSH6 and PMS2) [48–49]. Veeraraghvan et al. [50] recently employed contrast-enhanced CT to detect DNA MMR-D and/or tumour mutational burden-high (TMB-H) subgroups in ECs. This work used generalized linear regression (GLMNet) and recursive feature elimination random forest (RF) classifiers to successfully discriminate between MMR-D in ECs, as well as the growing rate of TMB-H in ECs.

10.6   LIMITATIONS OF MACHINE LEARNING APPROACHES IN EC

When training ML-based models, EC data is typically required to be sensitive and specific to safeguard privacy while also allowing for innovation and technical progress. To improve the performance, safeguards should be adopted to ensure data access is strictly managed. The following are some of the significant problems connected with ML deployment in EC data sets:

1. *Data imbalance in ML systems:* An abundance of data drives ML algorithms; however, it is equally crucial that there is no bias due to an imbalanced data set. A data set is said to be balanced if the label distribution is roughly equal. Labels show the class associated with each data point and if the output variable is qualitative in nature, the label is determined by assessing how the input data performs in a classification problem. Most categorization challenges include a class imbalance. However, when the dominant class is significantly larger than the minority class, the discrepancy is evident, best seen when one target class overshadows the other classes. Imbalance in data sets is quite prevalent in real-world classification settings, and the traditional techniques for tackling issues typically yield unsatisfactory results. Just the majority class should not be recognized and due attention must be paid to consequently grant the minority class the same importance, making it critical to appropriately establish the minority groups in uncommon scenarios. The class imbalance problem can be overcome by including resampling procedures and ensemble learning approaches. It can also be mitigated with the application of appropriate evaluation metrics, boosting techniques, one-class learning, cost-sensitive learning and active learning. In contrast, most ML algorithms have a major issue with unbalanced data sets. There is no single strategy that can be regarded as a panacea for dealing with unbalanced data sets and increasing the model's prediction accuracy. To select the optimum sampling mechanism, multiple methods may be necessary. The most effective solutions will vary based on the characteristics of the unbalanced data collection.
2. *Human obstacles:* There are major obstructions regarding the inclusion of AI in healthcare which, through a stronger understanding of human and

computer interactions, we can shed light on. It will be critical to retain an emphasis on clinical applicability and medical outcomes to make sure that this technology reaches and benefits individuals.

3. *Nature of metrics to not accurately portray clinical relevance:* Despite its extensive use in ML research in the EC literature discussed earlier, the AUC of a receiver operating characteristic is not always the best metric for capturing clinical validity and is difficult to understand in some cases. Patient treatment in the real world should be the benchmark to determine how an algorithm is made, but most articles do not attempt to do so; other methods, such as decision curve review, have been proposed.

4. *The importance of prospective research:* Prospective research is vital to determine the actual use case of the developed systems in a real-world setting, as a large population of the patients presented in the trials was recruited retrospectively using already labelled data for training and testing algorithms.

5. *Generalizing to new settings:* Significant variations in patient demographics and sickness conditions in real-world clinical settings should properly be represented in the system where it will be used. A core component is the evaluation of an AI system with scaled data sets, facilitating the evaluation of real-world clinical output and generalizability. This technique is scarcely used in the literature surveyed and is a major source of concern. A current systematic assessment of research that assessed AI algorithms for medical imaging diagnostic analysis discovered that only 6% of 516 relevant scientific publications completed external validation.

6. *Peer-reviewed controlled trials:* Peer-reviewed proof is critical in building confidence and acceptance of ML in the medical community. Furthermore, there have been relatively few randomized controlled studies reported so far. High-quality reporting is required for ML experiments. Only when all aspects of a diagnostic or prognostic model are completely presented can the possibility of bias and potential value of prediction models be reliably quantified.

7. *Defining the grounds for comparing different algorithms:* Clinicians will face great problems in identifying the most suitable algorithms for their EC patients as the output of each test is captured using different tools and methods, and quantitative comparison of these algorithms is challenging. To create a standard benchmark for fair comparisons, algorithms should be compared on the basis of a similar test set that accurately represents a target population using comparable metrics.

8. *Data set shift:* Because data is generated in a non-stationary environment with a continually shifting patient population, screening techniques and models for data quality vary. Novel algorithms may need operational changes, resulting in new data distributions.

9. *Algorithmic bias:* As subdivisions like gender and race form a core component of a population, when analysing the output, we should incorporate them. Algorithmic bias can be divided into three categories: model bias,

variance and ambiguity and noise in the output. Effective solutions should be communicated by researchers to ensure necessary protocols can detect bias and assist doctors in their objective involvement in system design and growth.

10. *Logistical issues associated with AI:* The limited access of medical data poses plenty of difficulties to the application of AI in clinical cases like the study of EC. Data is frequently divided into various archiving programmes and monitoring software, making integration hard.

REFERENCES

1. Kaur R, Kumar R and Gupta M. Food Image-based Diet Recommendation Framework to Overcome PCOS Problem in Women Using Deep Convolutional Neural Network. *Computers and Electrical Engineering* (2022) 103: 108298, ISSN 0045-7906, https://doi.org/10.1016/j.compeleceng.2022.108298.

2. Kaur R., Kumar R, and Gupta M. "Food Image-based Diet Recommendation Framework to Overcome PCOS Problem in Women Using Deep Convolutional Neural Network." *Computers and Electrical Engineering* (Oct-2022) 103:108298.

3. Njoku K, Chiasserini D, Whetton AD, Crosbie EJ. Proteomic Biomarkers for the Detection of Endometrial Cancer. *Cancers* (2019) 11(10):1572. doi: 10.3390/cancers11101572

4. Cheng S-C, Chen K, Chiu C-Y, Lu K-Y, Lu H-Y, Chiang M-H, … Lin G. Metabolomic Biomarkers in Cervicovaginal Fluid for Detecting Endometrial Cancer Through Nuclear Magnetic Resonance Spectroscopy. *Metabolomics* (2019) 15(11). doi: 10.1007/s11306-019-1609-z

5. Knific T, Osredkar J, Smrkolj Š, Tonin I, Vouk K, Blejec A, … Rižner TL. Novel Algorithm Including CA-125, HE4 and Body Mass Index in the Diagnosis of Endometrial Cancer. *Gynecol Oncol* (2017) 147(1):126–132. doi: 10.1016/j.ygyno.2017.07.130

6. Sun Y, Li Zhi, Gao Li, Yuan W, Yang F. Fertility-sparing Treatments Decision in Patients with Endometrial Cancer Based on Machine Learning. *Eur J Gynaecol Oncol* (2022) 43(5):91–99. doi: 10.22514/ejgo.2022.046.

7. Günakan E, Atan S, Haberal AN, Küçükyıldız İA, Gökçe E, Ayhan A. A Novel Prediction Method for Lymph Node Involvement in Endometrial Cancer: Machine Learning. *Int J Gynecol Cancer* (2019) 29(2):320–324. doi: 10.1136/ijgc-2018-000033

8. National Cancer Institute. *Uterine Cancer*, https://www.cancer.gov/.

9. Bishop CM, Nasrabadi NM. *Pattern Recognition and Machine Learning*. Vol. 4, No. 4. New York: Springer, 2006.

10. Yang CQ, Gardiner L, Wang H, Hueman MT, Chen D. Creating Prognostic Systems for Well-differentiated Thyroid Cancer using Machine Learning. *Front Endocrinol* (2019) 10:288.

11. Hart GR, Yan V, Huang GS, Liang Y, Nartowt BJ, Muhammad W, et al. Population-Based Screening for Endometrial Cancer: Human vs. Machine Intelligence. *Front Artif Intell* (2020) 3:539879. doi: 10.3389/frai.2020.539879

12. Hueman MT, Wang H, Yang CQ, Sheng L, Henson DE, Schwartz AM, et al. Creating Prognostic Systems for Cancer Patients: A Demonstration Using Breast Cancer. *Cancer Med* (2018) 7(8):3611–3621. doi: 10.1002/cam4.1629

13. Chandra V, Kim JJ, Benbrook DM, Dwivedi A, Rai R. Therapeutic Options for Management of Endometrial Hyperplasia. *J Gynecol Oncol* (2016) 27(1):e8. doi: 10.3802/jgo.2016.27.e8

14. Acs B, Rantalainen M, Hartman J. Artificial Intelligence as the Next Step Towards Precision Pathology. *J Intern Med* (2020) 288(1):62–81. doi: 10.1111/joim.13030

15. Constantinou IP, Koumourou CA, Neofytou MS, Tanos V, Pattichis CS, Kyriakou EC. An integrated CAD system facilitating the endometrial cancer diagnosis. *2009* 9th International Conference on Information Technology and Applications in Biomedicine (2009). doi: 10.1109/itab.2009.5394424

16. Yamamoto Y, Tsuzuki T, Akatsuka J, Ueki M, Morikawa H, Numata Y, et al. Automated Acquisition of Explainable Knowledge From Unannotated Histopathology Images. *Nat Commun* (2019) 10(1):5642. doi: 10.1038/s41467-019-13647-8

17. Wersäll OC, Razumova Z, Govorov I, Mints M. Dietary Habits and Daily Routines as Prognostic Factors in Endometrial Cancer: A Machine Learning Approach. *Nutr Cancer* (2022). doi: 10.1080/01635581.2022.2112241

18. Hodneland E, Dybvik JA, Wagner-Larsen KS, Šoltészová V, Munthe-Kaas AZ, Fasmer KE, et al. Automated Segmentation of Endometrial Cancer on MR Images Using Deep Learning. *Sci Rep* (2021) 11(1):179. doi: 10.1038/s41598-020-80068-9

19. Urushibara A, Saida T, Mori K, Ishiguro T, Inoue K, Masumoto T, et al. The Efficacy of Deep Learning Models in the Diagnosis of Endometrial Cancer Using MRI: A Comparison With Radiologists. *BMC Med Imag* (2022) 22(1):80. doi: 10.1186/s12880-022-00808-3

20. Stanzione A, Cuocolo R, Del Grosso R, Nardiello A, Romeo V, Travaglino A, Raffone A, Bifulco G, Zullo F, Insabato L, Maurea S, Mainenti PP. Deep Myometrial Infiltration of Endometrial Cancer on MRI: A Radiomics-Powered Machine Learning Pilot Study. *Acad Radiol.* (2021 May) 28(5):737–744. doi: 10.1016/j.acra.2020.02.028. Epub 2020 Mar 28. PMID: 32229081.

21. Dong HC, Dong HK, Yu MH, Lin YH, Chang CC. Using Deep Learning With Convolutional Neural Network Approach to Identify the Invasion Depth of Endometrial Cancer in Myometrium Using MR Images: A Pilot Study. *Int J Environ Res Public Health* (2020) 17(16):E5993. doi: 10.3390/ijerph17165993.

22. Chen X, Wang Y, Shen M, Yang B, Zhou Q, Yi Y, et al. Deep Learning for the Determination of Myometrial Invasion Depth and Automatic Lesion Identification in Endometrial Cancer MR Imaging: A Preliminary Study in a Single Institution. *Eur Radiol* (2020) 30(9):4985–4994. doi: 10.1007/s00330-020-06870-1

23. Pelikan HMP, Trum JW, Bakers FCH, Beets-Tan RGH, Smits LJM, Kruitwagen RFPM. Diagnostic Accuracy of Preoperative Tests for Lymph Node Status in Endometrial Cancer: A Systematic Review. *Cancer Imag* (2013) 13(3):314–322. doi: 10.1102/1470-7330.2013.0032

24. Xu X, Li H, Wang S, Fang M, Zhong L, Fan W, et al. Multiplanar MRI-Based Predictive Model for Preoperative Assessment of Lymph Node Metastasis in Endometrial Cancer. *Front Oncol* (2019) 9:1007. doi: 10.3389/fonc.2019.01007

25. Norimatsu Y, Kouda H, Kobayashi TK, Shimizu K, Yanoh K, Tsukayama C, et al. Utility of Liquid-Based Cytology in Endometrial Pathology: Diagnosis of Endometrial Carcinoma. *Cytopathology* (2009) 20(6):395–402. doi: 10.1111/j.1365-2303.2008.00589.x

26. Wang Q, Wang Q, Zhao L, Han L, Sun C, Ma S, et al. Endometrial Cytology as a Method to Improve the Accuracy of Diagnosis of Endometrial Cancer: Case Report and Meta-Analysis. *Front Oncol* (2019) 9:256. doi: 10.3389/fonc.2019.00256

27. Makris GM, Pouliakis A, Siristatidis C, Margari N, Terzakis E, Koureas N, et al. Image Analysis and Multi-Layer Perceptron Artificial Neural Networks for the Discrimination Between Benign and Malignant Endometrial Lesions. *Diagn Cytopathol* (2017) 45(3):202–211. doi: 10.1002/dc.23649

28. Clark TJ, Voit D, Gupta JK, Hyde C, Song F, Khan KS. Accuracy of Hysteroscopy in the Diagnosis of Endometrial Cancer and Hyperplasia: A Systematic Quantitative Review. *JAMA* (2002) 288(13):1610–1621. doi: 10.1001/jama.288.13.1610

29. Zhang Y, Wang Z, Zhang J, Wang C, Wang Y, Chen H, et al. Deep Learning Model for Classifying Endometrial Lesions. *J Transl Med* (2021) 19(1):10. doi: 10.1186/s12967-020-02660-x

30. Gao H, Zhang Z. Systematic Analysis of Endometrial Cancer-Associated Hub Proteins Based on Text Mining. *BioMed Research International* (2015) 2015:1–6. doi: 10.1155/2015/615825

31. Yin F, Shao X, Zhao L, Li X, Zhou J, Cheng Y, et al. Predicting Prognosis of Endometrioid Endometrial Adenocarcinoma on the Basis of Gene Expression and Clinical Features Using Random Forest. *Oncol Lett* (2019) 18(2):1597–1606. doi: 10.3892/ol.2019.10504

32. Burki TK. Predicting Lung Cancer Prognosis Using Machine Learning. *Lancet Oncol* (2016) 17(10):e421. doi: 10.1016/S1470-2045(16)30436-3

33. Akazawa M, Hashimoto K, Noda K, Yoshida K. The Application of Machine Learning for Predicting Recurrence in Patients With Early-Stage Endometrial Cancer: A Pilot Study. *Obstet Gynecol Sci* (2021) 64(3):266–273. doi: 10.5468/ogs.20248

34. Langarizadeh M, Moghbeli F. Applying Naive Bayesian Networks to Disease Prediction: A Systematic Review. *Acta Inform Med* (2016) 24(5):364–369. doi: 10.5455/aim.2016.24.364-369

35. Günakan E, Atan S, Haberal AN, et al. A Novel Prediction Method for Lymph Node Involvement in Endometrial Cancer: Machine Learning. *International Journal of Gynecologic Cancer*. Published Online First: 28 December 2018. doi: 10.1136/ijgc-2018-000033

36. Reijnen C, Gogou E, Visser NCM, Engerud H, Ramjith J, van der Putten LJM, et al. Preoperative Risk Stratification in Endometrial Cancer (ENDORISK) by a Bayesian Network Model: A Development and Validation Study. *PloS Med* (2020) 17(5):e1003111. doi: 10.1371/journal.pmed.1003111

37. Arora P, Boyne D, Slater JJ, Gupta A, Brenner DR, Druzdzel MJ. Bayesian Networks for Risk Prediction Using Real-World Data: A Tool for Precision Medicine. *Value Health* (2019) 22(4):439–445. doi: 10.1016/j.jval.2019.01.006

38. Meyers L. A New View of Sex Education. *J Natl Med Assoc* (1988) 80(2):129.

39. Praiss AM, Huang Y, St Clair CM, Tergas AI, Melamed A, Khoury-Collado F, et al. Using Machine Learning to Create Prognostic Systems for Endometrial Cancer. *Gynecol Oncol* (2020) 159(3):744–750. doi: 10.1016/j.ygyno.2020.09.047

40. Qi R, Wu D, Sheng L, Henson D, Schwartz A, Xu E, et al. On an Ensemble Algorithm for Clustering Cancer Patient Data. *BMC Syst Biol* (2013) 7 Suppl 4:S9. doi: 10.1186/1752-0509-7-S4-S9

41. Downing MJ, Papke DJ Jr, Tyekucheva S, Mutter GL. A New Classification of Benign, Premalignant, and Malignant Endometrial Tissues Using Machine Learning Applied to 1413 Candidate Variables. *Int J Gynecol Pathol*. (2020 Jul) 39(4):333–343. doi: 10.1097/PGP.0000000000000615. PMID: 31157686; PMCID: PMC6884662.

42. Chao A, Tang Y-H, Lai C-H, Chang C-J, Chang S-C, Wu T-I, ... Chang T-C. Potential of an Age-Stratified CA125 Cut-Off Value To Improve the Prognostic Classification of Patients with Endometrial Cancer. *Gynecologic Oncology* (2013) 129(3):500–504. doi: 10.1016/j.ygyno.2013.02.032

43. Bishop, C. *Pattern Recognition and Machine Learning*. Springer, (2006). https://www.microsoft.com/en-us/research/publication/pattern-recognition-machine-learning/

44. Kitson SJ, Evans DG, Crosbie EJ. Identifying High-Risk Women for Endometrial Cancer Prevention Strategies: Proposal of an Endometrial Cancer Risk Prediction Model. *Cancer Prev Res (Phila)* (2017) 10(1):1–13. doi: 10.1158/1940-6207.CAPR-16-0224

45. Hutt S, Mihaies D, Karteris E, Michael A, Payne AM, Chatterjee J. Statistical Meta-Analysis of Risk Factors for Endometrial Cancer and Development of a Risk Prediction Model Using an Artificial Neural Network Algorithm. *Cancers (Basel)* (2021) 13(15):3689. doi: 10.3390/cancers13153689

46. Njoku K, Chiasserini D, Whetton AD, Crosbie EJ. Proteomic Biomarkers for the Detection of Endometrial Cancer. *Cancers* 2019 11(10):1572. doi: 10.3390/cancers11101572

47. Cheng S-C, Chen K, Chiu C-Y, Lu K-Y, Lu H-Y, Chiang MH, … Lin G. Metabolomic Biomarkers in Cervicovaginal Fluid for Detecting Endometrial Cancer through Nuclear Magnetic Resonance Spectroscopy. *Metabolomics* (2019) 15(11). doi: 10.1007/s11306-019-1609-z

48. Haraldsdottir S, Hampel H, Tomsic J, Frankel WL, Pearlman R, de la Chapelle A, et al. Colon and Endometrial Cancers With Mismatch Repair Deficiency can Arise From Somatic, Rather Than Germline, Mutations. *Gastroenterology* (2014) 147(6):1308–1316.e1. doi: 10.1053/j.gastro.2014.08.041

49. Ryan NAJ, Glaire MA, Blake D, Cabrera-Dandy M, Evans DG, Crosbie EJ. The Proportion of Endometrial Cancers Associated With Lynch Syndrome: A Systematic Review of the Literature and Meta-Analysis. *Genet Med* (2019) 21(10):2167–2180. doi: 10.1038/s41436-019-0536-8

50. Veeraraghavan H, Friedman CF, DeLair DF, Ninčević J, Himoto Y, Bruni SG, et al. Machine Learning-Based Prediction of Microsatellite Instability and High Tumor Mutation Burden From Contrast-Enhanced Computed Tomography in Endometrial Cancers. *Sci Rep* (2020) 10(1):17769. doi: 10.1038/s41598-020-72475-9

11 Machine Learning Algorithm-based Early Prediction of Diabetes

A New Feature Selection Using Correlation Matrix with Heat Map

Salliah Shafi Bhat and Gufran Ahmad Ansari

11.1 INTRODUCTION

Diabetes mellitus (DM), generally known as diabetes, is a metabolic disorder that causes high blood sugar levels. It has become a serious issue in day-to-day life. The body's secreted insulin hormone enables the cells to store excess sugar in the blood as a source of energy. In diabetics, the body either produces insufficient insulin or is unable to absorb it properly to reduce glucose. Consequently, unchecked high blood sugar can harm the kidneys, eyes, nerves and other organs [1]. The pancreas's release of the hormone insulin is linked to the disorder. It can occur in different forms: type 1 diabetes (T1D), type 2 diabetes (T2D) and gestational diabetes. The immune system of the body attacks pancreatic beta cells, which develop into T1D. As an outcome, the body produces insufficient amounts of insulin, which affects the bloodstream's capacity to absorb glucose. Numerous factors, including obesity, an unhealthy lifestyle and hereditary transmission, are responsible. Hormonal changes in the body during pregnancy contribute to gestational diabetes. Impairment of glucose tolerance is another name for prediabetes. It is an instance of high blood sugar in comparison to type 2 diabetes. Type 2 diabetes and cardiovascular illnesses like stroke are risk factors. The glucose level is between 100 and 125 mg/dL. The HbA1c value ranges from 5.7 to 6.4. Prediabetes can cause a number of issues, including blood pressure, poor HDL cholesterol, high blood and high triglycerides. According to research, diabetes can exist for up to seven years before diagnosis [2]. Damage to important organs like the heart, kidneys, eyes and feet are just a few of the major

DOI: 10.1201/9781003378556-11

side effects of undiagnosed and uncontrolled diabetes. Ulceration is the death of pancreatic beta cells and causes weight loss. When there is as little time as possible between the development of the disease and the beginning of the treatment, these problems typically become less severe [3]. According to a global survey conducted in 2017 [4], 451 million individuals worldwide have been diagnosed with diabetes, and by the year 2045, that number is expected to increase to 693 million. Since the data imputation must be removed, they used a hybrid decision tree (CART) technique and genetic algorithm as part of their data pre-processing technique. Later, the author employed the conventional neural network and achieved an accuracy of 82.33%. It is clear from this research review that the PIDD data set scores differ with and without feature selection. Another study [5] demonstrates that between 1980 and 2021 the growth rate of diabetes cases among adults over 18 increased from 4.7% to 8.5% in second and third world nations. Diabetes is a dangerous long-term condition that has affected millions of people worldwide. Since the past ten years, the number of persons with diabetes has substantially increased, becoming a global threat. Some of the most significant statistical information on diabetes mellitus from various healthcare organizations shows the likelihood of having serious life-threatening complications. In recent research, ML has been used to predict numerous chronic illnesses, including diabetes, and has produced promising outcomes [6, 7] using PIIDD information to analyse the metrics based on ten-fold cross validation. According to the author, during the testing with various methodologies, the deep neural network (DNN) achieved the best accuracy of 77.86%. The goal of predicting diabetic disease utilizing soft computing is to offer an understanding of the large data used with ML algorithms. Early detection of diabetes mellitus is essential, and using machine learning techniques to increase accuracy is essential. Artificial intelligence (AI) is also called machine learning. It makes use of a computer's ability to learn automatically without being explicitly programmed and gets better with time. As research has shown that machine learning algorithms are effective for diagnosing diseases, numerous researchers are performing tests utilizing a variety of classification algorithms of machine learning approaches, such as J48, SVM, NB and decision table. The strength of machine learning algorithms comes from their capacity to manage vast amounts of data, mix data from several sources and integrate previous knowledge into the research. This research work focuses on the early prediction of diabetes. The authors of this chapter proposed a framework for the early prediction of diabetes. In this chapter, the authors have used different MLAs such as SVC, KNN, LR, RF, AdaBoost and DT and evaluated them on the PIDD data set to determine a patient's likelihood of having diabetes. They compared the experimental results of the six algorithms to various other algorithms and achieved good accuracy. The results also show that SVC has the highest accuracy of 94%.

The chapter is as divided as follows. Section 11.2 provides a literature review. Section 11.3 describes the methodology used for the proposed approach. Section 11.4 calculates the performance analysis. Section 11.5 analyses and discusses the results and finally in Section 11.6, the research work is concluded and suggestions for future work given in order to wrap up the research.

11.2 LITERATURE REVIEW

This section presents some earlier studies that used machine learning to predict and detect diabetes early. Research techniques, data sets and algorithms have all been covered. Recent scientific studies have demonstrated through their experimental methodology the importance of lifestyle, demography, psychosocial and genetic risk factors in managing and controlling diabetes, particularly early prediction of diabetes mellitus. Various researchers around the world have used different strategies for the early detection of diabetes using MLA. The authors in this chapter have used PIDD to predict diabetic risk using logistic regression [8, 9]. The number of pregnancies, BMI and glucose level were among the factors in PIDD that the researchers found to be most significant predictors of diabetes. Another researcher stated that the best algorithm, with an accuracy of 76.3021%, is naive Bayes. According to the literature study, each of these researchers examined particular techniques and made the best possible improvements to them. Pre-processing, feature selection and feature categorization are the three processes.For feature selection, techniques including k-means clustering, the genetic algorithm (GA), the harmony search algorithm (HSA) and the particle swarm optimization (PSO) are used. KNN is employed in classification techniques. Sensitivity, specificity, recall and precision are some of the criteria used to assess accuracy prediction. About 87.65% accuracy rate is achieved. DT classifier and SMOTE are used in a diabetic prognosis prediction model. The suggested system has two stages: SMOTE is used in stage 1 to remove data imbalance. DT classifier is used to diagnose diabetes in stage 2. A diagnostic lab in the Himalayan region provided a data set with 734 entries. About 87.7% accuracy rate is obtained to address problems brought on by data sets, such as imbalanced data sets and short training data sets, applying the ideas of transfer learning and data augmentation. Systematic analyses of several neural network topologies are used, including transfer learning tactics, augmentation strategies and various loss functions, such as mix up and generative models. The same network design for type 1 diabetes is created using the public T1DM data set. The International Review Board has authorized the use of the data set, which was obtained from Beth Israel Deaconess Medical Center. A total of 78% accuracy is acquired. The Pima data set from the UCI Repository was used. When comparing a well-balanced data set with a CNN classifier that has been trained with SAE for feature augmentation, the accuracy attained is 88.31%. Identification of ML, classification of DM and diagnosis of DM help to overcome classification limitations. Different supervised, unsupervised and clustering approaches are compared. There is a lot of work that needs to be done to increase the effectiveness of detecting various diabetic illnesses because different data sets provide different challenges. There are 1,157 samples in the data set. There are five predictors employed. They are linear, decision tree (DT), random forest, K-neighbour among many other types of regression analyses. Utilizing five-fold and ten-fold cross validation for training, we presented a method for DL network-based diabetes diagnosis. When ten-fold cross validation is applied, the prediction accuracy is 68.35% and the data set utilized is the Pima Indians data set. Most have concentrated on data pre-processing, which entails the following tasks: eliminating

TABLE 11.1
Literature Review

References	Year of Publication	Data Sets	Methods	Accuracy
[8]	2022	Real-world data set	Linear regression, random forest	72%, 56%
[9]	2022	Clinical data set	Random forest, extra tree Gaussian	70%, 69%, 81%
[10]	2021	PIDD	XG Boost, AdaBoost, random forest	70%, 83%, 69%, 68%
[11]	2021	PIDD	SVM, LR, KNN	74%, 63%, 71%
[12]	2020	Pima clinical data set	LR, RF, SVM	79.90%, 70%, 69%
[13]	2020	PIDD	LR, RF, SVM	70%, 84%
[14]	2019	PIDD	SVM, KNN, RF	70%, 72%, 71%
[15]	2019	PIDD	NB, DT, KNN	67%, 66%, 64%
[16]	2019	PIDD	DT, SVM, AdaBoost	74%, 70%, 70.86%
[17]	2018	PIDD	NB, CART, RF	72%, 70%, 70.86%
[18]	2017	Real-world diabetes data set	DT	79.90%
[19]	2017	Real-world clinical data set	RF, DT	70.69%, 80.1%

missing values, balancing the data and performing feature importance and data augmentation methods. In order to classify algorithms, RF and LR are utilized. When compared to data without pre-processing, the result achieved is 24% higher for recall and 20% higher for precision. The article introduces earlier studies on the identification of diabetes mellitus and several classifiers that have been employed to determine accuracy. A previous literature review is provided in Table 11.1.

11.3 METHODOLOGY FOR PROPOSED APPROACH

In this research, we used a novel hybrid feature selection methodology. There are various classification and regression issues that can be resolved in the field of machine learning. The implementation of ML-based data-driven methodologies has included the use of data collected from individual persons or patients. The focus of the methodology section is on the research methodologies. Numerous studies in the literature explain machine learning, data analysis, the data sets used, the suggested framework and the methodologies used to evaluate the framework. In this study, machine learning approaches are used to create a machine learning model that can determine from a variety of diagnostic parameters whether a patient has diabetes or not. Artificial intelligence in the form of machine learning allows software applications to become more accurate at making predictions without being specifically programmed to do

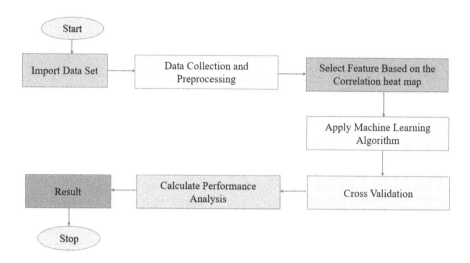

FIGURE 11.1   Proposed framework for early prediction of diabetes.

so. Finding inconsistencies, patterns and correlations within large data sets in order to forecast results is called data. The act of classifying a set of data into distinct categories is known as classification. Python has been chosen for this research because it contains reliable and effective libraries and packages for computational purposes. Preprocessed classification with supervised learning is the description of the problem raised here. The proposed architecture which includes various phases of data processing steps is depicted in Figure 11.1.

11.3.1   Data Collection

The diabetes data set is collected from the PIDD set for training and testing the model. It consists of 499 instances and 12 attributes. The data set descriptions are shown in Table 11.2. The purpose of data collection in this case is to forecast the development of diabetes using a novel hybrid feature selection technique. The suggested hybrid feature selection approach will reveal the key features in the prediction of diabetes illness. All observations are accurate, and there is just a missing value.

11.3.2   Data Pre-processing

Data pre-processing is a significant step in the implementation phase. It is the process of changing the data before putting it into the algorithm. It is a technique that converts unclean, unprocessed data into clean processed data. To produce a clearer output in a certain format, data preparation is done. Furthermore, it can be used to alter the data such that more than one kind of algorithm can be processed and implemented. The following are some of the steps in data preparation.

TABLE 11.2
Data Set Description

Attributes	Description
Thirst	The frequency of patient's water consumption during the day and at night
Glucose	The plasma glucose level
Blood pressure	The person having blood pressure low or high
Skinfold thickness	Triceps skin fold thickness
Insulin	2-hour insulin serum
BMI	Body Mass Index
Diabetes pedigree function	Family history of diabetes (a function which scores likelihood of diabetes based on family history)
Age	Age of a person
Smoker	Whether the person is a smoker or not
Fruits	Whether the person eats fruits or not
Veggies	Whether the person eats vegetables or not
Outcome	If the person is diabetic or not

11.3.2.1 Data Cleaning

Data cleaning is mostly used to ignore missing values and compute values in packed representations. Removal of outlier values that cannot be sorted into clusters is done along with offloading of noisy data, regression and grouping.

11.3.2.2 Data Integration

Multiple sources are combined and merged into one storage unit called the data garage using this method. It may involve attribute removal, object verification, schema unification, and the discovery and resolution of data conflict.

11.3.2.3 Data Transformation

By arranging and formatting the data and changing the values through procedures like aggregation, attribute selection, normalization and generalization it entails the procedure of grouping and consolidating the quality of data into alternative forms.

11.3.3 SELECT FEATURE BASED ON CORRELATION OF HEAT MAP

The correlation matrix shown in Figure 11.2 provides data on the relationships between features or the target value. Data are presented graphically in a correlation matrix to show which features are most closely related to the target feature. As a result of the fact that each feature in a data set is represented by a different colour, researchers can learn information about the relationships between features from the colour. We developed our correlation matrix heat map which is shown in Algorithm 1 in five phases.

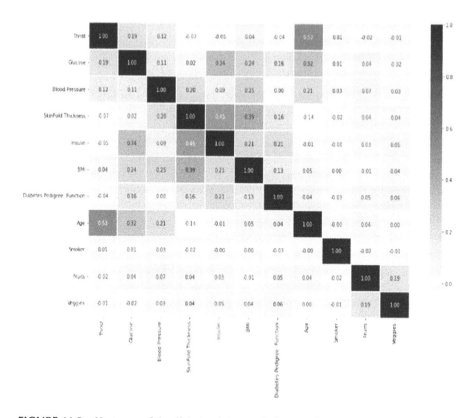

FIGURE 11.2   Heat map of the diabetes data correlation matrix.

ALGORITHM 1 CORRELATION MATRIX CREATION PROCESS USING HEAT MAP

1 Import data set
2 Determine the variable columns(x) and the target columns (y)
3 Generating a correlation matrix (finding correlation between each feature in a data set)
4 Create a heat map with dimensions (14,10)
5 Plot heat map and export.

11.3.3.1   Forward Sequential Selection

Algorithms involving feature selection are used to extract feature and unnecessary features. It was noted that selection of features is a useful tool for dimension reducing highly dimensional data. The 12 features were chosen and the forward sequential selection (FSS) algorithm was used to choose an ideal subset of data [20]. FSS was used for this research because it is a user-friendly wrapper technique and wrapper feature selection approaches are frequently used to identify fundamental relationships between variables. The initial result of the FSS algorithm is an infinite set. The empty set is filled with the feature with the highest feature attribute value. Algorithm 2 provides the FSS algorithm's pseudo-code.

ALGORITHM 2 PSEUDO-CODE FOR FORWARDED SEQUENTIAL SELECTION

Input: The entire set of dimension features $y = y1, y2, ..., yd$ is used as the input

Output: $XJ \in Y$, where $k = xy = xj|j = 1,2, ..., k$ $(0,1,2, ..., d)$

FSS returns a subset of features, a priority must be assigned to the number of features chosen (k)

where $k < d$.

1) Create an empty set $X0 = \alpha\ k = 0$

In order to set $k = 0$ (where k is the size of subset), we initialize the algorithm with an empty set (also known as null set).

(2) Choose the best process to improve the feature

$XT = \arg \max j(xk + x)$, where $x\alpha y\ xk$

$X_{K+1} = Xk + x +$

$K = k + 1$

Access step 2

(3) Conclusion $K = P$.

11.3.4 Apply Machine Learning Algorithms

Using a classification will help determine whether a patient is at risk for developing diabetes. A forecast for the test is then obtained after fitting training to the classification algorithm.

11.3.4.1 Support Vector Classification (SVC): One of the Most Well-known and Often Employed Machine Learning Methods Is the Support Vector Machine Method

Step 1: First we must choose the proper hyperplane.

Step 2: Making the spacing between neighbouring data points as large as possible comes after the first phase.

Step 3: Insert a feature.

$W = X^2\ 2 + Y\upsilon2$. It suggests that SVC can handle the problem.

Step 4: Classify the class using the SVC classifier. Binary is the group.

11.3.4.2 Logistic Regression

A supervised learning technique is logistic regression, often known as logit regression or the garch model taken from statistical analysis using predictive machine learning. A binary output in the forms of 0/1, yes/no and true/false is provided by the logistic method algorithm. The potential outcome for the two potential (y)-dependent qualities, i.e. output, and two or more nominally significant (x)-independent factors, i.e. input, is represented by logistic regression [21]. In mathematics, a prediction is generated using the logistic curve. An independent effort feature is required by LR for the prediction, and the task score is the monetary value of the distinct attribute. Associated multiplicate weights and activity ratings are also calculated using the logit algorithm. The score should be provided to the logistic function for the probability target class's achievement. To forecast whether a person has diabetes or not using the calculated logit, a protected class was given for each of its given features; the simple logistic regression form is provided as in Equation 11.1:

$$\text{Log} \frac{R(Y)}{1 - R(Y)} + \alpha + \beta(Y). \tag{11.1}$$

It is claimed that the logit is a natural logarithm (log) with the likelihood that the input ratios (x) and (y) will result in diabetes, the likelihoods of $(1 - R(Y))$ of (y) (i.e. non-diabetic patient).

11.3.4.3 K-Nearest Neighbour (KNN)

It is not a mathematical representation required to isolate the predicted regression from the data. Every time a pair is entered, the elements set the k-best nearby training instance from each pair as the input data [22]. KNN is one type of example showing learning. The outcome of KNN classification includes a set of members. The selection of a group's separation is made through data-based majority voting. If K is equal to 1, the class has a closest neighbour. The class has a bi or double closet if k = 2, and so forth. In general, the weighting decorations assert the signal neighbour to an amount of 1/x, where x is the distance from the separated point to the neighbouring point. A solid line is always the shortest distance between any two contacts, and this distance is known as the Euclidean distance. Before applying the KNN technique in the element's place, the extraction is performed on the raw data. The term for Euclidean distance in mathematics is

$$K(c,d) \sqrt{\sum_{i=1}^{n} (c_i - d_i)^2}. \tag{11.2}$$

Here k(c,d) means the distance in Euclid between c and d. To operate the system, we choose k = 5 with neighbours to analyse the data with the aid of KNN.

11.3.4.4 Random Forest

A collective learning technique called random decision forests (RDF) or random forests (RF) predicts a class or numbers (regression) according to the problem. During the training phase for classification, regression and other tasks many DT are built depending on [23]. The problem of DT over fitting training sets is addressed by random decision forests. The ability to predict type 2 diabetes was evaluated using different numbers of trees (50, 100, 250 and 500). With 500 trees, the best result was attained. Additionally, it plays a crucial part in collective machine learning and is frequently used in a variety of academic field, including healthcare.

11.3.4.5 AdaBoost

Adaptive Boosting, often known as "AdaBoost," focuses on classification problems and seeks to convert a group of unattractive classifiers into a dominant one. It is the initial workable boosting algorithm first proposed in 1996. The final equation for the classification issue can be shown as

$$F(y)\text{sign}\left(\sum_{n=1}^{n} \alpha nfn(x)\right),\qquad(11.3)$$

where F(y) stands for the appropriate weight, and n indicates the nth weak classifier.

11.3.4.6 Decision Tree

It is a technique that makes use of a tree's structure to map the system's likely outcomes in accordance with the outcome of an event, capacity to classify from their expenses and performance. It is organized like a tree. It has a collocation of nodes, where each leaf node represents a class label and each interior node represents features. And each branch represents a test result.

11.3.5 Cross-validation

The best resampling technique for evaluating the precision of ML models at small data samples is cross-validation. Since there are not many unbalanced data samples in PIDD, a structured fivefold cross-validation method was used to assess the performance of the model. At the beginning of the procedure, the data set was frequently partitioned into equal or substantially comparable K segments or folds, and the train and test data sets were selected using the stratified K-fold validation technique. The train data set which includes (K 1) folds and the error/accuracy was then fitted to the model. [24] was evaluated using the test data set, which has only one fold for each splitting independently in Equation (11.4). The equation was then used to get the model's average error (F) (2).

$$F = \frac{1}{K}\left(\sum_{I=1}^{n} FI\right).\qquad(11.4)$$

11.3.6 Calculate Performance Analysis

On a machine running the Windows 10 operating system with the following hardware configuration, the various recommended data preparation pipelines are implemented using the Python programming language and the Anaconda Distribution: Intel(R) CoreTM i5-3210M processor, clocked at 2 GHz with 8 GB of installed memory. The performance of the algorithms will be used to classify them, and all these characteristics will be measured. In any work the machine learning algorithm evaluation is a vital step. When the model is evaluated using one parameter, it might produce satisfactory results, but it might produce poor outcomes when assessed using another set of criteria or statistics. To evaluate a model's performance in our research, we primarily look at classifier although this is inadequate to make a definitive conclusion. The most popular classifiers are listed below. The Accuracy, ROC Curve, F1 score and Time taken are some of the performance indicators used to evaluate each experiment. Accuracy is determined by the number of accurate predictions to all input samples. When the target classes in the data are approximately balanced, accuracy is a good metric [25]. Since the area under the ROC curve is capable of predicting the odds of a tuple belonging to each target class instead of direct class prediction, it is also employed as a performance evaluation metric. The ROC curve is also better suited when the classification of the data set is balanced [26]. This explains how the ROC's points are obtained: with respect to various candidate threshold values between 0.0 and 1.0, the ROC curve is drawn using the points obtained through the false positive rate (x-axis) versus the true positive rate (y-axis).

11.4 ANALYSIS AND DISCUSSION

The classification model's effectiveness and accuracy were enhanced by incorporating filter and wrapper feature selection techniques. For the purposes of this research diabetes data were used.

11.4.1 Implementation

The proposed hybrid feature selection approach had two phases: filter and wrapper. To rank features between the features and the target class in the first phase, a correlation matrix with a heat map filter approach was used. To choose the k-best features, a minimum value for correlation heat map scores was created. If the correlation between two features and the target class is more than 0.5, then the features should be chosen. However, just the features are present. Thirst and age have correlation scores with the target class of greater than 0.53. Additionally, most of the features have correlation ratings that range from 0.1 to 0.4. Figure 11.2 displays a heat map of the correlation matrix for the diabetes data. The target classes of Thrist and age are displayed in sky blue when the correlation between their features and the target class is higher than 0.5. The significance of these two aspects in the identification of diabetes makes the association between them reasonable. The FSS method was used to choose the k-best features in the second phase. Based on the feature significance technique, the ideal number of features was chosen. It rates features and assigns scores to each data feature. A tree based classifier that extracts the feature's k-best number is the future importance technique. The best feature set was then chosen using the FSS wrapper feature selection approach. The selected best features' evaluations applied to evaluate are SVC, KNN, RF, LR, DT and AdaBoost. In order to evaluate the suggested strategy, four matrices were employed: accuracy, F1 score, ROC curve and time taken. The classification outcomes for the initial hybrid feature section technique FSS are shown in Table 11.3. A set of heat map displaying correlations alone and a correlation matrix FSS was used. Also, in Table 11.2 it shows SVC has the highest accuracy of 94%. To evaluate whether the classification method worked ten-fold cross validation was used.

11.4.2 RESULTS

We aim to come to the ultimate conclusion that is based on the crucial exploration by conducting various classification techniques. Cross validation is performed to

TABLE 11.3
Comparison of Performance Classifier

Algorithms	Accuracy	ROC Curve	FI Score	Time Taken
SVC	94	91	94	0.50
LR	83	79	83	0.14
KNN	89	86	89	0.29
RF	90	87	90	1.16
AdaBoost	75	73	75	0.80
DT	68	65	68	0.01

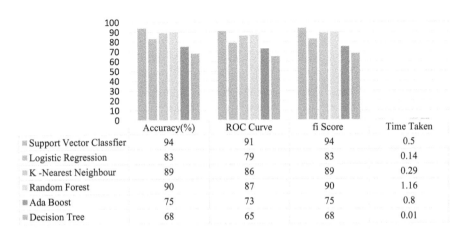

	Accuracy(%)	ROC Curve	fi Score	Time Taken
Support Vector Classfier	94	91	94	0.5
Logistic Regression	83	79	83	0.14
K -Nearest Neighbour	89	86	89	0.29
Random Forest	90	87	90	1.16
Ada Boost	75	73	75	0.8
Decision Tree	68	65	68	0.01

FIGURE 11.3   The graphical representation of performance analysis.

evaluate the suggested system in order to assess the performance of a model-fold. In this research, a variety of parameters are used, such as thirst, glucose, BMI, blood pressure, skin fold thickness, diabetes pedigree function, age, smoker, fruits, veggies and outcome for evaluating machine learning classification algorithm for predicting diabetes. In this chapter, we have used SVC, KNN, RF, LR, DT and AdaBoost for early prediction of diabetes. SVC has the highest accuracy of 94% as compared to KNN, RF, LR, DT and AdaBoost. The graphical representation of performance analysis is shown in Figure 11.3.

11.5 CONCLUSION AND FUTURE WORK

Early diabetes detection is essential for medical treatment. In order to create a strong predictive model, data sets can be chosen using important feature selection techniques. This is because not all feature selection techniques can take into account crucial features that would improve the prediction process. Be aware that important features are utilized to create accurate predictive models that aid healthcare professionals in treating patients. It could be appropriate to present several feature selection methods as a solution to this problem. In this case, a new hybrid feature selection methodology has been used to build a predictive model. Filter (correlation matrix with heat map) and wrapper (sequential forward selection) approaches utilized in the suggested hybrid feature selection process. To evaluate how well the recently proposed hybrid feature selection technique works for diabetes diagnosis, six different machine learning algorithms were applied to the chosen features (feature subsets), and then their performances were compared. This study found that using the SVC algorithm with a feature set created using the suggested hybrid feature selection strategy yielded the best classification accuracy (94%). Finally, the proposed hybrid feature selection is probably accurate. Strategy and machine learning algorithms have improved significantly our comprehension of the data. The combination of methods for feature selection and deep learning approaches will be the focus of our future research in order to increase classification accuracy using an image collection.

REFERENCES

1. Mahesh, T. R., et al. "Blended ensemble learning prediction model for strengthening diagnosis and treatment of chronic diabetes disease." *Computational Intelligence and Neuroscience* 2022 (2022).1–9

2. Islam, M. M., et al. "Likelihood prediction of diabetes at an early stage using data mining techniques." *Computer Vision and Machine Intelligence in Medical Image Analysis.* Springer, Singapore, 2020. 113–125.

3. Cui, Yangyang, et al. "Research on diabetes risk prediction model at early stage based on machine learning." *International Conference on Intelligent Automation and Soft Computing.* Springer, Cham, 2021.

4. Cho, Nam H., et al. "IDF diabetes atlas: Global estimates of diabetes prevalence for 2017 and projections for 2045." *Diabetes Research and Clinical Practice* 138 (2018): 271–281.

5. Trakarnvanich, Thananda, Tanun Ngamvichchukorn, and Paweena Susantitaphong. "Incidence of acute kidney injury during pregnancy and its prognostic value for adverse clinical outcomes: A systematic review and meta-analysis." *Medicine* 101.30 (2022).

6. Davazdahemami, Behrooz, Hamed M. Zolbanin, and Dursun Delen. "An explanatory analytics framework for early detection of chronic risk factors in pandemics." *Healthcare Analytics* 2 (2022): 100020.

7. Revathi, A., et al. "Early detection of cognitive decline using machine learning algorithm and cognitive ability test." *Security and Communication Networks* 2022 (2022): 1–9.

8. Suzuki, Yasuhiro, et al. "Exploratory analysis using machine learning of predictive factors for falls in type 2 diabetes." *Scientific Reports* 12.1 (2022): 1–10.

9. Bhat, Salliah Shafi, et al. "Prevalence and early prediction of diabetes using machine learning in North Kashmir: A case study of district Bandipora." *Computational Intelligence and Neuroscience* 2022, pp. 1–9(2022).

10. Taz, Nahid Hossain, Abrar Islam, and Ishrak Mahmud. "A comparative analysis of ensemble based machine learning techniques for diabetes identification." 2021 *2nd International Conference on Robotics, Electrical and Signal Processing Techniques (ICREST)*. IEEE, 2021.

11. Bhat, Salliah Shafi, and Gufran Ahmad Ansari. "Predictions of diabetes and diet recommendation system for diabetic patients using machine learning techniques." *2021 2nd International Conference for Emerging Technology (INCET)*. IEEE, 2021.

12. Gupta, Deepak, et al. "Computational approach to clinical diagnosis of diabetes disease: A comparative study." *Multimedia Tools and Applications* 80.20 (2021): 30091–30116.

13. Kaul, Surabhi, and Yogesh Kumar. "Artificial intelligence-based learning techniques for diabetes prediction: Challenges and systematic review." *SN Computer Science* 1.6 (2020): 1–7.

14. Varma, Kucharlapati Manoj, and Dr B. S. Panda. "Comparative analysis of predicting diabetes using machine learning techniques." *Journal of Emerging Technology and Innovative Research* 6.6 (2019): 522–530.

15. Saru, S., and S. Subashree. "Analysis and prediction of diabetes using machine learning." *International Journal of Emerging Technology and Innovative Engineering* 5.4 (2019).

16. Aada, Arvind, and Sakshi Tiwari. "Predicting diabetes in medical datasets using machine learning techniques." *International Journal of Scientific Engineering and Research* 5.2 (2019): 257–267.

17. Mir, Ayman, and Sudhir N. Dhage. "Diabetes disease prediction using machine learning on big data of healthcare." *2018 Fourth International Conference on Computing Communication Control and Automation (ICCUBEA)*. IEEE, 2018.

18. Bhargava, Neeraj, et al. "An approach for classification using simple CART algorithm in WEKA." *2017 11th International Conference on Intelligent Systems and Control (ISCO)*. IEEE, 2017.

19. Mercaldo, Francesco, Vittoria Nardone, and Antonella Santone. "Diabetes mellitus affected patients' classification and diagnosis through machine learning techniques." *Procedia Computer Science* 112 (2017): 2519–2528.

20. Vivek, Y., Ravi, V., and Krishna, P. R. "Scalable feature subset selection for big data using parallel hybrid evolutionary algorithm based wrapper under apache spark environment", *Cluster Computing*, 26.3 (2023): 1949–1983.

21. Obuchowski, N. A., Huang, E., Nandita, M. D., Raunig, D., Delfino, J., Buckler, A., ... and Pennello, G. "A framework for evaluating the technical performance of multiparameter quantitative imaging biomarkers (mp-QIBs)." *Academic Radiology* 30.2 (2022): 147–158.

22. Novakovsky, G., Dexter, N., Libbrecht, M. W., Wasserman, W. W., & Mostafavi, S. Obtaining genetics insights from deep learning via explainable artificial intelligence. *Nature Reviews Genetics* 24.2 (2023): 125–137.

23. Chen, Wei, et al. "Groundwater spring potential mapping using artificial intelligence approach based on kernel logistic regression, random forest, and alternating decision tree models." *Applied Sciences* 10.2 (2020): 425.

24. Kaur, Rajdeep, Rakesh Kumar, and Meenu Gupta. "Food image-based diet recommendation framework to overcome PCOS problem in women using deep convolutional neural network." *Computers and Electrical Engineering* 103 (2022): 108298.

25. Kaur, Rajdeep, Rakesh Kumar, and Meenu Gupta. "Food image-based nutritional management system to overcome polycystic ovary syndrome using deep learning: A systematic review." *International Journal of Image and Graphics* 23 (2022): 2350043.

26. Ansari, G. A., and Bhat, S. S. Exploring a Link Between Fasting Perspective and Different Patterns of Diabetes using a Machine Learning Approach. *Educational Research* 12.2 (2021): 500–517.

12 Analysing Factors for Improving Pregnancy Outcomes Using Machine Learning

Sarika Devi, Arpit Raj, Poonam Joshi and Sapna Rawat

12.1 INTRODUCTION

All pregnancies carry a risk, even though the majority of pregnancies and deliveries go smoothly. A life-threatening pregnancy problem will occur in about 15% of all pregnant women, necessitating specialized treatment. Some of these women will also require extensive obstetric intervention to survive (WHO, 2019). The World Health Organization (WHO) estimates that 800 women worldwide pass away every day from preventable diseases associated with pregnancy's inherent dangers. In 2017, almost 295,000 women lost their lives during, immediately after, or soon after childbirth. The vast majority of these fatalities (94%) happened in areas with few resources, and the bulk of them could have been avoided (WHO, 2019) [1, 2].

Studies have been conducted in recent years to forecast potential pregnancy risks and the delivery technique most appropriate for mothers' pregnancies. Pereira et al. [3, 4], for example, used supervised machine learning (ML) algorithms to predict the best delivery technique among vaginal, caesarean, forceps and vacuum delivery. In a different study, Chen et al. [5] used a neural network (NN) and decision tree (DT) algorithm to identify the factors linked to preterm birth. Similar to this, Rawashdeh et al. [6] used a random forest (RF), DT, K-nearest neighbour (KNN) and NN algorithm to predict the probability of premature birth. These studies used several machine learning approaches and had diverse results.

Once more, the type of information employed in these studies varied. Examples include demographic data, maternal information, obstetric characteristics, medical and obstetric history, ultrasound measures, behavioural data and the like. This study's main goal is to examine contemporary theories of research and development with a focus on ML to predict and identify various pregnancy conditions. The following secondary goals can be addressed by examining the study scopes and publication histories of current research (RO1) and examining the sorts of data utilized to predict pregnancy outcomes. (e.g. type of childbirth method, suitability of vaginal birth, vaginal birth after caesarean section and the like) (RO2); to investigate the use of various ML algorithms for anticipating the mode of birth, complications during childbirth etc. (RO3); to identify the gaps in the literature and suggest new areas for research (RO4). A systematic literature review (SLR) approach [7] is used to achieve these goals. The remainder of this chapter is structured as follows: The "theoretical background" section provides a description of the theoretical underpinnings of this review study. The study's methodology is briefly covered in the "Study methodology" section.

The "Analysis of extracted data" section analyses selected articles in terms of correlation among reviewed studies, publication year and article type, study objectives, type of features and algorithms used, the prevalence of ML algorithms, and the context (country) of these studies. The "Study Findings" section summarizes the findings from reviewed articles. Future research opportunities in relevant areas of pregnancy complications, along with an ML healthcare framework, are discussed in the "Future research implication" and "Future research framework" sections, respectively.

12.2 MACHINE LEARNING

Practically every industry uses ML from healthcare to cutting-edge technology, including smartphones, computers and robots for issues like disease diagnosis and safety. Many industries, including healthcare and illness diagnosis, are embracing machine learning. The promise of inexpensive and speedy machine learning-based disease diagnostics (MLBDD) has been demonstrated by numerous researchers and practitioners [8]. Traditional diagnosis procedures take a long time, are expensive and frequently include human interaction. Traditional diagnosis methods are constrained by the patient's capacity; however, ML-based algorithms are unrestricted and do not experience human fatigue. As a result, a technique for diagnosing diseases with unexpectedly high patient numbers in the healthcare setting might be created. X-ray and MRI images, as well as tabular information about the diseases and age and gender of patients, are used to create MLBDD systems [9]. Data is used as an input resource in ML, which is a subset of artificial intelligence (AI) [10]. When specified mathematical functions are used, classification or regression results are produced that are frequently challenging for people to achieve. For instance, detecting cancerous cells in a microscopic image using ML is generally easier than doing it manually, which is typically difficult to do. Furthermore, the most recent work demonstrates MLBDD accuracy of above 90% [8], thanks to breakthroughs in deep learning (a type of machine learning).

ML can be used to identify and diagnose diseases (including the prediction of kidney disease, breast cancer and diabetes); predict caesarean births; identify the best features for predicting different childbirth methods; find an unknown pattern in medical records; produce medicine by analysing genome data; and for other uses. It is feasible to anticipate several pregnancy issues before childbirth with the help of ML approaches [11].

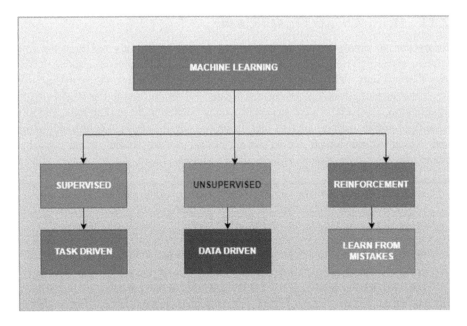

FIGURE 12.1   Types of machine learning.

12.2.1 Types of Machine Learning

There are numerous subcategories of ML, although there are three generally acknowledged categories of machine learning depending on the system (ML model or agent), as shown in Figure 12.1. Different types of ML in use today are as follows:

(a) Supervised learning
(b) Unsupervised learning
(c) Reinforcement learning

12.3 DEFINITION OF OBESITY

The term obese means the accumulation of excessive fat in specific areas of the body which may contribute to the transformation of normal cells into more severe conditions [12]. Therefore, according to the medical science, obesity is considered to be a severe situation that adversely affects the normal health of individuals. According to standard testing records for the fats, it was estimated that the accumulation of fat can be effectively measured using the Body Mass Index (BMI). Calculations indicate that a BMI exceeding 30 kg/m^2 is classified as obese, while a BMI under 25–30 kg/m^2 is considered to be overweight. This condition is more commonly seen in women than men [13].

12.3.1 Health Consequences of Obesity

The uneven accumulation of fat in various places in the body has now become the most alarming issue across the world as it leads to a number of associated diseases that not only significantly abrupt normal fluid flow across the body but also affects the normal physiology of certain organs [14]. According to the World Health Organization, most adults are overweight, young women more so than men, and this is due to improper maintenance of diet, improper care of physical health and many more associated problems that give rise of obesity. In many studies, it was seen that obesity may lead to the following associated diseases:

- *Cancer:* Obesity causes cancer. According to recent studies, it was estimated that excess fatty deposits inside the body signify the certain endocrine glands are big enough to be able to continuously release the biological signals that directly or indirectly affect normal metabolism, such as the reproductive cycle in case of the females. In recent studies, many researchers show that there are three distinct categories of conditions that directly link with the cause of cancers. Firstly, the most important cause of cancer is the excess accumulation of fat that leads to an increase in growth hormones like insulin-linked growth hormones; secondly, the excess of sex hormones in the case of females, such as oestrogens; and lastly, left untreated, fat accumulations lead to inflammation resulting in chronic conditions. So, the signals that are received due to the increase leads to cancer-developing conditions [15].
- *Cardiovascular diseases:* The leading causes that are associated with obesity are the deposition of fat which leads to sudden changes in metabolic rates and may lead to glucose tolerances, insulin resistance and many associated problems that affect the the body's lipid levels resulting in dyslipidaemia. Furthemore, in many studies it was found that the deposition of fat also affects blood pressure and blood vessels, which leads to hypertension and many other associated problems such as arrythmias and atherosclerosis. These directly or indirectly affect the normal cardiac physiology [16].
- *Type II diabetes mellitus:* This is also a leading cause of obesity. In many recent studies, it was found that more than 80% of relevant cases are due to type II diabetes mellitus, which causes disrupted insulin levels and results in patients being overweight or obesity of the patients which directly or indirectly causes cardiovascular diseases [17].
- *Obstructive sleep apnea:* This seems to be the most common type of the disease which occurs due to excess deposition of fat around blood vessels. It may lead to oxygen deprivation when sleeping which also leads to cardiac-related problems that result in poor sleep quality [18].
- *Non-alcoholic fatty liver (NAFLD):* This is a leading problem which is often seen in obesity patients. This usually occurs due to the excess deposition of fats around the liver which arises due to inadequate diet, manly seen in conditions that are caused by alterations in the metabolic activities of the

body. In most cases, it was found that NAFLD is seen during liver transplantations, liver cirrhosis and with cancer-related problems that affect the liver, which also leads to diabetic conditions [19].

- *Infertility:* This is the most common form of disease, often seen in women who are overweight, when the accumulatio of fat leads to the release of chemical hormones such as oestrogens which directly or indirectly leads to endometrial types of diseases called endometrial hyperplasia. Due to a lack of awareness in patients, certain types of cancers, such as uterine cancer, can lead to infertility [20].

12.4   CLINICAL EVALUATION OF OBESITY

Obesity is considered to be the most common form of disease worldwide, especially in youth of all genders, thos who are at socio-economic disadvantage and those who are unaware of their health issues. Obesity results from a lack of awareness about health and biological features. It is a major challenge for medical practitioners to classify obese and non-obese patients because the condition of obesity is not caused by a single process; it may be due to the decreased quality of fatty foods or it could arise due to side effects of many medicines and related diseases that cause obese conditions. In many recent studies, it was found that the early detection of obesity in children is a better way of controlling the condition and implementing proper treatment within a short amount of time [21]. To overcome this ever-growing problem across the globe, a special organization was established: the National Institute of Health (NIH). According to the NIH, obesity is defined as having a body weight that is more than 29.9 kg/m^2; those having body weight below 29.9 kg/m^2, i.e. those in the range of 25–29.69 kg/m^2, are considered overweight. According to the NIH, obese patients can be classified into three distinct classes: those patients whose body weight is 30–34.9 kg/m^2 and who are considered to be class I type obese, which signifies that the condition of obesity arose due to an unhealthy lifestyle, improper maintenance of diet and, as shown in some studies excessive use of medications whose side effects cause obesity and can be treated by maintaining a certain lifestyle; those patients whose body weight is 35–39.9 kg/m^2 and who are considered to be class II type obese, which occurs due to abnormal changes in the lifestyle or previously performed surgery for diseases, these patients come under the risk factors for obese and can be treated by maintaining healthy lifestyles or using proper medications; finally, there is extreme obesity, also called class III type of obese, which includes those patients whose body weight is more than 40 kg/m^2, which occurs in patients who have a genetic history of obesity and who can only be treated by surgery [22]. Apart from these medical consequences facing overweight patients, there were also effective testing of the obese through in vivo/in vitro techniques at the laboratory level through the effective determination of chemical messengers, such as unique hormonal levels, whose disturbance also leads to obese conditions. For example, a decrease in metabolism which is due to a sudden fall in T3 levels causes hypothyroidism which also results in obesity if left untreated. Many recent studies also suggest that using a high dose of steroids also leads to obesity as seen during

COVID-19. This is due to a massive alteration in hormone levels. Furthermore, recent studies and test results show that the levels of ALT is greater than 25 U/L in case of males while the level of ALTs (alanine transaminase) is greater than 22 U/L in case of the females. Due to the non-alcoholic fatty liver diseases (NAFLD), it is adversely shown in laboratory testing of the children and those adolescent who are affected by obesity [23]. There are also numerous ways to determine obese conditions using physical measurements of particular body parts like waist and hip size of patients. This process is often termed as the waist hip circumference, and, according to WHO, there are specific criteria that help medical practitioners to easily discriminate obese patients from non-obese patients, for exmaple, if the waist circumference is about 1.0 m or higher in the case of males or about 0.86 m or higher in the case of females, they are considered to be at high risk for conditions like heart-related problem or associated fluid-related problems which may also cause strokes or diabetes. Usually, the waist hip circumference is calculated by comparing the waist circumference with that of the hip circumference in centimetres. Apart from these, there are also some body parts whose physical appsearance can also assist in diagnosing patients as obese or overweight. These are abdominal region, such as the suprailium in the case of females, and the abdomen in the case of males; massive mass deposition on muscles like the thigh in the case of both males and females; upper portion of the body such as triceps in the case of females and the chest in the case of males. These areas of the body can be measured using specially designed tools in the form of callipers, also called skin fold instruments, which can measure suprailium skinfolds to determine the amount of fat on the belly region in diagonal positions or thigh skinfolds, to determe how much fat has been deposited the thigh region. A lot of researchers use specially designed callipers to measure fat [24].

12.5 AETIOLOGY OF OBESITY AND OVERWEIGHT

Obesity and overweight are caused by the deposition of fat on particular parts of the body. These two terms are often differentiated on the basis of the level of the fat deposition on particular body portions such as in the case of those patients whose body weight lies within the range of $25–29.9$ kg/m^2 who are considered overweight and those whose bodyweight is 29.9 kg/m^2 and above who are considered obese. The cause of obesity and overweight may be similar, i.e. due to overeating unhealthy foods or a lack of exercise [23]. The American Medical Association was instituted in 2013 to oversee the impact of obesity. According to a recent report, obesity is not only associated with disease but also with the combinatorial effects of many diseases which cause uneven deposits of fat on particular portions of the body [21]. Numerous aetiological factors contribute to the development of obesity. These factors involve changes in hormone levels, particularly those released by the endocrine glands, and a decline in the body's immune response against foreign substances. These changes result from the improper functioning of specialized adipose tissues responsible for maintaining fat deposition balance. Impairment in these tissues leads to deviations in the body's calorie levels from the normal range. Additionally, it has been observed that genetic factors play a role in the development of obesity, indicating inherited genetic problems. Furthermore, the excessive accumulation of fat in different body areas can lead to lipidemic conditions, such as dyslipidemia, non-alcoholic fatty liver disease (NAFLD), cholecystitis, lipomastia, and other associated diseases, which can ultimately increase the risk of cardiac problems [25].

12.6 FACTORS ASSOCIATED WITH OBESITY AND OVERWEIGHT

Numerous associated factors contribute to obesity conditions, as shown in Figure 12.2. These are associated with other disease forms, as summarized below:

1. *Genetics:* These are considered to be the most common cause of obesity, with specific genes identified as the main contributors. This link is often observed in individuals with a family history of obesity, as indicated by recent studies and clinical evaluations. Genetic causes of obesity can be classified based on the number of genes involved, as outlined below:
   a) *Polygenic disorders:* These cases involve multiple genes contributing to obesity, such as the PPAR-gamma (Proliferator-activated receptor-gamma) gene and adiponectin.
   b) *Monogenic disorders:* Obesity in these cases is caused by a single mutated gene, such as mutations in the POMC (Pro-Opio Melano Cortin) gene, leptin genes, or specific receptors like leptin receptors. In some instances, autosomal loss of mutations may result in mental retardation and uncontrollable polyphagia [26].
   c) *Others:* Obesity-related conditions may also give rise to other genetic disorders like Prader–Willi Syndrome and Laurence–Moon–Biedl syndromes [27].
2. *Environmental:* These occur due to changes in the normal lifestyles of the individuals like not having proper diets, not performing regular exercises, and many associated lifestyle problems which directly or indirectly

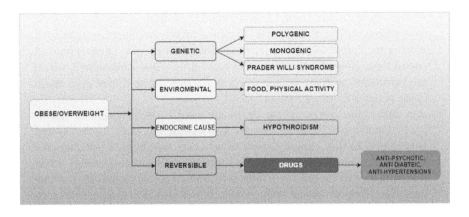

FIGURE 12.2   Classification of obese conditions.

increase the intake of food or beverages that are not burned off and are converted to fatty depositions. Poor digestion may also contribute to obesity conditions [28].

3. *Endocrine glands:* It includes the imbalance in the hormonal levels which gives rise to many associated problems like hypothyroidism, disturbance in normal sleeping, Cushing syndrome and many associated conditions that imbalance the reproductive organs, i.e. it gives rise to PCOS conditions.

4. *Reversible causes:* These are considered to be the most common cause of obesity conditions that are not only associated within vitro forms but also with the in vivo changes that accordingly are classified into two distinct categories listed below:

   (a) *Drugs:* Several studies show that many drugs have side effects that cause obesity such as those that treat anti-diabetic conditions and anti-hypertensive conditions. This can also be seen with psychotic patients who use anti-psychotic drugs, and in individuals using hormonal balancing contraceptives [29].

12.6.1 Medical Treatment of Obese and Overweight Patients

There are numerous traditional methods and in recent studies it was also found that there are certain medications that are helpful for weight gain and also provide better treatment of obesity conditions:

- *Anti-diabetic drugs*: These drugs are used specifically to control diabetic conditions that directly or indirectly lead to obesity conditions, mostly seen in diabetes type II conditions. In recent studies, it was shown that most drugs cause weight gain in patients, such as those that are part of the Thiazolidinediones category (e.g. Pioglitazone). On the other hand, there are also drugs like metformin and glucagon-controlling drugs (e.g. peptide-1 agonists) that significantly reduce body weight [30].

- *Anti-psychoti drugs:* These are considered to be those drugs that are used to treat neuronal types of disease. They are directly or indirectly associated with an increased risk of obesity in patients, for example, Olanzapine and risperidone. However, there are also some drugs, like Ziprasidone, which are considered to have no role in obesity conditions and may even cause obese patients to lose weight [31].

- *Anti-depressant drugs:* These drugs are used to treat hormonal imbalances that cause depression. they are also the leading cause of obesity and overweight. In this category, some drugs cause weight gain, for example, Doxepin and Imipramine, but some specially designed novel drugs act as inhibiting agents for serotonin reuptakes, and, as recent studies show, these drugs are likely to reduce body weight. In addition, Mirtazapine category drugs are also used to decrease body weight. In some studies, it was also seen that anti-depressants exhibit results during therapy for weight loss [32].

- *Anti-epileptic drugs:* These drugs are used to treat epileptic conditions and are considered to be major causes of obesity in patients that take them. They include Gabapentin, and Valproates when used regularly during drug therapy. However, some drugs also lead to weight loss, including Zonisamide and Topiramate [33].
- *Immunosuppressants drugs:* These are considered to be those drugs that are used for immunosuppressives therapy like glucocorticoids, Among them there are inhibiting agents like calcineurin which includes Tacrolimus and the mTOR (mammalian target of rapamycin) inhibitor such as Sirolimus which rsult in weight gain [29]. In recent times, the effective treatment of obese patients has become the most challenging task for emerging medical practitioners who need to effectively discriminate between overweight and obese patients. These problems can be effectively overcome when there are specially designed platforms that support effective communication between patients and medical practitioners. Results that are obtained using machines must achieve high accuracy rates for the determination of fat layers to make these conditions true and effective. Specially designed artificial intelligence (AI)–based machines were introduced in the field of medical science. These AI-based machines not only provide platforms for the patients to have better communication with specialists in hospitals but also achieve higher accuracy in discriminating the conditions of the fat layers that help medical specialists to provide better advice to patients. The introduction of these platforms is considered to be a way of linking traditional methods of obesity treatments with technology-based methods to effectively discriminate between patients with similar symptoms, as seen in the case of overweight and obese patients [34]. Usually this communication is based on specially designed machine learning programs that make effective communication between the patients and the medical specialists possible. Such processes are called natural language processing (NLP), which works by effectively converting one language to another with the help of several translators that are available on highly effective network systems like Google, GPT-3 (Generative Pretrained Transformer-3) and many associated networking systems. These systems are able to convert technical language understood by medical specialists and practitioners into language that is more easily understood by the patient, allowing for more effective treatment procedures [35]. On the other hand, recent studies have shown that in many cases, the specially designed machine learning programs popularly known as precision-based medicine tools effectively work by combining different data together and their results suggest that obesity is not caused by a single disease but by multivariant forms of the disease whose side effects lead to obesity conditions. So to effectively determine the distinct layers of the fats, patients are evaluated according to four distinct categories.
- *Hunger brain:* This refers to a condition where patients have difficulty recognizing their hunger levels. These individuals experience problems in

determining whether their stomach is empty or full which can lead to over-eating and discomfort [36].

- *Hunger gut:* Similarly to hunger brain, this condition can relates to patients who feel hungry after eating certain meals, leading to a constant desire to eat food at regular intervals. This also leads to overeating and discomfort [37].
- *Emotional hunger:* Apart from hunger brain and hunger gut, there is also the condition of emotional hunger. Patients with this condition feel hungry but may not be able to eat due to many emotional feelings like anxiety, depression and other feelings that directly or indirectly affect the patient's normal health [38].
- *Slow burn:* This is the most common condition among obese patients and means that they are unable to metabolize food qucikly at particular time periods and also have less tendency of effectively burn calories which results in discomfort after taking their meals [39]. The specially designed artificial intelligence programming classified the individuals by collecting information from different sources of the patients and distinctly classified it accordingly as per the above four distinct stages and effectively evaluated the individual information of the patients and better be able to provide the best treatment for a particular patients at each stage [40].

12.6.2   CLINICAL IMPLICATIONS OF THE STUDY

Reviewing the use of machine learning algorithms in obesity research and identifying the advantages and disadvantages of these approaches for the application of machine learning in obesity are key therapeutic implications of this work [41, 42]. Many people employ simple statistical methods like regression algorithms. Deep learning, neural networks, and random forests are less popular algorithms. Traditional data analysis techniques have been complemented by machine learning applications in a variety of industries, including healthcare and obesity [43]. Numerous machines learning algorithms, including regression, classification, clustering and neural network algorithms, have been used to study obesity. The use of machine learning in research on obesity reveals that ML offers a crucial and practical analytical tool for predicting obesity. The most recent ML algorithms have not, however, been effectively used in obesity research despite their promising performance. Overall, ML techniques including XGBOOST, random forest, deep neural networks and DT are among the best ways to enable early identification and clinical management of obesity [43, 44, 45].

12.6.3   LIMITATIONS OF THE STUDY

The application of machine learning to obesity and the use of various keywords to search the PubMed and Scopus databases were limitations of this study. We only included English-language articles about adult obesity. Additionally, only studies that concentrated on modifiable factors (such as food intake, dietary habits and/

or physical activity) were thoroughly reviewed. Studies on inherited or paediatric obesity were not included. Machine learning techniques were utilized in 20 peer-reviewed studies to determine the link between obesity-related contributing factors. We talked about the drawbacks of overfitting, hyperparameter optimization and data priority assumptions [41–68].

12.7   FURTHER WORK

One of the main objectives of this study was to identify the ML methods that are currently widely used to predict obesity.

Future researchers should evaluate the accuracy and robustness of each ML algorithm before attempting further research in this area. This study also briefly looked at the main causes or factors contributing to the worsening of obesity. However, further study is required in this difficult area, especially given the possibility that it will refocus on other important elements that have previously been recognized as contributing to obesity.

12.8   CONCLUSION

Obesity is considered to be an alarming issue that arises due to multiple factors such as the imbalance in the normal lifestyles across the world. In addition to the imbalance between caloric intake, which primarily consists of high-calorie foods, and caloric expenditure, obesity is thought to arise from the imbalance between white adipose tissue, which is thought to be the primary site of energy storage, and brown adipose tissue, which is used for energy expenditure. Infection is an atypical causative/inducing factor among the several aetiological causes for obesity that has just begun to draw more attention. Being diagnosed with obesity would be a relatively new but hugely important notion if it applied to people. The quality, effectiveness and affordability of care for persons who are obese have the potential to improve, thanks to digital health technologies, both now and in the future. The study of epigenetics is rapidly developing, and preliminary measures are being taken to identify potential biomarkers for obesity. Overall, significant progress has been made in understanding how the surrounding obesogenic environment is translated into different functions and phenotypes through the role of epigenetics. Yet, obesity is a complicated, multifaceted disease characterized by a complex interplay of multiple pathways connected to oxidative stress, inflammation, metabolism, hypoxia and other factors. In India, childhood obesity is a relatively recent yet pervasive pandemic that has likely received the least attention. So, in order to avoid long-term consequences, it is crucial to assess and identify these kids as soon as possible.

REFERENCES

1. Bertini, A. *et al.* (2022) "Using machine learning to predict complications in pregnancy: A systematic review," *Frontiers in Bioengineering and Biotechnology*, 9. Available at: https://doi.org/10.3389/fbioe.2021.780389.

2. Moran, M. (2021) "Suicide, overdose are significant contributors to pregnancy-related maternal deaths," *Psychiatric News*, 56(1). Available at: https://doi.org/10.1176/appi.pn .2021.1.11.

3. "The challenge of maternal mortality" (2021) *Proceedings in Obstetrics and Gynecology*, 10(2). Available at: https://doi.org/10.17077/2154-4751.1523.

4. Pereira, S. *et al.* (2015) "Predicting type of delivery by identification of obstetric risk factors through data mining," *Procedia Computer Science*, 64, pp. 601–609. Available at: https://doi.org/10.1016/j.procs.2015.08.573.

5. Chen, H.-Y. *et al.* (2011) "Exploring the risk factors of preterm birth using data mining," *Expert Systems with Applications*, 38(5), pp. 5384–5387. Available at: https://doi .org/10.1016/j.eswa.2010.10.017.

6. Rawashdeh, H. *et al.* (2020) "Intelligent system based on data mining techniques for prediction of preterm birth for women with cervical cerclage," *Computational Biology and Chemistry*, 85, p. 107233. Available at: https://doi.org/10.1016/j.compbiolchem .2020.107233.

7. Kitchenham, B. *et al.* (2009) "Systematic literature reviews in software engineering – A systematic literature review," *Information and Software Technology*, 51(1), pp. 7–15. Available at: https://doi.org/10.1016/j.infsof.2008.09.009.

8. Roy, D. D., & De, D. (2021) "Defining the best-fit machine learning classifier prediction model for diagnosis of heart disease." Available at: https://doi.org/10.21203/rs.3.rs -1152876/v1.

9. Ahsan, M. M. *et al.* (2020) "Deep MLP-CNN model using mixed-data to distinguish between COVID-19 and non-covid-19 patients," *Symmetry*, 12(9), p. 1526. Available at: https://doi.org/10.3390/sym12091526.

10. Stafford, I. S. *et al.* (2020) "A systematic review of the applications of artificial intelligence and machine learning in autoimmune diseases," *NPJ Digital Medicine*, 3(1). Available at: https://doi.org/10.1038/s41746-020-0229-3.

11. Islam, M. N. *et al.* (2022) "Machine learning to predict pregnancy outcomes: A systematic review, synthesizing framework and future research agenda," *BMC Pregnancy and Childbirth*, 22(1). Available at: https://doi.org/10.1186/s12884-022-04594-2.

12. *Obesity – Introduction – Clinical Obesity in Adults and Children ...* (no date) Available at: https://onlinelibrary.wiley.com/doi/abs/10.1002/9781119695257.ch1 (Accessed: March 3, 2023).

13. Haqq, A. M., Kebbe, M., Tan, Q., Manco, M., & Salas, X. R. (no date) *Complexity and Stigma of Pediatric Obesity, Childhood Obesity (Print)*. U.S. National Library of Medicine. Available at: https://pubmed.ncbi.nlm.nih.gov/33780639/ (Accessed: March 3, 2023).

14. Kaur, R., Kumar, R., & Gupta, M. (2022) "Food image-based nutritional management system to overcome polycystic ovary syndrome using Deeplearning: A systematic review," *International Journal of Image and Graphics*, 22(4), p. 2350043.

15. Kaur, R., Kumar, R., & Gupta, M. (2022) "Predicting risk of obesity and meal planning to reduce the obese in adulthood using artificial intelligence," *Endocrine*, 78(3), pp. 458–469.

16. Kaur, R., Kumar, R., & Gupta, M. (2022) "Food Image-based diet recommendation framework to overcome PCOS problem in women using deep convolutional neural network," *Computers and Electrical Engineering*, 103, p. 108298.

17. Lingvay, I., Sumithran, P., Cohen, R. V., & le Roux, C. W. (2022) "Obesity management as a primary treatment goal for type 2 diabetes: Time to reframe the conversation," *The Lancet*, 399(10322), pp. 394–405.

18. Rodrigues, M. M. *et al.* (2022) "How obesity affects nasal function in obstructive sleep apnea: Anatomic and volumetric parameters," *Brazilian Journal of*

Otorhinolaryngology. Elsevier. Available at: https://www.bjorl.org/en-how-obesity
-affects-nasal-function-articulo-S1808869420300987 (Accessed: March 3, 2023).

19. Wang, Y.-D. *et al.* (2022) "New insight of obesity-associated NAFLD: Dysregulated
    "crosstalk" between multi-organ and the liver?," *Genes & Diseases.* Elsevier. Available
    at: https://www.sciencedirect.com/science/article/pii/S2352304222000071 (Accessed:
    March 3, 2023).

20. *Obesity and Female Infertility—A Review on Mechanisms (endocrinology)* (no
    date) Available at: https://researchmgt.monash.edu/ws/portalfiles/portal/401298427
    /383495192_oa.pdf (Accessed: March 3, 2023).

21. Cuda, S. E. *et al.* (2022) "Withdrawn: Assessment, differential diagnosis, and initial
    clinical evaluation of the pediatric patient with obesity: An Obesity Medical Association
    (OMA) clinical practice statement 2022," *Obesity Pillars.* Elsevier. Available at: https://
    www.sciencedirect.com/science/article/pii/S2667368121000097 (Accessed: March 3,
    2023).

22. Khadilkar, V., & Shah, N. (2021) "Evaluation of children and adolescents with obesity,"
    Indian Journal of Pediatrics. Springer India. Available at: https://link.springer.com/
    article/10.1007/s12098-021-03893-4 (Accessed: March 3, 2023).

23. Chung, C. Y. *et al.* (2022) "The clinical evaluation of electroacupuncture combined
    with mindfulness meditation for overweight and obesity: Study protocol for a random-
    ized sham-controlled clinical trial," *Trials.* BioMed Central. Available at: https://trial-
    sjournal.biomedcentral.com/articles/10.1186/s13063-022-06725-8 (Accessed: March 3,
    2023).

24. Chew, H. S. J. (2022) "The use of artificial intelligence-based conversational agents
    (chatbots) for weight loss: Scoping review and practical recommendations," *JMIR
    Medical Informatics.* U.S. National Library of Medicine. Available at: https://www
    .ncbi.nlm.nih.gov/pmc/articles/PMC9047740/ (Accessed: March 3, 2023).

25. Archer, E., & Lavie, C. J. (no date) "Obesity subtyping: The etiology, prevention, and
    management of acquired versus inherited obese phenotypes," *Nutrients.* U.S. National
    Library of Medicine. Available at: https://pubmed.ncbi.nlm.nih.gov/35684086/
    (Accessed: March 3, 2023).

26. Socol, C. T. *et al.* (2022) "Leptin signaling in obesity and colorectal cancer,"
    International Journal of Molecular Sciences. U.S. National Library of Medicine.
    Available at: https://www.ncbi.nlm.nih.gov/pmc/articles/PMC9102849/ (Accessed:
    March 3, 2023).

27. Mahmoud, A. M. (no date) "An overview of epigenetics in obesity: The role of life-
    style and therapeutic interventions," *International Journal of Molecular Sciences.* U.S.
    National Library of Medicine. Available at: https://pubmed.ncbi.nlm.nih.gov/35163268/
    (Accessed: March 3, 2023).

28. *Walkable Neighborhoods Can Reduce Prevalence of Obesity, Diabetes* (2022) *Science
    Daily.* Available at: https://www.sciencedaily.com/releases/2022/02/220224091123
    .htm (Accessed: March 3, 2023).

29. May, M. *et al.* (no date) "Modern pharmacological treatment of obese patients,"
    Therapeutic Advances in Endocrinology and Metabolism. U.S. National Library of
    Medicine. Available at: https://pubmed.ncbi.nlm.nih.gov/32030121/ (Accessed: March
    3, 2023).

30. Muller, T. D. (no date) "Anti-obesity drug discovery: Advances and challenges," *Nature
    Reviews. Drug Discovery.* U.S. National Library of Medicine. Available at: https://
    pubmed.ncbi.nlm.nih.gov/34815532/ (Accessed: March 3, 2023).

31. Christensen, S. M. *et al.* (1970) "Stress, psychiatric disease, and obesity: An Obesity
    Medicine Association (OMA) clinical practice statement (CPS) 2022," *Semantic
    Scholar, Obesity Pillars.* Available at: https://www.semanticscholar.org/paper/Stress

%2C-psychiatric-disease%2C-and-obesity%3A-An-(OMA)-Christensen-Varney/4182c
c835e6b5e77f8371c621dd4ce6fec01b709 (Accessed: March 3, 2023).

32. Hinchliffe, N. *et al.* (2022) "The potential role of digital health in obesity care," *Advances in Therapy, SpringerLink.* Springer Healthcare. Available at: https://link.springer.com/article/10.1007/s12325-022-02265-4 (Accessed: March 3, 2023).

33. *In vitro Activity of Therapeutic Antibodies against SARS-COV-2 Omicron BA.1 and BA.2* (2022) *Home.* Available at: https://www.researchsquare.com/article/rs-1415749/v1 (Accessed: March 3, 2023).

34. Moidu, F., & Ovallath, S. (no date) "Deep brain stimulation-emerging indications and newer techniques: A current perspective," *International Neuropsychiatric Disease Journal.* Available at: https://journalindj.com/index.php/INDJ/article/view/356 (Accessed: March 3, 2023).

35. Alotaibi, M. *et al.* (2022) "Efficacy of emerging technologies to manage childhood obesity," *Diabetes, Metabolic Syndrome and Obesity: Targets and Therapy,* 15, pp. 1227–1244. Available at: https://doi.org/10.2147/dmso.s357176.

36. Zare, S. *et al.* (2021) "Use of machine learning to determine the information value of a BMI screening program," *American Journal of Preventive Medicine.* Elsevier. Available at: https://www.ajpmonline.org/article/S0749-3797(20)30513-4/fulltext (Accessed: March 3, 2023).

37. Khuda, I. E., Nazish, S., Zeeshan, M. A., Shariff, E., Aljaafari, D., & Alabdali, M. (no date) "Non-HDL cholesterol, obesity, and metabolic syndrome in epileptic patients," *The Primary Care Companion for CNS Disorders.* U.S. National Library of Medicine. Available at: https://pubmed.ncbi.nlm.nih.gov/35687885/ (Accessed: March 3, 2023).

38. Ghusn, W. *et al.* (1970) "Weight-centric treatment of depression and chronic pain," *Semantic Scholar, Obesity Pillars.* Available at: https://www.semanticscholar.org/paper/Weight-centric-treatment-of-depression-and-chronic-Ghusn-Bouchard/b782e56cbf33b0439f158b011b6d79cfe8634dd1 (Accessed: March 3, 2023).

39. *Sci-hub | Applications of Artificial Intelligence (AI) in Researches On ...* (no date) Available at: https://sci-hub.se/10.1007/s11154-021-09681-x (Accessed: March 3, 2023).

40. Pantelis, A. G. (2022) "Current and potential applications of Artificial Intelligence in metabolic bariatric surgery," *IntechOpen.* Available at: https://www.intechopen.com/online-first/82941 (Accessed: March 3, 2023).

41. Safaei, M. *et al.* (2021) "A systematic literature review on obesity: Understanding the causes & consequences of obesity and reviewing various machine learning approaches used to predict obesity," *Computers in Biology and Medicine,* 136, p. 104754. Available at: https://doi.org/10.1016/j.compbiomed.2021.104754.

42. Alkhalaf, M. *et al.* (no date) "A review of the application of machine learning in adult obesity studies," *Applied Computing and Intelligence.* Available at: https://aimspress.com/article/doi/10.3934/aci.2022002?viewType=HTML (Accessed: March 3, 2023).

43. Panaretos, D. *et al.* (2018) "A comparison of statistical and machine-learning techniques in evaluating the association between dietary patterns and 10-year cardiometabolic risk (2002–2012): The Attica Study," *British Journal of Nutrition,* 120(3), pp. 326–334. Available at: https://doi.org/10.1017/s0007114518001150.

44. Easton, J. F., Román Sicilia, H., & Stephens, C. R. (2018) "Classification of diagnostic subcategories for obesity and diabetes based on eating patterns," *Nutrition & Dietetics,* 76(1), pp. 104–109. Available at: https://doi.org/10.1111/1747-0080.12495.

45. Beam, A. L., & Kohane, I. S. (2018) "Big data and machine learning in health care," *JAMA,* 319(13), p. 1317. Available at: https://doi.org/10.1001/jama.2017.18391.

46. Pouladzadeh, P. *et al.* (2014) "Cloud-based SVM for food categorization," *Multimedia Tools and Applications,* 74(14), pp. 5243–5260. Available at: https://doi.org/10.1007/s11042-014-2116-x.

47. Cesare, N. *et al.* (2019) "Use of social media, search queries, and demographic data to assess obesity prevalence in the United States," *Palgrave Communications*, 5(1). Available at: https://doi.org/10.1057/s41599-019-0314-x.

48. JahaniHeravi, E., Habibi Aghdam, H., & Puig, D. (2015) "A deep convolutional neural network for recognizing foods," *SPIE Proceedings* [Preprint]. Available at: https://doi.org/10.1117/12.2228875.

49. DeGregory, K. W. *et al.* (2018) "A review of machine learning in obesity," *Obesity Reviews*, 19(5), pp. 668–685. Available at: https://doi.org/10.1111/obr.12667.

50. Easton, J. F., Román Sicilia, H., & Stephens, C. R. (2018) "Classification of diagnostic subcategories for obesity and diabetes based on eating patterns," *Nutrition & Dietetics*, 76(1), pp. 104–109. Available at: https://doi.org/10.1111/1747-0080.12495.

51. Heerman, W. J. *et al.* (2017) "Clusters of healthy and unhealthy eating behaviors are associated with body mass index among adults," *Journal of Nutrition Education and Behavior*, 49(5). Available at: https://doi.org/10.1016/j.jneb.2017.02.001.

52. So, H., McLaren, L., & Currie, G. C. (2017) "The relationship between health eating and overweight/obesity in Canada: Cross-sectional study using the CCHS," *Obesity Science & Practice*, 3(4), pp. 399–406. Available at: https://doi.org/10.1002/osp4.123.

53. PovalejBrzan, P., Obradovic, Z., & Stiglic, G. (2017) "Contribution of temporal data to predictive performance in 30-day readmission of morbidly obese patients," *PeerJ*, 5. Available at: https://doi.org/10.7717/peerj.3230.

54. Kanerva, N. *et al.* (2017) "Suitability of random forest analysis for epidemiological research: Exploring sociodemographic and lifestyle-related risk factors of overweight in a cross-sectional design," *Scandinavian Journal of Public Health*, 46(5), pp. 557–564. Available at: https://doi.org/10.1177/1403494817736944.

55. Green, M. A. *et al.* (2015) "Who are the obese? A cluster analysis exploring subgroups of the obese," *Journal of Public Health*, 38(2), pp. 258–264. Available at: https://doi.org/10.1093/pubmed/fdv040.

56. Kim, D. *et al.* (2019) "Factors affecting obesity and waist circumference among us adults," *Preventing Chronic Disease*, 16. Available at: https://doi.org/10.5888/pcd16.180220.

57. Figueroa, R. L., & Flores, C. A. (2016) "Extracting information from electronic medical records to identify the obesity status of a patient based on comorbidities and body-weight measures," *Journal of Medical Systems*, 40(8). Available at: https://doi.org/10.1007/s10916-016-0548-8.

58. Kupusinac, A., Stokić, E., & Doroslovački, R. (2014) "Predicting body fat percentage based on gender, age and BMI by using Artificial Neural Networks," *Computer Methods and Programs in Biomedicine*, 113(2), pp. 610–619. Available at: https://doi.org/10.1016/j.cmpb.2013.10.013.

59. Disse, E. *et al.* (2018) "An artificial neural network to predict resting energy expenditure in obesity," *Clinical Nutrition*, 37(5), pp. 1661–1669. Available at: https://doi.org/10.1016/j.clnu.2017.07.017.

60. *Data Mining: Potential Applications in Research on Nutrition and Health ...* (no date). Available at: https://onlinelibrary.wiley.com/doi/full/10.1111/1747-0080.12337 (Accessed: March 3, 2023).

61. Daud, N. A. *et al.* (2018) "Predictive analytics: The application of J48 algorithm on grocery data to predict obesity," *2018 IEEE Conference on Big Data and Analytics (ICBDA)* [Preprint]. Available at: https://doi.org/10.1109/icbdaa.2018.8629623.

62. Sarafis, I. *et al.* (2019) "Assessment of in-meal eating behaviour using fuzzy SVM," *2019 41st Annual International Conference of the IEEE Engineering in Medicine and Biology Society (EMBC)* [Preprint]. Available at: https://doi.org/10.1109/embc.2019.8857606.

63. Dunstan, J. *et al.* (2019) "Predicting nationwide obesity from food sales using machine learning," *Health Informatics Journal*, 26(1), pp. 652–663. Available at: https://doi.org/10.1177/1460458219845959.

64. Batterham, M. *et al.* (2017) "Using data mining to predict success in a weight loss trial," *Journal of Human Nutrition and Dietetics*, 30(4), pp. 471–478. Available at: https://doi.org/10.1111/jhn.12448.

65. Feng, Z., Mo, L., & Li, M. (2015) "A random forest-based ensemble method for activity recognition," *2015 37th Annual International Conference of the IEEE Engineering in Medicine and Biology Society (EMBC)* [Preprint]. Available at: https://doi.org/10.1109/embc.2015.7319532.

66. Khosravi, P., Newton, C., & Rezvani, A. (2019) "Management innovation: A systematic review and meta-analysis of past decades of research," *European Management Journal*, 37(6), pp. 694–707. Available at: https://doi.org/10.1016/j.emj.2019.03.003.

67. Shameer, K. *et al.* (2018) "Machine learning in cardiovascular medicine: Are we there yet?," *Heart*, 104(14), pp. 1156–1164. Available at: https://doi.org/10.1136/heartjnl-2017-311198.

68. Goldstein, B. A., Navar, A. M., & Carter, R. E. (2016) "Moving beyond regression techniques in cardiovascular risk prediction: Applying machine learning to address analytic challenges," *European Heart Journal* [Preprint]. Available at: https://doi.org/10.1093/eurheartj/ehw302.

13 Future Consideration and Challenges in Women's Health Using AI

C. Prakash, L. P. Singh, A. Gupta,
R. Kumar and A. Bhardwaj

13.1 INTRODUCTION

The term "artificial intelligence" (AI) is frequently used in society; the term relates to the use of machines for learning data, performing human-like tasks and making decisions for specific tasks. Nowadays, AI is widely used in different sectors, including agriculture, transportation, industrialization, banking, education and entertainment. AI is capable of building models from collective data; further, it accurately categorizes the provided data. Moreover, AI models use real-time predictions and recommendations which help them to make better decisions. These decisions are made via machine learning (ML), a subset of AI. ML techniques make decisions based on previous data by applying algorithms. For example, if something happened in the past, then it is easy to predict an effective decision on the basis of that past situation [1]. An overview of AI, ML and deep learning (DL) is shown in Figure 13.1.

It has recently become popular to use AI in modern healthcare applications. This is because AI allows computer systems to learn from data and improve their performance without being explicitly built. The digital healthcare system is enabled with smart sensors and real-time prediction models [3]. In the fifth revolution of healthcare, medical communities expect the interconnection of millions of Internet of Thing (IoT)-based sensors, which drive innovative business solutions in this sector [4]. The IoT combines with AI in modern healthcare practices and allows for wearable smart sensors to be integrated with mobile communication which provides easy and remote healthcare delivery [5]. The current scenario that contains AI revolves around an advanced technique known as deep learning. It uses a strong prediction technique in ML which allows a computer system to learn or predict decisions based on previous data. Deep learning is also contributing to different health sectors and aiding in differential diagnosis and disease treatments [6].

Today, our everyday lives are completely reliant on mobile devices and the internet. Apps like Google Maps, Amazon's Alexa, Apple's Siri, Microsoft's Cortana and Google's own OK Google are indispensable for our daily lives. The weather for today and the following several days may also be predicted using various AI-based

DOI: 10.1201/9781003378556-13

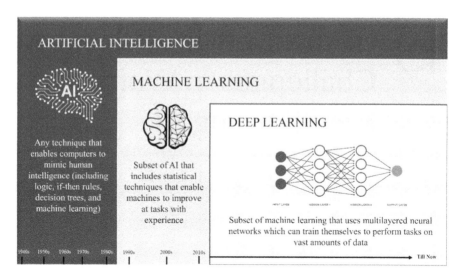

FIGURE 13.1 Overview of the concepts AI, ML and DL [2].

technologies. Furthermore, several studies have shown that AI is superior to humans in essential healthcare activities such as illness diagnosis. When it comes to detecting cancerous tumours, algorithms are already more accurate than radiologists, and they are also helping researchers build demographics for expensive clinical studies. Studies suggest that AI is increasingly being used in most medical activities for human healthcare [7, 8]. The current coronavirus (COVID-19) pandemic is the worst global disaster in a generation, and it has struck at a time when AI is being more widely used in the real world [9]. AI is a revolutionary healthcare system that possesses immense capabilities for bringing about paradigm shifts and analysing large amounts of data in a short timeframe [10, 11]. In addition, AI methods may prove useful in times of crisis and when decisive action is required [12].

Currently, there is a need to explore the potential of new technologies (such as AI and ML) to manage such crises [13]. Each country has taken a unique approach to the problem, but they have all been employing state-of-the-art, revolutionary AI-based technology to share information and collaborate on finding the best strategies to combat the epidemic [14]. Consequently, several academics have highlighted the promise of employing AI applications to help health organizations serve huge numbers of patients more efficiently and reliably as compared to a human. This does not imply that human interaction is unnecessary, but rather that healthcare providers will be more equipped to make the right diagnoses and choices [15]. AI-based healthcare technologies can be put to a variety of practical uses, including tracking and monitoring cases, stopping the spread of infection and facilitating the sharing of knowledge between doctors and specialists for problem-solving and decision-making [16].

AI systems help doctors and nurses give the right care to their patients by observing live health status as stated by some scientific journals [17]. The inevitable diagnostic and therapeutic mistakes made by humans in clinical practice can be mitigated by using an AI system [18]. In addition, an AI system can collect useful data from multiple patients and make accurate decisions based on their current health status [19].

Women's bodies change significantly throughout their lives, which means that different age groups have different health concerns. During periods of physiological transition, women suffer from mental health difficulties such as sadness, anxiety and eating disorders. As a person gets older, things like fertility, avoiding STDs and using safe birth control become more important. Prevalence rates of mental health problems including sadness and anxiety are much higher in postpartum mothers [20]. The results of a recent meta-analysis have shown that 15% of postpartum women reported experiencing anxiety symptoms, and anxiety is frequently seen along with postpartum depression (PPD) [21]. Fetal and maternal mental illness is a major public health concern because it hurts the health of both the mother and the baby [22]. The uses of AI to analyse the vitals and performance of active women to make training, recovery and nutrition suggestions that are best for their bodies. In the medical research context, AI research has been used to predict a wide range of health problems, including diabetes [23], cardiovascular diseases [24], obesity [25], cancer [26] and disorders related to pregnancy [27]. However, for a number of reasons, we think it will be several years before AI replaces humans in medical process areas. Prediction studies are categorized into different groups: (1) to study the risk factor with the prediction of age, disease stage or biomarkers; (2) prediction model studies, in which the purpose is to design, validate or enhance prediction models to guide individualized patient care; and (3) prediction model impact studies, in which researchers investigate what happens when a model is used to guide patient care [28]. Tinker et al. [29] elaborated on the various health issues in females during the different years of their life cycle as shown in Figure 13.2.

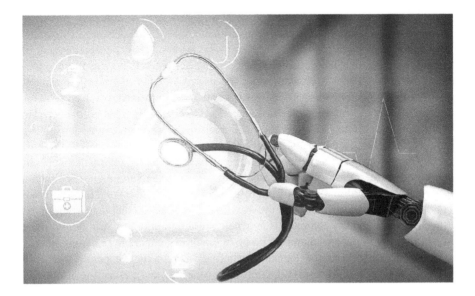

FIGURE 13.2   AI in healthcare technology

Moreover, AI offers a practical way to analyse endometrial histology, producing data that is both objective and complete. During different parts of a woman's cycle, the number of endometrial leucocytes and the rate at which they multiply change. This change seems to be the same in both ovulating women with polycystic ovary syndrome (PCOS) and healthy women [30]. Besides this, AI algorithms, especially those that use deep learning, have made a lot of progress in image-recognition tasks. In an even more recent study, it was found that an AI system could predict breast cancer better than radiologists using screening mammography [31–34].

AI will completely change the healthcare system in a variety of ways, including clinical applications in areas like imaging and diagnostics; hospital workflow optimization; and symptom assessment via mobile health apps. The market for AI in healthcare is expected to expand rapidly in the next years, with some estimates predicting a tenfold rise in size between 2014 and 2021. There will be many new obstacles to overcome as a result of this expansion, hence AI must be used ethically and lawfully within the healthcare system. Concerns remain about the applicability and effectiveness of emerging systems in dealing with COVID-19, especially in underdeveloped countries like India. It is very difficult to implement on-ground and additional resources would be required to implement government investment in AI-based technology, especially in the medical and health sector. As a result, it is important to have a complete picture of all the factors involved in implementing an AI-based public healthcare system, as well as how these new systems might improve efficiency in finding solutions to problems and making decisions.

13.2   FEMALE HEALTH PROBLEMS WITH POSSIBLE AI SOLUTIONS ACROSS THE LIFE CYCLE

In a world that is continually transforming, unanticipated global crises can significantly and rapidly alter conventional behavioural norms. AI is the development of computer systems that are capable of performing activities that typically necessitate human intelligence. It also describes the use of systems that mimic the intelligence of human-run processes. These strategies can be utilized to solve problems affecting a variety of intelligent behaviour-related applications. This is connected to an individual's aptitude for observation and learning, in addition to their capability of making specific decisions on matters relating to intelligent reasoning. For this reason, researchers from a wide range of fields have found AI and related applications to be fruitful areas of study. The fields of E-government and digital healthcare have received particular attention from researchers in AI. The current literature will elaborate on the meaning of AI and the consequences of its use that may occur in the future. The use of AI in healthcare is now being tested in pilot programmes with the goals of improving the speed and accuracy of diagnosis, enhancing imaging, reducing errors caused by human exhaustion, bringing down medical expenses, assisting with and replacing dull, repetitive, labour-intensive activities, performing minimally invasive surgery and lowering death rates.

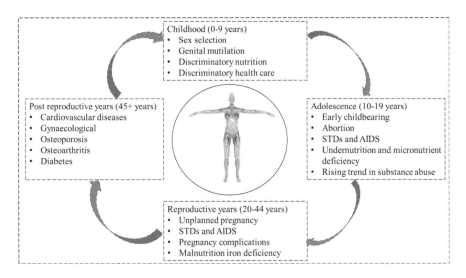

FIGURE 13.3   Health problems among females during the entire life cycle.

There are many aspects of women's health that need to be addressed to make improvements. This chapter addresses some of the most important concerns in the developing world, including unsafe parenting, sexually transmitted diseases (STDs) (including HIV/AIDS), malnutrition, gender-based violence and female genital mutilation. Several issues that need fixing to improve women's health are shown in Figure 13.3[29].

13.2.1   Childhood (0–9 years)

Childhood is mainly considered to be from birth to 9 years. Common problems that occur in childhood and appropriate solutions with AI are discussed in the following subsections.

13.2.1.1   Sex Selection

Sexual selection is a key part of the science of evolution. It represents a biological mechanism in which one sex chooses a mate for the best reproductive success. Generally, sexual selection in non-human animals differs greatly from that in humans since they are subjected to greater evolutionary pressures to reproduce and can readily decline a mate [35]. With AI technology, it is possible to determine an infant's age and gender by analysing their personality. But gender imbalance is a key issue in AI. It was found to be good for the determination of the health of the infants. It is possible to determine a patient's age and sex using just an electrocardiogram and some other AI-embedded system. Attia et al. suggested that an AI algorithm might someday serve as a measure of overall health if its capacity to assess physiological age was further validated [36].

13.2.1.2   Genital Mutilation

Genital mutilation (GM) is a harmful practice that has been around for a long time. It is the practice of causing physical harm to a woman's genitalia or removing her external genitalia without any reason. Sexual assault against women is rarely discussed [37]. . It is an age-old taboo that people adhere to out of respect for the past. Mumkin, an app that uses AI to help people start conversations about female genital cutting (FGC) in their communities, is a step towards using AI for social change. The software, which is still in its experimental phase, intends to expand its conversational AI to include issues such as domestic abuse, consent and good touch–bad touch [38].

13.2.1.3   Discriminatory Nutrition

This ingrained systemic nutritional violence causes major health difficulties such as anaemia, stunted growth, eye problems, diabetes and heart disease, and is often handed down from mother to daughter, who, if raised in the same societal norms of gender discrimination and violence in access to food, become trapped in the cycle. On the other hand, food insecurity makes gender-based violence worse, making women and girls more likely to be abused as they deal with a hard life of hunger and poverty. With such a large and complicated data set to work with, nutrition research is one area of medicine that is increasingly benefiting from new computational tools. In the context of varied dietary exposures, AI-based methodologies have improved health outcome prediction and led to the enhancement and development of dietary assessment tools [39]. AI-based technologies are employed in various "omics"-related nutrition studies, as well as in the processing and analysis of social media data.

13.2.1.4   Discriminatory Healthcare

Discrimination against women in the medical field is defined as adverse actions or disregard for an individual woman or a group of women based on an irrational and stereotypical assumption. AI research in healthcare is moving quickly and potential uses are being shown in many different areas of medicine and decision-making [40]. Traditional techniques of developing intelligent systems, such as rule-based systems, were ineffective until it was realized that computers can measure more than just numbers. AI has the potential to change the way people receive medical care because it seems to have no limits. The expanding availability of healthcare data and the quick advancement of analysis methodologies are causing a paradigm shift in the healthcare industry. AI is used to obtain information, streamline clinical orders and assess high-risk patients in healthcare. The findings in [41] confirmed the importance of these new technologies in epidemiological surveys, analyses, predictions and case tracking [41].

13.2.2   Adolescence (10–19 years)

Adolescence is a time of physical and mental transition that normally occurs between youth and adult life stages. Physical, psychological and cultural aspects of adolescence may begin and end before or beyond the teenage years. In addition to sexual assault, other issues that begin in childhood and adolescence include an unhealthy diet plan and a lack of physical activity [42]. Intimate relationships and violence disproportionately affect older adolescent girls. Complications during pregnancy and unsafe abortions are the primary causes of death in the age group 15–19 years among girls [43].

13.2.2.1   Early Childbearing

Around the world, 15% of births occur to women under the age of 18. A girl's education, career opportunities and health may all be negatively impacted by having a child at a young age or having a baby while she is still a teenager [44]. Pregnant women under the age of 20 are at a greater risk of mortality and illness, especially from complications of pregnancy such as bleeding, toxaemia, haemorrhage, a protracted and difficult birth, severe anaemia and disability, compared to women between the ages of 20 and 35. Birth at a young age may cause social and economic problems throughout a person's life [45]. There has been a dramatic uptick in the deployment of AI systems across a wide range of medical subfields in recent years, in both the private and public healthcare sectors. Recently, AI-driven technologies have been incorporated into prenatal care [46].

13.2.2.2   Abortion

Abortion is the termination of a pregnancy before viability (in human beings, usually about the 20th week of gestation). Abortions may occur naturally, sometimes known as a miscarriage, or they can be created artificially, in which case known as induced abortions. Miscarriages, or spontaneous abortions, may happen for numerous reasons, including the woman's health, the fetus' health, a genetic defect or the mother and fetus' metabolism. It is widely agreed that providing information on methods of contraception is an important part of post-abortion care. The Act of Contraception ensures a woman's right to obtain and use contraception after an abortion. The medical sector does not support any measures that would make it harder for women to get prenatal care, abortions and other medical services they need when they need them [47]. All of this will be possible, thanks to the collaboration of service provider organizations. Surgical evacuation management and uterine expectations have been provided for women who need post-abortion care.

Both of these methods have been used [48]. The majority of research sectors, including large-scale medical research and pharmaceutical development, have begun to make use of AI, which can threaten the lives of both mother and unborn child. In the course of pregnancy, a woman may experience headaches or illness. There is substantial medical evidence to support the notion that emotional issues (such as anxiety, tension, depression etc.) can be associated with pregnancy-related risk factors. Pregnant women's mental health and computer/AI technology were examined together with scientific articles published over the last decade (2010–2020) to determine the framework's tactics, approaches and algorithms [49]. Figure 13.4 depicts evidence indicating that misoprostol is a safe, effective and acceptable technique for women who have been released from a hospital's post-abortion care system [50].

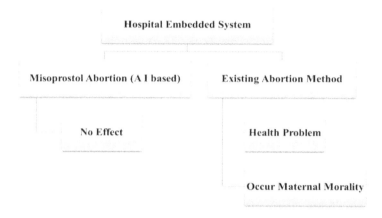

FIGURE 13.4 A straight comparison between the AI-based method and the existing abortion method. hierarchy

13.2.2.3 STDs and AIDS

More than half of the world's 37.7 million AIDS sufferers are women and girls. To successfully end AIDS by 2030, it is crucial to focus on girls and women, recognizing their unique contributions in a heterosexual interaction, which is a major risk factor for HIV transmission among the women. According to a recent study [51], females are more likely to get HIV from male partners during sexual activity. Currently, 0.22% of women and 0.36% of males in India between the ages of 15 and 49 live with HIV, according to newly revealed national data [52]. Few female patients undergo anti-retroviral therapy, although they have a greater risk of Steven Johnson syndrome and hepatic problems from nevirapine. A few studies have provided some AI-based solutions, including some that identify ways to prevent HIV in patients [53, 54]. Moreover, youth experiencing homelessness (YEH) demonstrate a benefit in PCA (Principle component analysis) models that encourage HIV understanding and condom usage among youth which may connect interventionists with their communities [55].

13.2.2.4 Undernutrition and Micronutrient Deficiency

There is sufficient food for everyone on the planet, but maternal and child malnutrition is still prevalent and is related to millions of deaths annually. Maternal nutrition refers to the nutritional requirements of women during the preconception, antepartum and postpartum periods, and often also before conception (i.e. during adolescence). Women who are malnourished at the time of conception are unlikely to improve their nutrition during pregnancy when their nutritional needs increase due to the growing fetus [56]. They may not gain enough weight during pregnancy and have an increased risk of mortality compared to healthy mothers. In most developing countries, mothers' malnutrition is a common cause of illness, death and adverse birth outcomes, such as low birth weight, neonatal death and later malnutrition in children. With AI, malnutrition screening methods are used to detect individuals with specific nutritional deficiencies. The use of assessment tools allows doctors to obtain a deeper understanding of the patient's condition and facilitates the implementation of tailored treatment plans [57].

13.2.2.5   Rising Trends in Substance Abuse

A great amount of attention has been paid to female alcoholism on a global scale. There are significant variations between the problems associated with illicit substance abuse and their treatment and the problems associated with alcohol abuse, necessitating distinct research [58]. The primary advantages of AI-based approaches to healthcare are the reduction of human error and the saving of both time and resources. While AI has been utilized extensively in numerous healthcare situations, psychiatry has been neglected. Given the growth of psychiatric problems, this is a fairly disturbing trend. From the earliest stages of drug discovery to the approval phase, AI-based tools and techniques have the potential to accelerate and enhance drug research. Simultaneously, access to high-quality data for model training and validation is emerging as a significant barrier, resulting in an increased emphasis on data, metadata and data stewardship [58].

13.2.3   Reproductive Years (20–44 Years)

Females in their 20s have the greatest potential for bearing children. When a woman reaches her 30s, her fertility begins to diminish, especially beyond the age of 35. A 30-year-old healthy, fertile woman has a 20% chance of becoming pregnant. In other words, only 20 out of every 100 fertile women aged 30 will get pregnant in a given cycle. By the time a woman reaches the age of 40, her monthly chances of conceiving decrease to below 5%, meaning that fewer than 5 out of every 100 women are expected to be successful [59].

13.2.3.1   Unplanned Pregnancy

In low- and middle-income countries/regions, unintended pregnancy is a public health concern. Every year, there are 74 million unplanned pregnancies that occur among women all over the world. Moreover, in India, there are around 53.8 million unintended births every year [60]. Recent research shows that ML and deep learning may greatly enhance prediction performance. Significant markers of unplanned pregnancy in married women have been identified using several statistical approaches (binary logistic regression analysis). Therefore, policies and recommendations should be established to increase the use of modern methods of contraception and to enhance communication between married partners about potential pregnancies [61].

13.2.3.2   STDs and AIDS

Sexually transmitted diseases (STDs) are diseases that may be passed between partners during sexual activity. Pathogens like bacteria, parasites and viruses are responsible for these. The human immunodeficiency virus (HIV) is a sexually transmitted illness that, if left untreated with HIV medications, may cause acquired immunodeficiency syndrome (AIDS). Sexually transmitted diseases include chlamydia, gonorrhoea, HPV infection and syphilis [62]. Surveillance and treatment for sexually transmitted infections both may benefit from the use of AI. Researchers into sexually transmitted infections (STIs) have previously shown that AI can predict the county-level prevalence of syphilis by evaluating publically accessible social media data on people's sexual attitudes and behaviours linked with syphilis. Inaccuracies in STI data collecting, such as long delays in receiving reports of new cases, may be mitigated with the use of AI techniques [63].

13.2.3.3 Pregnancy Complications

The process of pregnancy is not always smooth for some women. These issues may affect either the mother or the developing baby. Complications during pregnancy may occur in women of any health status [64]. By using ML-based algorithms, it may be possible to create a personalized, dynamic model for predicting delivery outcomes and aiding in intrapartum decision-making. AI has been used in gynaecology and obstetrics, as reported in recent research [27].

13.2.3.4 Malnutrition Iron Deficiency

The condition known as anaemia develops when either the total number of red blood cells or the quantity of haemoglobin inside those cells falls below normal. Lack of haemoglobin or defective red blood cells reduces the blood's oxygen-carrying ability, which has detrimental effects on the body's tissues. Dizziness, weakness, weariness and shortness of breath are among the symptoms that may occur in a person with anaemia. The incidence of disorders like anaemia may be predicted using several ML methods. Time, money and access prevent most hospitals from measuring serum iron [65].

13.2.4 Post-reproductive Years (45+ Years)

Post-reproductive lifespan (PRLS) (age 45 years to end of life) refers to the phenomena of individuals or cohorts surviving beyond the age at which they can no longer be expected to reproduce [66].

13.2.4.1 Cardiovascular Disease

Women who experience a heart attack have a greater mortality rate than men. Heart attack is one of the top causes of death around the world. This has been a concern for cardiologists for decades and has sparked disagreement in the medical community regarding the origins and ramifications of potential therapy gaps. It mostly occurs during the post-reproductive age. The problem starts with symptoms. Unlike men, who usually have chest pain that spreads to the left arm, a heart attack in women often shows up as stomach pain that spreads to the back or as nausea and vomiting. These symptoms are often misunderstood by both patients and doctors [67]. According tothe European Society of Cardiology Congress in Barcelona, an algorithm made with AI could help doctors diagnose heart attacks in women faster and more accurately than ever before.

13.2.4.2   Gynaecological Diseases

Gynaecological diseases affect the female reproductive system as a whole. Some of these diseases are benign/malignant tumours, diseases caused by pregnancy, infections and diseases of the endocrine system. Malignant tumours are the most common cause of death among these [68, 69]. AI improves the accuracy of diagnosis, reduces the amount of work doctors have to do and improves the effectiveness of therapy and prognosis. AI will play a crucial role in the area of gynaecological cancer and will stimulate the development of medicine and the shift from conventional to precision and preventive treatment [70].

13.2.4.3   Osteoporosis

Osteoporosis is a systemic skeletal disease associated with low bone mass, micro-architectural degradation of bone tissue leading to bone fragility and a consequential increase in fracture risk. It is the most common cause of bone fractures in elderly individuals [71]. The vertebrae of the spine, the bones of the forearm and the hip are regularly broken bones [72]. Here, we examine the most recent studies on the application of AI to osteoporosis prediction, published in recent years. Approximately half of the included papers predict (via classification or regression) a sign of osteoporosis, such as bone mass or fragility fractures; the other half employ approaches for automated segmentation of images of individuals with or at risk for osteoporosis. These investigations use a variety of signal sources, including acoustics, MRI, CT and X-rays.

13.2.4.4   Osteoarthritis

Millions of individuals all around the globe are suffering from osteoarthritis. It results in the gradual deterioration of the lubricating cartilage at the bone ends. Finding the joints in X-rays, MRIs and CT scans is one of the most important and difficult parts of automatically diagnosing arthritis. Assisted by AI, doctors may be able to treat osteoarthritis with drugs instead of surgery one day. Lezcano-Valverde et al. [73] showed how ML can predict the death rate of rheumatoid arthritis patients based on demographic and clinical variables.

13.2.4.5   Diabetes

Diabetes is a chronic disease caused by inadequate insulin synthesis by the pancreas or inappropriate insulin use by the body. Because sometimes blood sugar levels rise too high, insulin is secreted to bring them back down [74]. Diabetic retinopathy may now be automatically diagnosed, thanks to the development of deep learning algorithms. Screening for diabetic retinopathy using AI has shown to be a practical, reliable and well-recognized procedure. Automated retinal screening has been found to have a high sensitivity of 92.3% and a specificity of 93.7%. Over 96% of patients have reported being happy or extremely satisfied with automated screening [75].

13.3 SWOT (STRENGTHS, WEAKNESSES, OPPORTUNITIES, AND THREATS) ANALYSIS FOR AI-ASSISTED HEALTHCARE SYSTEMS

A SWOT analysis is a strategic planning methodology that offers testing techniques. The identification of a sector's or organization's core strengths, weaknesses, opportunities and threats provides the way for fact-based analysis, fresh perspectives and inventive ideas.

A SWOT analysis highlights significant achievements or objectives that the healthcare industry should strive to achieve. It assists the whole sector in determining ways to improve or enhance its performance. It also provides information on the current status of each area.

13.3.1 STRENGTHS

There are multiple ways in which the application of AI in healthcare can be beneficial, as shown in Figure 13.5. For instance, in patient demographics (i.e. simplifying person-wise data and adherence monitoring) as well as risk predictions for physicians or pharmacists; for healthcare systems, in the provision of cost and time savings; and, finally, for patients, so that they can monitor their health status on their own [76]. In addition, the requirements of emerging markets contribute to an increase in the demand for AI-assisted devices that can assist patients in improving their health status. The application of AI in the healthcare sector also yields immediate and impactful results. In pharmacovigilance studies [1, 2], the use of AI in this particular aspect of the field of women's healthcare is frequently observed and has proven to be an effective application. In addition, the combination of big data and ML algorithms may be able to assist with the recruitment and selection of patients for clinical trials. AI may also make it possible for patients to independently seek enrolment in clinical trials [3]. Additionally, it boosts productivity at work. Employees may set up AI to easily handle tasks rather than wasting hours of labour

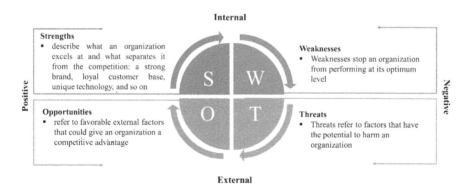

FIGURE 13.5 SWOT analysis of artificial intelligence implementation in the healthcare sector.

on monotonous, repeated activities. Even though we have used robots on manufacturing lines in the past, AI allows us to do a range of tasks more efficiently than ever before. Last but not least, AI is currently utilized in a variety of fields, from digital marketing to healthcare. Depending on the activity, the type and level of AI required will vary; for example, email automation will demand less processing power than looking through a medical data database. In addition to classifying information, AI is used for academic research and face recognition.

13.3.2 WEAKNESSES

Weaknesses prevent an organization from operating at its best. However, the limitations of AI have already been identified, and some challenges must be addressed (Figure 13.6). As AI is driven by enormous data sets, gathering such data may be difficult. Another issue is the expensive price of AI-assisted gadgets, which makes them inaccessible to some people. Furthermore, given the risk assessment involved in the AI healthcare industry, the government is directly involved (through policies and conditions). AI developers are always attempting to push the boundaries of the technology. It can now accomplish a task, learn and remember information. But maybe, in the future, it will reach the stage of upgrading and redesigning without human input. In addition, there is a lack of understanding among the general public regarding AI-assisted medical devices, which contributes to their lack of popularity. Even while AI contributes something beneficial to the clinical decision-making process, it is impossible to overestimate the significance of human intellect. For instance, drug interaction databases do exist as a clinical decision support tool; however, a human explanation is still necessary to evaluate the numerous clinical factors that

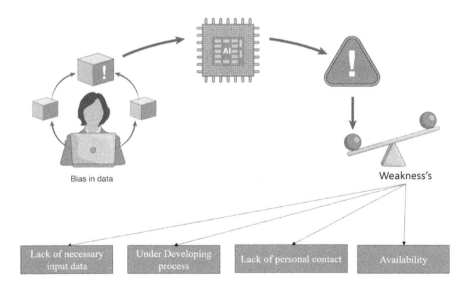

FIGURE 13.6   Major weakness of AI-assisted healthcare system.

may influence a patient's response to a drug and to weigh the advantages and disadvantages of certain drug combinations. This is the case even though drug interaction databases already exist [77].

Moreover, AI has the potential to become an essential instrument for the improvement of healthcare in nations and populations that have limited resources. In situations when resources are scarce, AI may become a potent ally by lending a hand in the processes of prediction, diagnosis and therapy. Figure 13.6 also highlights the major weakness of the AI-assisted healthcare system.

13.3.3 Opportunities

There are several opportunities available in the AI-assisted women's healthcare sector; for example, undiscovered realms of treatment and diagnostics regions that can unlock many secret doors of the future world. Furthermore, enabling AI technology reduces costs and improves functioning in the women's healthcare industry. The most significant prospects in an AI-powered healthcare system is shown in Figure 13.7.

13.3.3.1 AI-assisted Predictive Care

Tracking social human determinants enables healthcare providers to anticipate the development of chronic risk in humans. Predictive care uses modelling and forecasting techniques to predict what is likely to occur in the future. The projections can then be used by physicians, researchers, medical specialty societies, pharmaceutical corporations and everyone else involved in healthcare to provide the best possible care for specific patients.

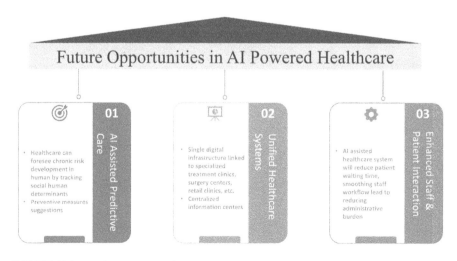

FIGURE 13.7   Main prospects of AI-powered healthcare system.

13.3.3.2   Unified Healthcare Systems

There can be a single digital unified infrastructure linked to specialized treatment clinics, surgery centres, retail clinics etc. which can encompass the healthcare system with systematic single-way communication among doctors, patients as well as pharmacists.

13.3.3.3   Enhanced Staff and Patient Interaction

In the prospect, AI-assisted healthcare systems enhance the productivity of staff as well as enhance the doctor–patient interaction by reducing patient waiting time, direct communication and by streamlining staff workflow which can lead to reduced administrative burden.

13.3.4   Threats

There are many known problems and dangers associated with AI. First and foremost, the risk of unauthorized access to the patient's protected health information as well as the likelihood that such access may be exploited in a manner that would result in adverse effects. To lessen the impact of these dangers, there need to be laws enacted at the national level, along with appropriate policy and advocacy.

There is also a danger to employment since some believe that the introduction of AI would result in job losses. In all honesty, this only happens occasionally. Consider your local Walmart's self-service check-out lanes. There are a lot of them, but only one or two people are on hand to help customers if there is a problem. There is also the issue of patients' distrust and scepticism of medical practitioners.

13.4   FUTURE INDIAN SCENARIO

The use of AI in India's healthcare system has the potential to significantly improve both the efficiency and quality of treatment provided. Inadequate financing, lax regulation, a lack of healthcare infrastructure and entrenched sociocultural habits are all contributing factors to the sector's inadequacies and problems. AI-only solutions will not suffice to address these challenges. Additionally, technical potential is not the same as widespread use. The adoption of AI is expected to be delayed and very heterogeneous in India due to the country's weak digital infrastructure; big, diversified and unregulated private sector; and varying capacities between states and medical practitioners. These same considerations also suggest that large, privately owned hospitals are more likely to lead the way in adopting this practice. As a result, the dominant narrative or justification for the development of AI in healthcare, namely improving fairness and quality, is unlikely to be addressed solely by market forces. These solutions are more likely to benefit populations that already have access to high-quality treatment, as is the case in cities with well-developed digital infrastructure. Basic information and communication technology (ICT) solutions, such as invoicing and billing platforms, are still far from being widely adopted in India's many small hospitals and single-provider practices. The success of these systems will depend on how well problems are identified and how well they are matched with the right solutions. The current state of affairs poses a threat of technology-led, rather than problem-led, solutions, which are often oblivious to particular contextual demands or limits. For digital goods aimed towards usage in underserved regions, such as those without reliable access to the internet, real-time or synchronous solutions may not be the best option. The digital gap between the technology developer and the user might make it difficult to design effective digital interventions [78]. In conclusion, much more in-depth study is needed before AI can provide safe and equitable healthcare solutions, such as privacy, utilization and responsibility. Some of the suggestions for addressing future scenarios can be adopted in the Indian context. A close working relationship between scientific and medical institutions is necessary to advance research, which, if successful, could open the door for more effective communication in the healthcare industry. In addition, data have to be gathered in real-time, and institutions have a responsibility to encourage the transformation of data into processes that can be understood. Government funding should be more focused on results rather than medical data collection. Additionally, clinical findings should be open-sourced and shared, and aggregated data should be displayed for easy access by medical professionals and researchers. The current status of medical records should be updated for AI collaboration.

In conclusion, this chapter offers guidance for academics and practitioners interested in learning more about the use of AI and effective computing in female healthcare. These insights will aid in the creation of future innovations in this rapidly evolving field.

REFERENCES

1. N. Mehta and M. V. Devarakonda, "Machine learning, natural language programming, and electronic health records: The next step in the artificial intelligence journey?," *J. Allergy Clin. Immunol.*, vol. 141, no. 6, pp. 2019–2021.e1, 2018, doi: 10.1016/j.jaci.2018.02.025.
2. https://www.usoft.com/blog/difference-between-ai-ml-and-deep-learning, assessed on 21 December 2022.
3. D. Saraswat *et al.*, "Explainable AI for healthcare 5.0: Opportunities and challenges," *IEEE Access*, vol. 10, no. July, pp. 84486–84517, 2022, doi: 10.1109/ACCESS.2022.3197671.
4. E. Mbunge, B. Muchemwa, S. Jiyane, and J. Batani, "Sensors and healthcare 5.0: Transformative shift in virtual care through emerging digital health technologies," *Glob. Heal. J.*, vol. 5, no. 4, pp. 169–177, 2021, doi: 10.1016/j.glohj.2021.11.008.
5. C. F. Pasluosta, H. Gassner, J. Winkler, J. Klucken, and B. M. Eskofier, "An emerging era in the management of Parkinson's Disease: Wearable technologies and the internet of things," *IEEE J. Biomed. Heal. Informatics*, vol. 19, no. 6, pp. 1873–1881, 2015, doi: 10.1109/JBHI.2015.2461555.
6. A. Esteva *et al.*, "A guide to deep learning in healthcare," *Nat. Med.*, vol. 25, no. 1, pp. 24–29, 2019, doi: 10.1038/s41591-018-0316-z.
7. W. G. de Sousa, E. R. P. de Melo, P. H. D. S. Bermejo, R. A. S. Farias, and A. O. Gomes, "How and where is artificial intelligence in the public sector going? A literature review and research agenda," *Gov. Inf. Q.*, vol. 36, no. 4, p. 101392, 2019, doi: 10.1016/j.giq.2019.07.004.

8. D. Bunker, "Who do you trust? The digital destruction of shared situational awareness and the COVID-19 infodemic," *Int. J. Inf. Manage.*, vol. 55, p. 102201, 2020, doi: 10.1016/j.ijinfomgt.2020.102201.

9. Y. K. Dwivedi *et al.*, "Setting the future of digital and social media marketing research: Perspectives and research propositions," *Int. J. Inf. Manage.*, vol. 59, p. 102168, 2021, doi: 10.1016/j.ijinfomgt.2020.102168.

10. Y. Chung *et al.*, "Role of visual analytics in supporting mental healthcare systems research and policy: A systematic scoping review," *Int. J. Inf. Manage.*, vol. 50, pp. 17–27, 2020, doi: 10.1016/j.ijinfomgt.2019.04.012.

11. K.-H. Yu, A. L. Beam, and I. S. Kohane, "Artificial intelligence in healthcare," *Nat. Biomed. Eng.*, vol. 2, no. 10, pp. 719–731, 2018, doi: 10.1038/s41551-018-0305-z.

12. Y. K. Dwivedi *et al.*, "Artificial Intelligence (AI): Multidisciplinary perspectives on emerging challenges, opportunities, and agenda for research, practice and policy," *Int. J. Inf. Manage.*, vol. 57, p. 101994, 2021, doi: 10.1016/j.ijinfomgt.2019.08.002.

13. K. Raza, "Artificial Intelligence against COVID-19: A meta-analysis of current research BT - Big data analytics and artificial intelligence against COVID-19: Innovation vision and approach," A.-E. Hassanien, N. Dey, and S. Elghamrawy, Eds. Cham: Springer International Publishing, 2020, pp. 165–176. doi: 10.1007/978-3-030-55258-9_10.

14. T. Davenport and R. Kalakota, "The potential for artificial intelligence in healthcare," *Future Healthcare Journal*, vol. 6, no. 2, pp. 94–98, Jun. 2019. doi: 10.7861/futurehosp.6-2-94.

15. S. Lalmuanawma, J. Hussain, and L. Chhakchhuak, "Applications of machine learning and artificial intelligence for Covid-19 (SARS-CoV-2) pandemic: A review," *Chaos, Solitons & Fractals*, vol. 139, p. 110059, 2020, doi: 10.1016/j.chaos.2020.110059.

16. R. Vaishya, M. Javaid, I. H. Khan, and A. Haleem, "Artificial Intelligence (AI) applications for COVID-19 pandemic," *Diabetes Metab. Syndr. Clin. Res. Rev.*, vol. 14, no. 4, pp. 337–339, 2020, doi: 10.1016/j.dsx.2020.04.012.

17. T. Q. Sun and R. Medaglia, "Mapping the challenges of Artificial Intelligence in the public sector: Evidence from public healthcare," *Gov. Inf. Q.*, vol. 36, no. 2, pp. 368–383, 2019, doi: 10.1016/j.giq.2018.09.008.

18. A. H. Sodhro, Z. Luo, A. K. Sangaiah, and S. W. Baik, "Mobile edge computing based QoS optimization in medical healthcare applications," *Int. J. Inf. Manage.*, vol. 45, pp. 308–318, 2019, doi: 10.1016/j.ijinfomgt.2018.08.004.

19. J. C. Sipior, "Considerations for development and use of AI in response to COVID-19," *Int. J. Inf. Manage.*, vol. 55, p. 102170, 2020, doi: 10.1016/j.ijinfomgt.2020.102170.

20. R. Cantwell, "Mental disorder in pregnancy and the early postpartum," *Anaesthesia*, vol. 76, no. S4, pp. 76–83, Apr. 2021, doi: 10.1111/anae.15424.

21. C.-L. Dennis, K. Falah-Hassani, and R. Shiri, "Prevalence of antenatal and postnatal anxiety: Systematic review and meta-analysis," *Br. J. Psychiatry*, vol. 210, no. 5, pp. 315–323, 2017, doi: 10.1192/bjp.bp.116.187179.

22. F. Abdollahi and M. Zarghami, "Effect of postpartum depression on women's mental and physical health four years after childbirth," *East. Mediterr. Heal. J.*, vol. 24, no. 10, pp. 1002–1009, 2018, doi: 10.26719/2018.24.10.1002.

23. H. Yang *et al.*, "Risk prediction of diabetes: Big data mining with fusion of multifarious physical examination indicators," *Inf. Fusion*, vol. 75, pp. 140–149, 2021, doi: 10.1016/j.inffus.2021.02.015.

24. K. Seetharam, S. Shrestha, and P. P. Sengupta, "Artificial Intelligence in cardiovascular medicine," *Curr. Treat. Options Cardiovasc. Med.*, vol. 21, no. 5, p. 25, 2019, doi: 10.1007/s11936-019-0728-1.

25. P. Jin *et al.*, "Artificial Intelligence in gastric cancer: A systematic review," *J. Cancer Res. Clin. Oncol.*, vol. 146, no. 9, pp. 2339–2350, 2020, doi: 10.1007/s00432-020-03304-9.

26. P. Singh and A. Kaur, "A systematic review of artificial intelligence in agriculture," *Deep Learn. Sustain. Agric.*, pp. 57–80, 2022, doi: 10.1016/B978-0-323-85214-2.00011-2.

27. A. M. Oprescu, G. Miró-amarante, L. García-Díaz, L. M. Beltrán, V. E. Rey, and M. Romero-Ternero, "Artificial Intelligence in pregnancy: A scoping review," *IEEE Access*, vol. 8, pp. 181450–181484, 2020, doi: 10.1109/ACCESS.2020.3028333.

28. R. F. Wolff *et al.*, "PROBAST: A tool to assess the risk of bias and applicability of prediction model studies," *Ann. Intern. Med.*, vol. 170, no. 1, pp. 51–58, Jan. 2019, doi: 10.7326/M18-1376.

29. A. Tinker, K. Finn, and J. Epp, "Improving women's health: Issues and interventions," TT, no. June, 2000 [Online]. Available: http://www.worldbank.org.

30. M. H. Kangasniemi *et al.*, "Artificial intelligence deep learning model assessment of leukocyte counts and proliferation in endometrium from women with and without polycystic ovary syndrome," *F&S Sci.*, vol. 3, no. 2, pp. 174–186, 2022, doi: 10.1016/j.xfss.2022.01.006.

31. A. Hosny, C. Parmar, J. Quackenbush, L. H. Schwartz, and H. J. W. L. Aerts, "Artificial intelligence in radiology," *Nat. Rev. Cancer*, vol. 18, no. 8, pp. 500–510, 2018, doi: 10.1038/s41568-018-0016-5.

32. A. Rodríguez-Ruiz *et al.*, "Detection of breast cancer with mammography: Effect of an artificial intelligence support system," *Radiology*, vol. 290, no. 3, pp. 305–314, 2019, doi: 10.1148/radiol.2018181371.

33. A. Rodriguez-Ruiz *et al.*, "Stand-Alone Artificial Intelligence for breast cancer detection in mammography: Comparison with 101 radiologists," *JNCI J. Natl. Cancer Inst.*, vol. 111, no. 9, pp. 916–922, Sep. 2019, doi: 10.1093/jnci/djy222.

34. S. M. McKinney *et al.*, "International evaluation of an AI system for breast cancer screening," *Nature*, vol. 577, no. 7788, pp. 89–94, 2020, doi: 10.1038/s41586-019-1799-6.

35. Y. Vogt, "Large testicles are linked to infidelity," *Phys. org*, 2014.

36. Z. I. Attia *et al.*, "Age and sex estimation using artificial intelligence from standard 12-lead ECGs," *Circ. Arrhythmia Electrophysiol.*, vol. 12, no. 9, pp. 1–11, 2019, doi: 10.1161/CIRCEP.119.007284.

37. E. K. Mpinga *et al.*, "Female genital mutilation: A systematic review of research on its economic and social impacts across four decades," *Glob. Health Action*, vol. 9, no. 1, p. 31489, Dec. 2016, doi: 10.3402/gha.v9.31489.

38. J. Mayhew and H. Jahankhani, "Current challenges of modern-day domestic abuse BT – Policing in the era of AI and smart societies," H. Jahankhani, B. Akhgar, P. Cochrane, and M. Dastbaz, Eds. Cham: Springer International Publishing, 2020, pp. 267–282. doi: 10.1007/978-3-030-50613-1_12.

39. M. Côté and B. Lamarche, "Artificial intelligence in nutrition research: Perspectives on current and future applications," *Appl. Physiol. Nutr. Metab.*, vol. 47, no. 1, pp. 1–8, Sep. 2021, doi: 10.1139/apnm-2021-0448.

40. J. G. Rivenbark and M. Ichou, "Discrimination in healthcare as a barrier to care: Experiences of socially disadvantaged populations in France from a nationally representative survey," *BMC Public Health*, vol. 20, no. 1, p. 31, 2020, doi: 10.1186/s12889-019-8124-z.

41. M. E. Matheny, D. Whicher, and S. Thadaney Israni, "Artificial Intelligence in health care: A report from the national academy of medicine," *JAMA*, vol. 323, no. 6, pp. 509–510, Feb. 2020, doi: 10.1001/jama.2019.21579.

42. Bimrew Sendekie Belay, "Flow experience, stress, and mindfulness as predictors of internet addiction among university students in Malaysia," *Univ. Tunku Abdul Rahman*, no. 8.5.2017, pp. 2003–2005, 2022.

43. D. A. Grimes *et al.*, "Unsafe abortion: The preventable pandemic," *Lancet*, vol. 368, no. 9550, pp. 1908–1919, 2006, doi: 10.1016/S0140-6736(06)69481-6.

44. M. G. Phipps and M. Sowers, "Defining early adolescent childbearing," *Am. J. Public Health*, vol. 92, no. 1, pp. 125–128, Jan. 2002, doi: 10.2105/AJPH.92.1.125.

45. A. Monroy De Velasco, "Consequences of early childbearing," *Draper Fund Rep.*, no. 11, pp. 26–27, Dec. 1982.

46. R. Ramakrishnan, S. Rao, and J.-R. He, "Perinatal health predictors using artificial intelligence: A review," *Women's Heal.*, vol. 17, p. 17455065211046132, Jan. 2021, doi: 10.1177/17455065211046132.

47. B. Dempsey, M. Connolly, and M. F. Higgins. ""I suppose we've all been on a bit of a journey": a qualitative study on providers' lived experiences with liberalised abortion care in the Republic of Ireland," *Sexual and Reproductive Health Matters*, vol. 31, no. 1, p. 2216526, 2023.

48. A. Kulczycki, *The Abortion Debate in the World Arena*. Routledge, 1999 [Online]. Available: https://books.google.co.in/books?id=kEUFcBGjUOcC.

49. L. Davidson and M. R. Boland, "Towards deep phenotyping pregnancy: A systematic review on artificial intelligence and machine learning methods to improve pregnancy outcomes," *Brief. Bioinform.*, vol. 22, no. 5, p. bbaa369, Sep. 2021, doi: 10.1093/bib/bbaa369.

50. B. M. Chakhame, E. Darj, M. Mwapasa, U. K. Kafulafula, A. Maluwa, J. Ø. Odland, and M. L. Odland. "Women's perceptions of and experiences with the use of misoprostol for treatment of incomplete abortion in central Malawi: a mixed methods study," *Reproductive Health*, vol. 20, no. 1, p. 26, 2023.

51. J. Brown *et al.*, "Routine HIV screening in the emergency department using the new US centers for disease control and prevention guidelines: Results from a high-prevalence area," *JAIDS J. Acquir. Immune Defic. Syndr.*, vol. 46, no. 4, 2007 [Online]. Available: https://journals.lww.com/jaids/Fulltext/2007/12010/Routine_HIV_Screening_in_the_Emergency_Department.4.aspx.

52. "Comparison of female to male and male to female transmission of HIV in 563 stable couples. European Study Group on Heterosexual Transmission of HIV," *BMJ*, vol. 304, no. 6830, pp. 809–813, 1992, doi: 10.1136/bmj.304.6830.809.

53. J. L. Marcus, W. C. Sewell, L. B. Balzer, and D. S. Krakower, "Artificial Intelligence and machine learning for HIV prevention: Emerging approaches to ending the epidemic," *Curr. HIV/AIDS Rep.*, vol. 17, no. 3, pp. 171–179, Jun. 2020, doi: 10.1007/s11904-020-00490-6.

54. C. K. Mutai, P. E. McSharry, I. Ngaruye, and E. Musabanganji, "Use of machine learning techniques to identify HIV predictors for screening in sub-Saharan Africa," *BMC Med. Res. Methodol.*, vol. 21, no. 1, p. 159, 2021, doi: 10.1186/s12874-021-01346-2.

55. E. Rice *et al.*, "A peer-led, Artificial Intelligence–Augmented social network intervention to prevent HIV among youth experiencing homelessness," *JAIDS J. Acquir. Immune Defic. Syndr.*, vol. 88, no. S1, 2021 [Online]. Available: https://journals.lww.com/jaids/Fulltext/2021/12151/A_Peer_Led,_Artificial_Intelligence_Augmented.4.aspx.

56. T. Ahmed, M. Hossain, and K. I. Sanin, "Global burden of maternal and child undernutrition and micronutrient deficiencies," *Ann. Nutr. Metab.*, vol. 61 (suppl 1, no. Suppl. 1), pp. 8–17, 2012, doi: 10.1159/000345165.

57. V. Sharma *et al.*, "Malnutrition, health and the role of machine learning in clinical setting," *Front. Nutr.*, vol. 7, no. April, pp. 1–9, 2020, doi: 10.3389/fnut.2020.00044.

58. S. Zaami, E. Marinelli, and M. R. Varì, "New trends of substance abuse during COVID-19 pandemic: An international perspective," *Front. Psychiatry*, vol. 11, no. July, pp. 1–4, 2020, doi: 10.3389/fpsyt.2020.00700.

59. S. Deatsman, T. Vasilopoulos, and A. Rhoton-Vlasak, "Age and fertility: A study on patient awareness," *J. Bras. Reprod. Assist.*, vol. 20, no. 3, pp. 99–106, 2016, doi: 10.5935/1518-0557.20160024.

60. M. I. Hossain *et al.*, "Performance evaluation of machine learning algorithm for classification of unintended pregnancy among married women in Bangladesh," *J. Healthc. Eng.*, vol. 2022, p. 1460908, 2022, doi: 10.1155/2022/1460908.

61. M. N. Islam, S. N. Mustafina, T. Mahmud, and N. I. Khan, "Machine learning to predict pregnancy outcomes: A systematic review, synthesizing framework and future research agenda," *BMC Pregnancy Childbirth*, vol. 22, no. 1, p. 348, 2022, doi: 10.1186/s12884-022-04594-2.

62. F. N. Samkange-Zeeb, L. Spallek, and H. Zeeb, "Awareness and knowledge of sexually transmitted diseases (STDs) among school-going adolescents in Europe: A systematic review of published literature," *BMC Public Health*, vol. 11, no. 1, p. 727, 2011, doi: 10.1186/1471-2458-11-727.

63. S. D. Young, J. S. Crowley, and S. H. Vermund, "Artificial intelligence and sexual health in the USA," *Lancet Digit. Heal.*, vol. 3, no. 8, pp. e467–e468, 2021, doi: 10.1016/S2589-7500(21)00117-5.

64. F. Galtier-Dereure, C. Boegner, and J. Bringer, "Obesity and pregnancy: Complications and cost," *Am. J. Clin. Nutr.*, vol. 71, no. 5, pp. 1242S–1248S, May 2000, doi: 10.1093/ajcn/71.5.1242s.

65. J. Wang *et al.*, "The influence of malnutrition and micronutrient status on anemic risk in children under 3 years old in poor areas in China," *PLoS One*, vol. 10, no. 10, p. e0140840, Oct. 2015 [Online], doi: 10.1371/journal.pone.0140840.

66. K. Hill and A. M. Hurtado, "The evolution of premature reproductive senescence and menopause in human females," *Hum. Nat.*, vol. 2, no. 4, pp. 313–350, 1991, doi: 10.1007/BF02692196.

67. K. Chayakrit, Z. HongJu, W. Zhen, A. Mehmet, and K. Takeshi, "Artificial Intelligence in precision cardiovascular medicine," *J. Am. Coll. Cardiol.*, vol. 69, no. 21, pp. 2657–2664, May 2017, doi: 10.1016/j.jacc.2017.03.571.

68. A. M. Miniño, J. Xu, and K. D. Kochanek, "Deaths: Preliminary data for 2008," *Natl. Vital Stat. Rep.*, vol. 59, no. 2, pp. 1–52, 2010 [Online]. Available: http://europepmc.org/abstract/MED/25073655.

69. B. Favrat, A. Pécoud, and A. Jaussi, "Teaching cardiac auscultation to trainees in internal medicine and family practice: Does it work?," *BMC Med. Educ.*, vol. 4, no. 1, pp. 87–90, 2004, doi: 10.1186/1472-6920-4-5.

70. J. Zhou, Z. Y. Zeng, and L. Li, "Progress of Artificial Intelligence in gynecological malignant tumors," *Cancer Manag. Res.*, vol. 12, pp. 12823–12840, 2020, doi: 10.2147/CMAR.S279990.

71. I. Ofotokun *et al.*, "A single-dose zoledronic acid infusion prevents antiretroviral therapy–induced bone loss in treatment-naive HIV-infected patients: A phase IIb trial," *Clin. Infect. Dis.*, vol. 63, no. 5, pp. 663–671, Sep. 2016, doi: 10.1093/cid/ciw331.

72. A. Rashid, S. C. Hauge, C. Suetta, and D. Hansen, "'Sarcopenia and risk of osteoporosis, falls and bone fractures in patients with chronic kidney disease: A systematic review,'" *PLoS One*, vol. 17, no. 1, pp. 1–11, Jan. 2022, doi: 10.1371/journal.pone.0262572.

73. M. Imtiaz, S. A. A. Shah, and Z. ur Rehman, "A review of arthritis diagnosis techniques in artificial intelligence era: Current trends and research challenges," *Neurosci. Informatics*, vol. 2, no. 4, p. 100079, 2022, doi: 10.1016/j.neuri.2022.100079.

74. B. He, K. I. Shu, and H. Zhang, "Machine learning and data mining in diabetes diagnosis and treatment," *IOP Conf. Ser. Mater. Sci. Eng.*, vol. 490, no. 4, 2019, doi: 10.1088/1757-899X/490/4/042049.

75. S. Keel *et al.*, "Feasibility and patient acceptability of a novel artificial intelligence-based screening model for diabetic retinopathy at endocrinology outpatient services: A pilot study," *Sci. Rep.*, vol. 8, no. 1, p. 4330, 2018, doi: 10.1038/s41598-018-22612-2.

76. Mistry, P. (2015). *A Knowledge Based Approach of Toxicity Prediction for Drug Formulation. Modelling Drug Vehicle Relationships Using Soft Computing Techniques* (Doctoral dissertation, University of Bradford)

77. P. Shah *et al.*, "Artificial intelligence and machine learning in clinical development: A translational perspective," *NPJ Digit. Med.*, vol. 2, no. 1, p. 69, 2019, doi: 10.1038/s41746-019-0148-3.

78. M. M. Hossain *et al.*, "Digital interventions for people living with non-communicable diseases in India: A systematic review of intervention studies and recommendations for future research and development," *Digit. Heal.*, vol. 5, pp. 1–18, 2019, doi: 10.1177/2055207619896153.

Index